The
ANCESTRAL POwer
of
AMULETS, TALISMANS,
and
MASCOTS

"This is a very well-researched and well-written book, presenting great information through many photos of artifacts with annotations to help decode the meaning of the signs, numbers, and symbols used in witchcraft practices and esoteric traditions in general. It certainly is an inspirational work, and it sparks your interest in other topics. This book gives what is surely the most authoritative account of symbolism and practices in witchcraft available."

NATASHA HELVIN, AUTHOR OF *SLAVIC WITCHCRAFT*

"Written by one of the great wisdom keepers of British lore, this book is the most wonderful treasury of amulets, protective emblems, and the folklore by which people have kept themselves safe against plagues, envy, and evils of many kinds. Very highly recommended as an authentic sourcebook of protective wisdom."

CAITLÍN MATTHEWS, COAUTHOR OF *THE LOST BOOK OF THE GRAIL*

"The wise words of Nigel Pennick are amplified by the feast for the eyes in the images cataloging the ability of human beings to imbue power into objects as well as the innate 'manna' contained in certain shapes, words, and symbols. I am grateful for Nigel's valuable insights in this historical, multicultural, spiritual archive of fetishes and how they empower individuals in the face of authoritarian oppressive decrees. If you thought you knew everything about sigils, seals, talismans, and symbols, get ready to expand—thanks to Nigel's masterful scholarly work contained within these pages."

MAJA D'AOUST, AUTHOR OF *FAMILIARS IN WITCHCRAFT*

"This substantial compendium, documenting amulets and talismans' myriad manifestations, is pure Pennick and *sans pareil*. It is not only based upon a lifetime of learning but also the author's own artistic craftsmanship and keen-eyed collecting, as evidenced by the wealth of accompanying images. The result is a gem-studded wizard's chest of living folklore, overflowing with contents that cannot fail to fascinate and enchant."

MICHAEL MOYNIHAN, PH.D., COAUTHOR OF *LORDS OF CHAOS*

"The breadth and depth of Pennick's knowledge of folklore and magic never fails to deliver, and his latest work is no exception. Reaching across multiple cultures and spanning time from ancient history into the modern era, this book covers all aspects of the magic that deals with created objects and symbols of all varieties. The creation of amulets, talismans, and charms is the meeting of the numinous and the practical, embodying the desire and vision of the maker into a manifested creation, and this book covers all aspects of this most practical form of magic. Accompanied by numerous illustrations, this would be a welcome addition to any collection."

ALICE KARLSDÓTTIR, AUTHOR OF *NORSE GODDESS MAGIC*

"This book will inspire the reader to create sacred and magical objects, using media such as knotwork, ropes, bells, feathers, roots, bones, stones, and herbs. Numbers, colors, glyphs, and signs are offered as suggestions to add potency to these creations. Artists, magicians, witches, and Druids who seek to create physical objects of power and protection will find herein a treasure trove of historically grounded practices."

ELLEN EVERT HOPMAN, AUTHOR OF *THE SACRED HERBS OF SAMHAIN*

"What we have in Pennick is a modern-day cunning man. He is not only an authority in the field of folk magic but an active magical practitioner who is in tune with the energies and rhythms of landscape, symbol, and the timeless rituals and traditions that have helped to bolster man's connection to a universe that is alive. *Ancestral Power of Amulets, Talismans, and Mascots* is a boon to students of folklore and practitioners alike."

JOHNNY DECKER MILLER, AUTHOR OF *DARK MAGIC*

The
ANCESTRAL POWER
of
AMULETS, TALISMANS,
and
MASCOTS

Folk Magic in Witchcraft
and Religion

NIGEL PENNICK

Destiny Books
Rochester, Vermont

Destiny Books
One Park Street
Rochester, Vermont 05767
www.DestinyBooks.com

Text stock is SFI certified

Destiny Books is a division of Inner Traditions International

Cataloging-in-Publication Data for this title is available from the Library of Congress

ISBN 978-1-64411-220-5 (print)
ISBN 978-1-64411-221-2 (ebook)

Printed and bound in the United States by Lake Book Manufacturing, Inc.
The text stock is SFI certified. The Sustainable Forestry Initiative® program
promotes sustainable forest management.

10 9 8 7 6 5 4 3 2 1

Text design by Virginia Scott Bowman and layout by Debbie Glogover
This book was typeset in Garamond Premier Pro with Hermann, Mordova, Gill
Sans MT Pro, and Myriad Pro used as display fonts

To send correspondence to the author of this book, mail a first-class letter to the
author c/o Inner Traditions • Bear & Company, One Park Street, Rochester, VT
05767, and we will forward the communication.

Contents

Lucky Charms, Amulets, and Mascots

The great truth, or the absolute truth, makes itself visible to our mind through the invisible.

GEORGES VANTONGERLOO

TALISMANS AND AMULETS

Amulets and talismans, which include lucky charms and mascots, are carried or worn for essentially magical purposes. They are carried, worn, or displayed for their efficacy in preserving the wearer from hurt, bodily or spiritual. People who use them believe they are protected, assisted, or healed by a benevolent influence that is inherent within the objects, whose forms and variants compose a "code of symbols, accompanied by traditions which explain them" (Lethaby 1891, 2). However there is a difference between amulets and talismans.

An amulet may be a natural object possessing a particular intrinsic power: it may be a notable mineral object like a gem, a naturally holed stone, or a fossil, or it may be a whole or part of an animal or a plant, a human-made artifact, or a found object. Amulets exert their power whether or not they have been consecrated. An amulet or talisman may be seen as bringing luck, health, wealth, and happiness while preempting and averting harm. The mechanism by which luck, health, wealth, and happiness are achieved may be protective, by deflecting, blocking, or impeding demonic interference, or attractive, by bring-ing in or creating positive energies. Of course an amulet may do both. Writing about Flemish amulets early in the twentieth century, W. L. Hildburgh noted that some may be amuletic in their original intention while others may not, but be used as amulets nevertheless (Hildburgh 1908b, 200). Amuletic lucky charms, whose intrinsic power comes from their shape and associations, need not be empow-ered through ritual. Their forms often symbolize spiritual principles, and they give an opportunity for master craftspeople to produce work of exceptional beauty and power.

The word *talisman* has the meaning of objects bearing sigils, seals, or magical or religious texts that have been empowered by consecration or ritual. Like amulets, their function is to protect the person from evil, illness, and bodily harm. Talismans are material supporters of spiritual powers. They are artifacts charged by ceremonial consecration to pos-sess specific energies. The nature of a talisman depends entirely on the ritual actions enacted during its preparation and the intent put into it. If it is a written text, the intention of the scribe and the meaning of the inscription endow it with their power. Each talisman is individual. It embodies a specific function known to the user, so that, when carried or worn on the person, it evokes its powers within the user internally

Fig. I.1. Shield-knot tile amulet

as well as externally. Talisman makers strive to ensure that the magical virtues of the materials they use relate to the intended use. Only when inner powers and purpose are in perfect alignment can a talisman function properly.

Elizabeth Villiers proposed a theory on "how mascots gain their power": that they do not contain intrinsic power but rather attract influences. "Originally the word 'influence,'" she wrote, "was used astrologically and referred only to the occult power, the virtue, that was believed to flow from the planets to affect all things on earth. Thus the word is used in its strictest sense if we say that mascots have no power of their own, but serve to attract the influence of the Unknown and thus they benefit mankind" (Villiers 1923, 6). She claimed that no mascot will bring good fortune to one who is unworthy of it (Villiers 1923, 1).

Chapter 1

Functions

The functions and uses of amulets, talismans, charms, and mascots are numerous. Because something is labeled as one or the other does not mean that it has the same use as another similarly labeled. The meaning ascribed to a particular amulet or class of amulet at one place and time may not be the same that it had at another place and time. Meanings are a matter of cultural agreement, and even something like a religious text encapsulated in a charm can have a number of different meanings and interpretations in different places and at different times. Talismans created for individuals for a specific purpose have a known meaning to the maker and owner. But even they may pass to another by gift, sale, inheritance, or theft and thereafter be thought of in other ways.

Usually amulets, talismans, and charms are ascribed a specific function, such as to attract good luck, to preserve good luck, to avoid bad luck, to block evil spirits, and to deflect or divert the evil eye. They may invoke the assistance of divine or supernatural beings, guard against plague and pestilence, ward off wild animals, and be a safeguard against sudden or violent death. They may serve to alleviate suffering, assist in childbirth, and heal illnesses. They can remind the carrier of religious beliefs and obligations. They can increase confidence, suppress fear, and bring hope to the owner. They have many functions; even the ubiquitous lucky horseshoe may be used to boost the chances of a gambler, deter evil spirits, assist a bride, keep a wild horse away from the stable, or frustrate the machinations of ill-wishers.

But even in the days when almost everyone had faith in amulets, charms, and talismans, it was recognized that wearing or carrying them did not absolve the user from using common sense, taking care, and being aware of signs, both physical and otherworldly. In the nineteenth century the coal miners of the Black Country in the West Midlands of England were on the lookout for "the seven deadly signs." Originating before the eighteenth century, these were bad omens, some in dreams, which, if foolishly ignored on the way to work in the mine, would certainly lead to the death of the miner down below. Here is a list called the Colliers' Guide of Signs and Warnings, which formerly hung in the Cockfighters' Arms public house in Wednesbury, Staffordshire.*

1. To dream of a broken shoe is a sure sign of danger.
2. If you meet a woman at the rising of the sun, turn again from the pit. A sure sign of danger.
3. To dream of a fire is a sure sign of danger.
4. To see a bright light in ye mine is a sure sign to flee away.
5. If Gabriel's Hounds bin aboute, do not work that day.
6. When foule smells be aboute, ye pit, a sure sign that the imps *bin anneare* [in standard English, "are near"—NP].
7. To charm away ghosts and ye like, take a Bible and a key. Hold both in ye right hand and say ye Lord's Prayer and they will right speedily get farre away.

The seventh of these signs is a means of driving away evil spirits, and the seventh "deadly sign" proper is to see a robin on the handle of the local water pump. On the south coast of England, the quarrymen of the Isle of Portland watched out for similar deadly signs and, although almost everyone carried an amulet of one kind or another, refused to work for the day if one appeared on their way to work. It was better to have no pay that day than to be injured or killed.

---

*[Because this is a work particularly about historical magic in England, the places discussed are mostly places in England. Readers can assume any place named is in England unless it is otherwise designated (e.g., Perugia, Italy) or universally known (e.g., Paris, Berlin). —. *Ed.*]

Chapter 2

The Attitude of Authority toward Amulets

Whether by default or deliberately, the contemporary world attempts, usually successfully, to force the calculating mind on us all. The meditative, eldritch mind is prevented from manifesting by external forces that compel the individual to be constantly calculating what to do in order to conform and not be punished for doing spontaneously something that is disapproved of currently. Consequently the mind is closed to spontaneity, oblivious to the appearance of *ostenta* of any kind. The mind is attached compulsorily to the contingent needs of society thrust on it during every waking moment. Totalitarian religion and politics operate on this principle, not allowing anyone within their grasp to escape from this state of mind, which requires continuous and unbroken awareness of avoiding thinking or doing anything contrary to the authorities' requirements.

But centralized authorities in the most dictatorial of states cannot "win the hearts and minds" of every person under their jurisdiction. Even if autonomy and dissidence is silenced by force and threat of force, proscribed feelings and beliefs will persist among those who cannot or will not go along with the official belief system. The medieval church, in its periodic outbursts of zeal, persecuted astrologers, fortune-tellers, alchemists, magicians, and amulet makers for practicing in areas of human experience forbidden by religious doctrine. Those who did not follow church teachings—Jews, pagans, atheists, and those who held nonstandard Christian ideas that got them branded as superstitious heretics—were persecuted and often killed in church-sponsored witch hunts and pogroms. But as Reverend Christopher Wordsworth observed in 1903, "Amulets were forbidden in centuries the sixth to the tenth. But they still survived" (Wordsworth 1903, 397). As it had been in European countries, in colonial territories, indigenous religion was extirpated, sacred images were burned, and the wearing of amulets and talismans was prohibited. Despite these totalitarian attempts over centuries, policing beliefs and practices ultimately proved futile.

Fig. 2.1. A runic bracteate, twentieth century

The Latin word for superstition, *superstitio,* from which contemporary concepts come, originated in Roman pagan times, describing the excessive performance of religious rites and ceremonies. Cicero described it as empty fear of the gods, rather than proper observances. To do more than is strictly necessary is to be superstitious. Seneca even wrote a whole treatise on superstitio, but it is lost. The word *superstitio* was absorbed into the terminology of the early Roman Catholic Church, which was then attempting to extinguish practices and beliefs that stemmed from the pagan religions that it supplanted. It also took on the meaning of "things that stand over" (from a previous time), that is, things that are considered worthless or even harmful anachronisms. The idea of superstition was taken up later by Protestants and applied to the practices of Catholic religion, such as the veneration of images. Following the Protestant denunciation of "popery" as superstitious, the word was taken up by atheist rationalists and positivists who claimed that because science now explained the world, all magic and religion were superstition and thus worthless things that had to be abolished before "mankind" could progress.

During the imperialist period the magical, religious, and symbolic practices of native cultures were decried as superstition by the Christian missionaries and the many rationalist anthropologists from Europe and the United States who reported them. Similarly the customs, rites, and ceremonies of indigenous Europeans, such as witchcraft, folk magic, and the use of charms and divination, were seen as superstition by the ruling classes, who attempted to destroy them. The name of one African religious cult, Mumbo-Jumbo, even became a word in English that means meaningless superstition.

This historical background means that when the word *superstition* is used by someone, there is a wealth of attached meaning. It carries connotations of primitivity, not in the meaning of unsophistication, but as something rendered obsolete and unnecessary by rational civilization. Given its religious gloss, it also designates a degree of provocative willfulness, a deliberate and perverse intention by the practitioner not to see the truth and to continue in error.

The use of amulets, shunned as witchcraft, was actually fueled by preachers in their own countries and the colonies who warned of imminent visitations by the devil and his infernal legions if their congregations did not conform to impossibly strict religious regulations. Accidents, illnesses, and misfortunes were blamed on the activities of evil spirits acting under the orders of the devil. The world was teeming with evil spirits just waiting for a chance to do harm to those human beings who were not pious enough. Clearly it was a dangerous world, and a few hours in church on Sundays and holy days were not enough to protect against the ever-present danger of demonic attack.

Fig. 2.2. Runic cross of Johannes Bureus

Although it was strictly against early Christian teachings, the church catered to the need for protection against the Demonic Empire by issuing consecrated talismans that included crosses, medallions of saints, and religious texts to be carried by individuals wherever they went. Pilgrim badges depicting the saint to whose shrine the devotee had traveled were prized for their protective qualities. These talismans also functioned as shields against ill-wishing by witches and attacks by people possessing the evil eye. To be empowered, they were touched against the relics of the shrine. Parallel to this service, which was provided (at a cost) by the Catholic Church, there were traditional amulets whose nature varied with place and era, an "underground" magical practice in parallel with the church's. Often, as today, they appeared as ornamental jewelry, not overtly magical or religious in function to the casual observer. The *cimaruta* of Naples is perhaps the most persistent of these charms.

In Protestant countries, once Catholic images and practices had been destroyed, there were no priests to consecrate religious talismans against these spiritual and magical dangers. The veneration of saints, once the bedrock of sacred talismans, was abolished, and their shrines were dug up, looted, and dispersed. Fragments of these shrines and parts of saints' bodies were taken away clandestinely by believers and

Fig. 2.3. Locators' guild tin with Masonic square and compass sigil

preserved, becoming amulets in the process. Amulets and talismans (consecrated by special rites) of underground magical practice took on a greater significance. Rites and ceremonies of secret rural fraternities also employed symbolic amulets and talismans known only to sworn initiates.

Chapter 3

Amulets in Rationalism and Modernism

In the late nineteenth century, rationalists, positivists, socialists, and communists decried religion and superstition as hindrances to social progress. Campaigns were also waged against vanity, conspicuous consumption, and the use of ornament and finery that had no mundane, functional purpose. In his 1899 book *The Theory of the Leisure Class,* Thorsten Veblen linked delinquency with "a superstitious habit of mind." The delinquent, he asserted, "is a great believer in luck, spells, divination, and destiny, and in omens and shamanistic ceremony" (Veblen [1899] 1973, 75). A few years later, echoing the Italian criminologist Lombroso, the Austrian architect Adolf Loos railed against ornament in a highly influential polemic titled *Ornament und Verbrechen* (Ornament and crime), in which he equated the intimidating tattoos of criminals with ornament in general. Loos presented ornament as a symbol of deviant behavior that must be eliminated. It was very much part of the theory of degeneracy of people and society that was fashionable in the early twentieth century. In its most extreme form, this thinking led to the gulags and the Holocaust.

What Loos either chose to ignore or was actually ignorant of was that *ornament,* properly applied, has a spiritual meaning. The Latin word *ornare* has a meaning of "preparation, to make ready," that is, to prepare a sacred place, making it fit and ready for the entry of the deity. Ornament properly means making something spiritually acceptable,

Fig. 3.1. Wheat sheaf amulet of abundant harvest, horse brass (also see color plate 1)

not just something arbitrary that pleases the human eye. To ornament meant to bedeck a shrine with offerings that would invoke the deity, to make it fit for the spirit to enter. Ornament was not something inessential added arbitrarily to please the eye; it was an intrinsic part of the rite of sanctification.

The possibility of this very process was forgotten and denigrated by those who held modernism to be a progressive break from all tradition and sought to wipe out all remembrance of spiritual practice in the furtherance of a brave new world. Even those who collected and studied amulets and charms saw their continued use in the modern age as somewhat unexpected. "Strange to say," wrote the archaeologist Sir W. M. Flinders Petrie in 1914, "a large part of the children of the lower classes wear them; and the extent to which persons of supposed education will wear charms and mascots is an extraordinary revelation of the real fatuity and savagery of the mind of modern man" (Petrie 1914, 1). Their proliferation in the Great War that began in the year Petrie published his book was a matter of concerned study and comment. In 1920 Giuseppe Bellucci noted that Italian soldiers in that war had carried all sorts of traditional amulets but also new ones fashioned from fragments of munitions (Bellucci 1920, 14). A. R. Wright, in 1928, echoed Bellucci: "Much more astonishing than the revival of some ancient amulets, is the enormous outburst of new ones, and importation and adoption of foreign amulets, under the less 'superstitious' name of mascots" (Wright 1928, 73).

By this time religious images that somehow had escaped destruction were seen as "works of art" to be looked at rather than venerated. Even venerable relics were taken from working cathedrals and put in museum cabinets. This process applied also to sacred items taken from the colonies and displayed in museums as examples of primitive exotic artistry. But this approach denies the perception of the eldritch, the supernatural, that makers and users know is present in sacred images, amulets, and talismans. As Frederick Thomas Elworthy noted, "The monks of old saw the goblins they carved through the eye of undoubting belief" (Elworthy 1895, 231). André Malraux noted that when the images were made, to both artisan and devotee, Venus *was* Venus and a crucifix *was* Christ crucified (Malraux 1954, 52). For the concept of art to come into being, such artifacts need to be desacralized—removed from their context and put on show elsewhere in a secular place.

The architectural movement tellingly called *purism,* founded in 1918, actively promoted the faith that ornament, amulets, and mascots were outmoded remnants of primitive barbaric societies and had been rendered unnecessary by the new, clean, scientific-rational, concrete-and-glass world of the twentieth century. War had cleansed the old world, just as the futurist Filippo Tommaso Emilio Marinetti had promised. At the same time, the Weimar-era Bauhaus movement in Germany sought to "start again from zero" and make a clean sweep of all reference to the past. The main protagonists of purism were Amedeé Ozenfant, whose nickname was "Saugnier," and Charles-Édouard Jeanneret, who tellingly took the pseudonym "Le Corbusier," after the medieval workmen who were employed to clean crow droppings from churches. The purists saw ornament as the equivalent of abhorrent bird droppings and so produced sterile, blank surfaces, which, they believed, would raise human society to a higher level. The use of such pseudonyms was prevalent among Marxists of the period—Lenin, Trotsky, and Stalin being the best known. There was no place in modernism for natural energies or divine powers, let alone talismans and amulets. The brave new world would stride forward toward a bright shiny rational future where the "new man" would be forged. But they failed. Lucky charms, amulets, and talismans continued to be made, found, and used.

It is a matter of consciousness. The contemporary world attempts, usually successfully, to force the calculating mind on us all. The meditative, eldritch mind is prevented from manifesting by external forces that compel the individual to be constantly calculating what to do in order to conform. The possession and use of charms, amulets, and talismans is an antidote to this, for they serve no one but the user. The pig charm described on page 123 expresses this perfectly.

Fig. 3.2. Equal-armed cross with sigils of the four seasons,
Alsace, France

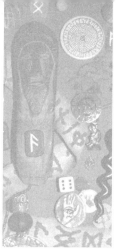

Chapter 4

Amulets, Talismans, Charms, and the Law

Over many centuries in the West, charms have come into conflict with the law. Christian prohibitions on pagan sacred items and magical texts were enforced from the beginning. Accounts of the successful attempts by missionaries to obliterate indigenous practices are sometimes the only record of them. The texts that record these events are written in glowing praise of what can now be seen as cultural genocide, so they must be read accordingly. Also practices by Christian priests that were identical in principle with the things they deplored are described in different terms by their apologists. A new terminology was invented to describe them so that they appeared different from the pagan and magical practices they supplanted. Magical and talismanic texts, written by priests, were permissible because they had new Latin names. They could be used in exactly the same way their pagan forerunners had been. But they were presented as good and godly, while the forerunners were condemned as evil and satanic.

In Flanders, like all the other missionaries, Saint Eligius (588–660) attempted to destroy the indigenous pagan religion and practices, including the use of amulets and talismans. He prohibited *vetulae* (straw plaits) and amulets hung around the necks of humans and animals. Women were forbidden to hang amber from their necks and to call on their goddess in their weaving and dyeing of cloth. But around the same time in pagan Zealand, where missionaries had not arrived

Fig. 4.1. Bindrune Gibu Auja,
meaning good luck

to destroy the local culture, a runic pendant was being made with the inscription "*Harihua* I am called I give good luck" (Macleod and Mees 2006, 94). The Gibu Auja "good luck" formula was never destroyed and appears now on contemporary runic amulets.

Six hundred years later, in 1224, Saint Francis of Assisi was producing similar amulets to be hung round the neck—written Christian religious texts bearing divine names and blessings. It was deemed proper to do this for people, so long as no payment was made for the service (Skemer 2006, 176). Such texts were assembled in various ways, often in a small pouch containing paper folded in an intricate manner. These items were called variously a *chartula, litterula,* or *schedula* (Skemer 2006, 172). They were bound to the body as phylacteries. Sometimes a number of them were assembled as kits and kept in special boxes. Printed Austrian *Breverls* from the seventeenth century onward are a later example of religious textual amulets.

Many Christian literary amulets and talismans originated in the Jewish tradition, and this connection was recognized and disapproved of by hard-line priests. Hebrew magic squares and grids such as the Aiq Beker, "the Qabalah of Nine Chambers," were significant models for non-Jewish magic squares, both numerical and literary (Pennick 1992a, 8–42). Magic letters squares such as the SATOR and others associated with medieval magic entered folk tradition and produced local variants such as the RATS (fig. 4.2). Historically such homemade amulets were in competition with the official exorcisms of priests, which cost money. The diminishing triangle amulet ABRACADABRA, which has a Hebrew counterpart, and the smaller Wattish'ka triangle of letters, an amulet against fire, are other examples of vernacular tradition (Pennick 1992a, 38).

Fig. 4.2. Literary magic square amulet to drive away rats, circa 1990

In fourteenth-century England the *Fasciculum morum,* a Franciscan textbook manual for preachers, warned of Tilsters, laypeople who attempted to effect cures by the laying on of "false charms." These charms included Christian textual amulets. But this was deemed to be witchcraft inspired by the devil (Wenzel 1989, 576). However, according to Raymundus de Peñafort, it was permissible for people to use Christian texts in an amuletic way, so long as they honored God and did not promise immediate results (Skemer 2006, 192). In the early fifteenth century, Ulrich von Pottenstein preached that using amulets was a sign of complicity with the devil. In this he was following the teachings of certain sects of Islam that wearing a *taweez* is a form of *shirk,* that is "ascribing partners to God," hence, is forbidden.

In Iceland the tradition of runic knowledge continued from the settlement times and is unbroken until the present day. Talismanic sigil-magic is extant in a number of medieval magical manuscripts, including the *Galdrabók,* the *Hlíðarendabók,* the *Huld Manuscript,* and the *Kreddur Manuscript,* all preserved in the National Library in Reykjavik. Specific sigils were written on parchment and used to assist people in various walks of life. Some are recognizable from widespread European magical traditions, while others are specific to Iceland. Some

Fig. 4.3. Vegvísir, pyrography on birch wood, Norfolk, 2019 (also see color plate 2)

incorporate runes. *Vegvísir* helped mariners keep on course at sea and ride out storms (fig. 4.3), *veiðistafur* gave success to fishermen, *kaupaloki* helped merchants to close deals and prosper, *Þjófastafur* warded off thieves or exposed their deeds, *angurgapi* was carved on the ends of barrels to prevent leakages, while farmers used *tóustefna* to keep foxes away. Thieves could gain access through locked doors with a *lásabrjótur* (see fig. 4.4.).

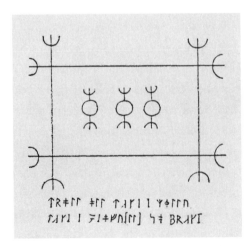

Fig. 4.4. Lásabrjótur, an Icelandic lock breaker amulet used by thieves to gain entry

The use of these and other talismans in playing chess and backgammon and to win wrestling matches was punished heavily. A number of people were burned at the stake for using them (Davídsson 1903, passim; Flowers 1989, 59–103).

The prosecution of amulet sellers and users has a very long history in Europe. In France in 1445 the council at Rouen ordered that people who hung notes and textual amulets around their or their animals' necks should serve a month's imprisonment and practice fasting. In England in 1590 James Sykes from Guiseley, Yorkshire, was brought before the Archbishop's Court in York and accused of having prepared and hung paper amulets on the manes of sick horses in an attempt to cure them (Flowers 1989, 169). In France people nailed Billets de Sainte-Agathe to the walls of houses and stables to defend against fire. Almost three hundred years later, during the First World War (1914–1918), people in Britain and France were being prosecuted for selling charms and amulets to wives and girlfriends of soldiers serving on the front line (Davies 2018, 105–7). Charms came to the notice of the law in England in 1926 when a gypsy named Smith was brought before the magistrates at Higham Ferrers in Northamptonshire and convicted for selling "charms to burn, wear, and put under her pillow." The charm seller was given one month's imprisonment with hard labor (Thompson 1927, 305).

Examples of criminals carrying amulets are, understandably, rare. William Jones noted a piece in *The Graphic* (June 14, 1879) that reported a trial of a burglar in London. He had been caught with a large stash of stolen goods in his house at Mile End, East London. At his trial a police officer noted that a piece of coal had been found on him because "every burglar who carries in his pocket a piece of charmed coal may defy the authorities" (Jones 1880, 193). The Imperial War Museum in London has a coal amulet sent in 1917 during the First World War to a soldier of the City of London Yeomanry by his sister (Davies 2018, 143). The blackness of coal, reflecting the blackness of night in which the burglar cannot be seen, may also have been thought to render the soldier able to defy the enemy's munitions.

Although some charm sellers were prosecuted into the twentieth century, jewelers and industrial manufacturers who did the same thing were not. They were only subject to the ministrations of the taxman.

In 1913 in the United States, a hearing was held by the U.S. Treasury Department about the status of charms for taxation purposes. Four witnesses were called for the government side and six for the importers of jewelry. The Treasury stated that "emblem charms, locket charms, neck-chain charms or pendants, seal charms, and signet charms are included within the class of 'charms.'" But the importers argued that "a charm is an article that is symbolic of something, such as a good-luck charm, a swastika charm, or a horse charm, and that lockets and pendants were never known as charms, but always bought and sold under the specific names." The importers' argument prevailed (McAdoo 1913, 127).

British law also has something to say about mascots. Car mascots (hood ornaments) are subject to legal sanction in the United Kingdom. UK Regulation 53 Road Vehicles (Construction and Use) Regulations 1986 (SI 1986 No. 1078) states that "no mascot, emblem, or other ornamental object shall be carried by a motor vehicle first used on or after 1 October 1937 in any position where it is likely to strike any person with whom the vehicle may collide unless the mascot is not liable to cause injury to such person by reason of any projections thereon." Physical safety is the consideration now, rather than religious fears that mascots and talismans might attract divine retribution.

Chapter 5

Things, Objects, and Places

Things worn around the neck as pendants or carried somewhere on the person are generally amulets. As C. J. S. Thompson characterized them: "the belief that certain objects, natural or artificial, composed of metals, stone, clay, or other materials sometimes possess occult powers capable of protecting those who carry them from danger, disease, or evil influences" (Thompson 1932, 229). Often collections of amulets and talismans are worn together, as on "charm bracelets." They may include beads, objects of stone, coral, amber, silver, and gold, and the claws of eagles and bears, wolves' teeth, toads' bones, and snake vertebrae. Teeth, claws, and bones link the wearer to the corresponding animal powers. In traditional societies animal powers are incorporated into personal identity. The *úlfheðnar* and *berserkir* of Viking times were warriors who drew on the power of the wolf and the bear, respectively, and in later medieval times, kings such as Heinrich der Löwe (Henry the Lion) of Saxony, Richard Cœur de Lion (Lionheart) of England, and Henry the Lion of Scotland drew on the power of the lion for their fighting prowess.

Charms are amulets that have the power to hold the unknown at bay. They serve as protection against unknown and unprecedented events. Elizabeth Villiers, writing in 1923, described the universal attraction of luck-bringing charms:

The airman carries his luck bringer in his "bus" when he attempts his greatest flights; the motorist has a mascot on his car. Tennis players, even the most celebrated champions, go to the courts thus protected, so boxers enter the ring. Cricketers and footballers go to the ground with their mascots, while the thousands of spectators who watch the matches carry the chosen luck-bringers of their favourites, hoping to give them victory. In racing it is the same, and it is well known that gamblers have the greatest belief in luck bringers. . . . The lover places his ring—a mascot—on his sweetheart's finger; the bride goes to the altar carrying her mascot of white flowers; the mother buys her baby the coral and bells, which are the mascots of childhood. The businessman has a paper-weight on his desk, and its shape is that of a horseshoe or a stag or an elephant—all-important mascots to bring commercial success. Recently an explorer set sail after having been presented with so many mascots by admirers that he was obliged to leave most of them behind, while a man tried for his life at the Old Bailey, stood in the dock with a row of mascots behind him. (Villiers 1923, 9–10)

Thompson had this to add concerning wartime talismans:

During the Great War, many of the German prisoners were found to be in possession of talismans, chiefly consisting of written charms or cabalistic letters inscribed on paper, which they carried both to protect them from harm, disease or death. . . . Such talismans were probably of ancient origin and appear to have been handed down in country districts in Germany from one generation to another. (Thompson 1932, 253)

Villiers defined the spiritual rules that govern the use of luck-bringers. She asserted that only a charm that had been given as a gift to the owner could be effective. If one bought one for one's own use or obtained it unjustly, then its power would be ineffective. Furthermore, if one is an unworthy person, it will not bring good fortune (Villiers 1923, 1). Mascots are said to be most powerful if they are worn on the left side

(Villiers 1923, 1). The meaning of the word *mascot* has altered since Villiers's time. *Mascot* originated in France around 1867, with a general meaning of "a lucky charm, an amulet, or talisman." Popularized by Edmond Audran in his opera *La Mascotte* (1880), it was absorbed into English with the same meaning. Subsequently the meaning of the word has become restricted to a lucky image, often a person in costume who functions as a cheerleader at sporting events. From the 1970s the rock bands the Grateful Dead and Iron Maiden have had skeletal images as their logos, mascots called Skeleton Sam and Eddie, respectively.

PLACES OF SPIRIT

During the ninth and tenth centuries, the uninhabited island of Iceland was colonized by Norse settlers from Norway and Scotland. Their response to the ensouled landscape is recorded in the *Landnámabók,* the book of land-taking. It is a unique record, for all other historic colonizations were of lands already inhabited by indigenous peoples whom the incoming settlers fought and conquered. Also the Norse settlers were not Christians, so they were acutely aware of the spiritual qualities of the land they had entered. Certain areas were not settled at all because they were reserved for the *landvættir,* the "land wights" or local spirits. At notable places, rites and ceremonies were performed in honor of the landvættir, and offerings were left for them. Some continue to honor the land wights today. Religions that view the local spirits as spiritual vermin to be extirpated do not relate to the land in the same way.

This was the way in pre-Christian Europe in general, for ancestral holy places—homesteads, grave mounds, tombs, and battlefields—were venerated as dwelling places of ancestral spirits, which were not seen as necessarily malevolent. Sagas, legends, and folktales recounted notable events that occurred there, which explained the meaning of their names. Gods, heroes, spirits, demons, events of death and destruction, apparitions, and accidents are recalled in place-names and their associated stories. Some remain today, places where people can experience transcendent states of timeless consciousness, receive spiritual inspiration, and accept healing. Materials from such places, such as dust scraped

Fig. 5.1. Castlerigg Stone Circle, Cumbria

from standing stones, were (and are) considered somehow to contain some of the power.

It is possible to carry away the inherent magical properties of materials from specific places deemed sacred. Twigs, cones, fruit, seeds, and fragments of wood from holy trees can be made into amulets, either unaltered or by transformation into images. Likewise pieces of stone chipped from sacred megaliths or other images contain the sacred power. Even cloths dipped in the blood of slain heroes or martyrs. Even in a secular context, the Socialist hymn "The Red Flag" expresses the symbolism of the cloth stained with the blood of those who have died for the cause.

For thousands of years small sacred images and talismans have been sold at places of pilgrimage to be taken back home by pilgrims as a token that they have been there and also as powerful objects in their own right. Tourists' souvenirs are a secular continuation of these relics of pilgrimage. This is what André Malraux called the persisting life of certain forms reemerging again and again like specters from the

Fig. 5.2. Bottle of water
from the Marian shrine
at Walsingham, Norfolk,
circa 1995

past (Malraux 1954, 13). Dust from standing stones and graveyards, pieces of sacred trees, wood from trees in Nazareth and Jerusalem or the British Royal Oak, Irish stones, or water from the river Jordan, the Zamzam Well at Mecca, Holywell, or Walsingham are all instances of this. Grave dirt, imbued with the essence of the dead, is an important ingredient in certain powders used by practitioners of hoodoo.

Chapter 6

Lucky Numbers, Randomness, and Numerology

In ancient times and in traditional cultures today, there are no concepts of randomness and mathematical probability. All events are seen within the bounds of a theory of total control, as acts of invisible divine or supernatural beings. Religions that teach of a transcendent, all-knowing, all-powerful god cannot conceive of randomness. Mathematics is seen as a manifestation of the god, essentially carrying out his will. The concept of probability is unthinkable, for every event that occurs must be

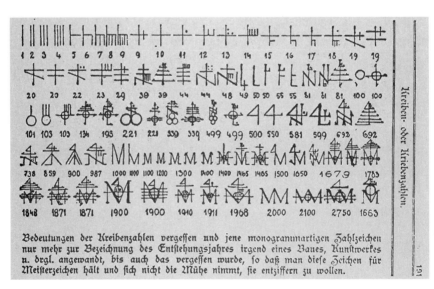

Fig. 6.1. Stave numbers as recorded by Guido von List, 1917

an act of God. Nothing can happen without God's agency. God's will controls everything down to the last speck of dust and drop of rain. The inevitable consequence of this theory is that everything that happens is preordained. Everything has been decided in advance by God and so is unchangeable. Prohibitions of divination to determine the future are always part of religions that teach infallible total control of everything by God. But because this deterministic belief denies all free will, it is arguable that those who carry out acts prohibited by religion are actually acting under the aegis of God's will as much as those who follow the precepts. They can do no other.

As a concept randomness lies outside this deterministic belief system. Often the word *random* denotes unpredictable, haphazard, incoherent, or chaotic happenings—actions done without conscious choice, without objective or purpose. Mathematically the concept of randomness is not chaotic, but it signifies a lack of predictability that nevertheless obeys the laws of probability. It is this sort of randomness that exists in divination systems using numbers to denote readings. Randomness is described formally in mathematics and statistics. Assigning a numerical value to each possible outcome of an event produces what is known as a random variable. This allows the probabilities of any event to be calculated.

Pythagoras taught that number was the first principle of all things. Pythagorean principles saw numbers as the source of geometrical figures. Lucky numbers are explained in Pythagorean symbolism.

1. **The Monad:** A single point; the essential, primal, indivisible beginning, and the source of all numbers, perfection, and goodness.
2. **The Dyad:** Departure from unity, doubling, loss of singleness, excess, and the beginning of imperfection in duality. The line joining two points.
3. **The Triad:** The restoration of harmony through the triangular balance of forces; the plane surface.
4. **The Tetrad:** Foursquare stability in the square and the cross. The first feminine square: 2×2.

5. **The Pentad:** The pentagram, uniting the first female number, two, with the first male, three, in mystic union. It is the origin of the golden section, and the pentagram is its sigil.

Fig. 6.2. Pentagram amulet with beads and bells
(also see color plate 3)

6. **The Hexad:** The first perfect number. Six is the perfect number because it reflects nature in that it is composed of nothing but its own parts. Six is the sum of 1 + 2 + 3, and the product of the multiplication of the first feminine and masculine numbers, 2 × 3. In square measure it is the area of the 3, 4, 5 triangle, and the division of the circumference of a circle by its own radius. Geometrically it is the hexagon. Its sigil is the hexagram.

Fig. 6.3. Hexagram with Hebrew texts on the gate of a Jewish graveyard, Middelburg, the Netherlands (also see color plate 4)

7. **The Heptad:** This is the virgin number, for 7 has neither factors nor is it a product.

8. **The Octad:** This is the first cube, the product of 2 × 2 × 2.

Fig. 6.4. Octagram amulet, England, circa 1960

Fig. 6.5. A Tibetan Buddhist amulet with nine amuletic emblems

9. **The Nonad** (shown above): This is the first masculine square: 3 × 3.

10. **The Decad:** This contains all the archetypal numbers, 1 + 2 + 3 + 4, as the *tetraktys*.

Other significant numbers according to Pythagoras include:

- **Twenty-seven:** The first masculine cube: 3 × 3 × 3.
- **Twenty-eight:** The second perfect number: 1 + 2 + 3 + 4 + 5 + 6 + 7.
- **Thirty-five:** The sum of the first feminine and the first masculine cubes: 8 + 27.
- **Thirty-six:** The product of the first square numbers: 4 × 9; the sum of the first three cubes: 1 + 8 + 27; and, as the sum of the first eight numbers, 1 + 2 + 3 + 4 + 5 + 6 + 7 + 8, and as the square of the first perfect number, 6 × 6, is the third perfect number.

Magic squares, where sequential numbers are arranged in a square so that lines of numbers all add up to the same sum, are amuletic. They are related to the astrological planets and used for both amulets and in talismanic magic. The smallest is the square of Saturn, with nine numbers, whose lines all add up to fifteen. The sixteen-number square is Jupiter's, Mars's is twenty-five, the Sun thirty-six, Venus forty-nine, Mercury sixty-four, and the moon has eighty-one numbers (Pennick 1992a, 34–37).

Fig. 6.6. Ceramic amuletic plaque with magic square of Saturn and labyrinth, England, 1985

Fig. 6.7. Talisman with magic square and planetary sigils (also see color plate 5)

The belief in lucky numbers is ancient and persists today in everyday life as well as in the more specialized area of gambling. Several ancient alphabets had no separate numbers, but used letters to represent them. The Roman alphabet is different because it is the least symbolic of the Western alphabets, having no special names and meanings for each letter. Hence Roman numerals, still in use today, were developed. Hebrew, Greek, and the runic alphabets all have names for the letters, with particular meanings and connections. Any amulet or talisman using a single letter in any of these three character sets will embody both the given meaning of each character as well as its numerical value. Although Roman characters can stand for their numbers in the alphabetical sequence, it is more a code than a symbolic system. Numerology using the Roman alphabet simply numbers the letters in sequence from one to twenty-six, then adds the numbers of a name together in order to get a single figure. So if, for instance, a name adds up to 351, 3 + 5 + 1 = 9.

The Hebrew system, however, is both different and filled with symbolic meaning. The first nine are single figures; the second 1 Aleph; 2 Bayt; 3 Ghimel; 4 Daleth; 5 He; 6 Vau; 7 Zayn; 8 Hayt; 9 Tayt; 10 Yod; 20 Kaph; 30 Lamech; 40 Mem; 50 Nun; 60 Samekh; 70 Ayn; 80 Fay; 90 Tzadde; 100 Qoph; 200 Raysh; 300 Shin; 400 Tau.

As there are only twenty-four characters, the final five are given to the modified characters forming final letters. Thus 500 is the final Kaph; 600 final Mem; 700 final Nun; 800 final Fay; and 900 final Tzadde.

The Greek system follows the Hebrew, with digits, tens and hundreds. The final numbers use Greek letters that had become obsolete even in Classical times. In both Jewish and Greek number-magic, names that add up to any particular number have a mystic link. The word is symbolic of the number it represents. Thus, in Greek, the names of the chief god, Zeus, ΔΙΟΣ "Dios" and ΘΕΟΣ "Thios," both have the same numerical value, 284. The number of the name of the marine god ΠΟΣΕΙΔΟΝ (Poseidon) is 1219, the same number as his fish, ΙΧΘΥΣ (ichthus). Correspondences such as this are believed to demonstrate links and are used on a magical level.

There are several alternative systems of runic numerology. One is given here. The most used runic numerological system ascribes a sequential number to each rune, as in the Roman alphabet. Scandinavian and Baltic runic calendars used runes in this way. The first sixteen numbers were the runes of the sixteen-character Younger Futhark, while numbers seventeen to nineteen were represented by three further exclusively numerical runes. In the earlier twenty-four-rune Common Germanic Futhark, which is used by most runesters today, the runes signify the numbers from one to twenty-four. Because the letter sequence is different in the runes, these numbers do not correspond with phonetically similar characters in other alphabets. Unlike the Roman alphabet, as in Hebrew and Greek numerology, the runic system does not reduce the final number to a single figure by addition. According to this particular system, the numerical meanings of the twenty-four runes can be given as follows:

1. **Fehu:** Unity
2. **Uruz:** Two horns, spiritual substance
3. **Thurisaz:** Triangle, enclosed energy
4. **Ansuz:** Universal coming-into-being, the soul of the cosmos
5. **Raidho:** Universal life
6. **Kenaz:** Divine intelligence/illumination
7. **Gebo:** A gift (lucky seven)
8. **Wunjo:** Balance
9. **Hagalaz:** The substance of being, the nine worlds
10. **Nauðhiz:** Potential force
11. **Isa:** Static force
12. **Jara:** The twelve months of the year, harvest
13. **Eihwaz:** Destruction/creation (unlucky 13)
14. **Perdhro:** Involution, entry of spirit into matter
15. **Elhaz:** Destiny
16. **Sowilo:** Divine power
17. **Teiwaz:** Wisdom, judgment, immortality
18. **Berkana:** New beginnings, a higher plane (twice nine)
19. **Ehwaz:** The solar/lunar number, transmission, correspondence
20. **Mannaz:** Actualized force
21. **Laguz:** Flow, facilitation of the will
22. **Inguz:** Connection, expansion

23. **Othala:** The "weird" number, things beyond conscious experience

24. **Dagaz:** Day, the twenty-four-hour cycle.

The total of the rune row adds up to 300 (see Pennick 1992b, 136–37).

Fig. 6.8. *Ex-Voto XI* of Nigel Pennick's *Ex-Voto* series of amuletic artworks, exhibited at the Walkers' Gallery, San Marcos, Texas, 2013 (also see color plate 6)

In addition to numerical equivalents, alphabetic and runic characters also possess numerous other correspondences that must be taken into account when making amulets with them. A combination of letters can have a significant and specific esoteric meaning, and one must take care to enhance a letter amulet's qualities by recognizing this.

Fig. 6.9. Runic amulet for wealth,
polymer clay and metal,
made by Nigel Pennick, 2019

Chapter 7

The Meaning of Numbers

In numerology all numbers have a meaning. But in common usage in the West, only particular numbers are considered lucky or unlucky, the most significant being seven and thirteen, lucky and unlucky, respectively. The symbolic meaning of each number may be linked to its use as a lucky number or not, depending on the individual's belief and knowledge. Some, such as thirteen, have a wealth of associations and meanings.

Five: The Quincunx

Five, the Pythagorean pentad, is "a peculiar and a magical number used by the Greeks and Romans, as an amulet to protect the wearer from evil spirits" (Thompson 1927, 178). Belgian soldiers in World War I had lucky charms with the number five. As a quincunx, one dot surrounded by four others arranged in a square, it is a protective sigil.

Lucky Seven

Astrologically ascribed to the sign of Cancer, seven is said to be "the number of lofty self-sacrifice and of all the higher virtues" (Villiers 1923, 119). Seven is the biblical number of divine abundance, punishment, purification, and penitence. It appears 507 times in the Bible. The Christian religion taught that the Holy Spirit confers seven gifts on the believer: wisdom, understanding, blessing, strength, honor, glory, and true godliness. The Orthodox and Roman Catholic churches also recognize seven sacraments. They are baptism, confirmation, the Eucharist, penance, anointing the sick, holy orders, and matrimony (Chapman 2007, 103). In traditional magical belief, a seventh son of a seventh son possesses the power of healing, and the seventh daughter of a seventh daughter, the power of seeing into the future. The Theosophist C. W. Leadbeater taught that there are seven jewels that channel the Seven Rays of Development through which evolution occurs. On a more prosaic level, "lucky seven" is a talisman for luck in all eventualities, most especially in gambling. In the 1950s a high-speed train in Italy was called Il Settebello (the Lucky Seven).

In their 1908 book *The History of Signboards*, Jacob Larwood and John Camden Hotten explained the preeminence of the number seven. Writing about a woman who claimed to be a seeress and who told fortunes at Seven Dials in London, Larwood and Hotten wrote:

> Generally they proclaimed themselves the seventh daughter of a seventh daughter, a relationship that is still thought to be accompanied by powers not vouchsafed to ordinary mortals. This belief in the virtue of the number seven doubtless originated from the Old Testament, where that number seems in greater favour than all others. The books of Moses are full of references to it; the creation of the world in seven days, sevenfold vengeance on whosoever slayeth Cain; Noah had to take seven males and females of every clean beast, seven males and females of every fowl of the air, for in seven days it would begin to rain; the ark rested in the seventh month, &c. From this the Middle Ages borrowed their predilection for this number, and its cabalistic power. (Larwood and Hotten 1908, 1985, 182)

Nine: The Magic Number of the North

Nine is the sacred number of the Northern Tradition, of prime importance. It is "the power of three times three" invoked in traditional magic. Nine is the runic number of Hagalaz, the substance of being, the nine worlds (Pennick 1992b, 137). Odin hung on the windswept tree for nine days and nine nights in order to obtain the runes. Traditional lore tells that the waves of an incoming tide come in groups of nine. The cat, a magical animal, is said to have nine lives. Writing in 1834 John Graham Dalyell noted, "In Scotland nine seems to have been always a mystical number." He goes on to describe nine in various Scottish folk magic ceremonies: "Nine enchanted stones were cast or laid for the destruction of a crop. Nine ridges were passed over in the course of a mystical ceremony; a cat was drawn nine times through the crook of a chimney; and a woman was drawn nine times back and forward by the leg for a cure" (Dalyell 1834, 392).

Unlucky and Lucky Thirteen

Thirteen at the table, reflecting Jesus's Last Supper, where he was betrayed by Judas Iscariot, is considered most unlucky. A remarkable means of overcoming this unlucky number is recounted in the section about black cats and Kaspar of the Savoy Hotel, London (see page 131). During World War I soldiers on the Allied side used the number thirteen as a lucky number. There are a number of French postcards issued during that war depicting *porte bonheur* (portable lucky charms). They have a number of talismanic figures, including the number thirteen. In gambling lore, especially in the United States, the principle of reversal is adopted. Things that appear unlucky, such as the skull, skeleton, the number thirteen, and the dead man's hand, become lucky in this "reverse luck" system. French soldiers in the First World War carried amulets of the number thirteen. Originating with gamblers thirteen was adopted by motorcyclists, among which the "outlaw bikers" also took to using "1%" as a badge of honor to signify that they were members of the 1 percent of motorcyclists who gave the others a bad reputation.

Higher Numbers

- **Fifteen:** "Was generally regarded as evil in magic, and was associated with the witches' Sabbath, which was sometimes held on the fifteenth day of the month" (Thompson 1927, 179).
- **Twenty-three:** A number that some have claimed appears with more-than-average frequency in movies. Robert Anton Wilson wrote copiously about the bizarre appearances of the number in life and fiction, as it had been used by Aleister Crowley in his *The*

Book of Lies, where it means "get out" (Crowley [1911] 2018, 676). The term *23 skidoo* was used by U.S. airmen in World War II to denote a shooting-down of an enemy aircraft. The British Royal Air Force sometimes used this number.

- **Forty-three:** "Is a very unlucky number and is associated with death, failure, and destruction" (Thompson 1927, 180). It appears rarely in amulets, but if the principle of reversal were applied, it could be used as one.

"His Number's Up"

A number of military veterans I knew in years past who had fought in various wars on various sides often talked about their fallen comrades in terms of their number "coming up." This is an image taken from gambling, for survival in war is a matter of chance. When a number turns up from a roll of the dice or on the gambling wheel of fortune, that is a moment of definition, an irreversible change, like death. The idea of having a personal number comes from the military practice of giving each recruit a service number upon enlistment. When a soldier died on the battlefield, his comrades would say "his number's up." Being killed in battle is a personal event, the slain seemingly fated to be hit fatally at that particular moment by that particular bullet with his number on it. Just as lucky charms in gambling are believed to assist the punter toward the right number coming up, so mascots carried by soldiers bring luck by not allowing their personal number to come up.

Chapter 8

Lucky and Symbolic Colors

Each color has a symbolic meaning that can be used in making amulets and talismans. The colors of birthstones and planetary connections have meaning to individuals, and that is where amulets, talismans, and mascots get their personal connections. Astrologically particular colors and metals correspond with the planets: gold (yellow) for the sun, silver (white) the moon, blue (copper) Venus, red (iron) Mars, tin (gray) Jupiter, and black (lead) Saturn. Mercury's metal is, of course, quicksilver, another silver color. In astrology the sun and the moon are termed planets. These colors are used in Anglo-French heraldry with the planetary allusions.

Colors in Anglo-French heraldry have specific meanings and are related to corresponding planets, spiritual beings, gems, and talismanic functions. In the fifteenth-century *Boke of St Albans,* Dame Juliana Berners described the origin and meaning of the color system in Anglo-French heraldry.

> The law of arms, the which was effigured and begun before any law in the world, both the law of nature and before the commandments of God. And this law of arms was grounded upon the nine diverse orders of angels in heaven encrowned with nine diverse precious stones of colours and of virtues diverse also of them are figured the nine colours in arms [spelling modernized]. (Berners 1905)

Anglo-French heraldry uses nine specific colors. There are two variant forms of this. One has two metals, five tinctures, and two furs, while the second has no furs but two additional tinctures. Sometimes the word *tincture* is used wrongly as a general term for all heraldic colors. The two heraldic metals are *or* (gold) and *argent* (silver). For practical purposes the colors yellow and white are generally used. The five tinctures are *azure* (blue), *gules* (red), *sable* (black), *vert* (green), and *purpure* (purple). The two furs are *ermine* and *vair*. They imitate the pelts of the stoat in wintertime and the blue-gray squirrel, respectively. An alternative tincture scheme removed vair and ermine and substituted them with the colors *tenné* (tawny) and *sanguine* or *murrey* (blood red), which did not have planetary correspondences.

Berners relates the seven planetary gems to their corresponding metals and tinctures: *or* is topaz; argent, pearl; sable, diamond; gules, ruby; azure, sapphire; vert, emerald; and purpure, amethyst. The form the color takes is important, for there are special names for jewel-like roundels. Golden roundels are *bezant;* those of silver, *plate;* red, *torteaux;* blue, *hurts;* black, *pellet;* green, *pomeis;* and purple, *golpe.* The final two, tenné and sanguine, are called *orange* and *guzes,* respectively. The color known as tawny was later renamed orange in popular usage, and in the twentieth century, a specific hue was called tango. The color remains only in modern English usage in the name of the tawny owl.

The traditional geocentric view of the cosmos sees it as nine spheres surrounding the Earth concentrically. Outermost is the Primum Mobile (Prime Mover), otherwise called Empyrean or Ninth Heaven. This is the realm of God. Inside this is the Stellar Heaven, the sphere of the Fixed Stars. Below this rotate, respectively, the spheres of Saturn, Jupiter, Mars, the sun, Venus, Mercury, and the sphere of the moon. At the lowest, innermost point is the Earth. Originating in archaic Europe these nine heavens appeared in later Christian cosmology and as the Nine Worlds of Norse myth. The system of Anglo-French heraldry ascribes the metals and tinctures with spiritual virtues related to the powers of the planetary spheres. *Or* signifies and relates to the sun; argent, the moon; sable, Saturn; azure, Jupiter; gules, Mars; vert, Venus; and purpure, Mercury.

The text *Einseignemens notablez aulx poursuivans,* preserved in the College of Arms in London, fits the heraldic tinctures into the scheme of the heavenly hierarchy described by Dionysius the Pseudo-Areopagite. The silvery argent seraphim are "full doughty and glorious." The "unfaint and durable" cherubim reflect the dark sable tincture. Next the Thrones, who are "wise and virtuous in working," bearing the "true blue" loyal tincture azure. Following the Thrones are the Principalities, "hot of courage," who bear the color of the Martian gules. The Dominations, carrying the blood-red sanguine, are "mighty of power," and the Powers, which are tenné, are "fortunate of victory." The Virtues are "knightly of government," with their imperial purpure. The Archangels, who carry vert, are "keen and hardy in battle." Finally the Angels, the "sure messengers," bear the noble solar metal *or.* These are the virtues that empower amulets.

In heraldry, as well as the planetary powers of traditional cosmology, the colors symbolize particular elements, virtues, and qualities. *Einseignemens notablez aulx poursuivans* lists them. The first color, azure, signifies loyalty, and the sanguine humor; the second, gules, valiant action, fire, and the choleric temperament. The third color, sable, represents the devil and the Earth. In the human sable signifies the melancholic humor. *Sinable* (green) represents the powers of plants and trees, and in the human, love and courtesy. Purpure signifies riches, abundance, and largesse. The first metal, *or,* represents the golden sun and noble goodwill in a person; the second, argent, signifies water, humility, and the phlegmatic temperament.

Another heraldic text, *The Blazon of Gentrie* by Sir John Ferne (1586), describes the spiritual correspondences of tinctures and metals with particular numbers, human age groups, seasons, and virtuous herbs:

> **Azure (blue)** corresponds with the planet Jupiter, the metal tin, and the weekday Thursday; the virtues of justice and loyalty or purity; the zodiac signs of Taurus and Libra; the month of September; the blue lily; the element of air; the season of spring; the sanguine humor; the numbers four and nine; and in the Ages of Man, boyhood (seven to fourteen years).

Gules (red/vermilion) corresponds with Mars, iron, and Tuesday; charity and magnanimity or power; the zodiac signs of Aries and Cancer; March, June, and July; the gillyflower; fire; summer; the choleric humor; the numbers three and ten; and the human quality of virility (the ages of thirty to forty).

Sable (black) has Saturn as its planet and Saturday as its day, prudence and constancy its virtues. Its metal is lead. The sable zodiac signs are Capricorn and Aquarius, with December and January its months. Its flower is the aubifaine, its element earth, and its season winter. The black humor is melancholy, its age decrepit or crooked old age, and its numbers five and eight.

Vert or sinable (green) is the copper planet Venus and Friday; love, loyalty, affability, and courtesy; Gemini and Virgo; the month of August; all kinds of green plants; spring, water, the number six and lusty green youth (twenty to thirty years of age). The green temperament is phlegmatic.

Purpure (purple) corresponds with the planet Mercury, the metal quicksilver, and Wednesday. Purpure virtues are temperance and prudence; its zodiac signs Sagittarius and Pisces. The violet is the purpure flower. Elementally it corresponds with water and earth, while its season is winter. It signifies the choleric humor, the age of gray hair in human life. It rules the numbers seven and twelve.

Or (gold/yellow) corresponds with the sun and Sunday, the metal gold, the virtues of faith and constancy, the zodiac sign Leo, the month of July, the marigold flower, the element of air, the season of summer, the sanguine humor, the numbers one, two, and three, and in the Ages of Man, the young age of adolescence (fourteen to twenty years).

Argent (silver/white) corresponds with the moon, silver, and Monday; hope and innocence or, alternatively, joy; Scorpio/Pisces; October/November; the white rose and lily flowers; autumn; the phlegmatic humor; the numbers ten and eleven; and human infancy, the first seven years of life.

By means of these colors, the heraldic artists were enabled to indicate certain virtues and particular meanings that other heralds could recognize readily. Amulets and talismans made with an understanding of these correspondences will embody all of their connected principles. They can be created with precision incorporating combinations of letters (or runes), numbers, colors, metals, and gems that will accomplish the desired results. But the maker needs a high level of knowledge, understanding, and competence to reach this level of achievement.

Chapter 9

Modernity's Approach to Colors

Many people have a lucky color, of which they may wear or carry an amulet. But over a century, the wearing of lucky colors has been overridden more and more by pressure groups adopting them for their own ends. During the nineteenth and twentieth centuries, colors became progressively politicized. Perhaps the earliest was the adoption of red by the Socialist and Communist Parties, the Red Flag of revolution. Supporters of this political tendency have always been called "reds." The song "The Red Flag" is still sung at Labor Party meetings in the United Kingdom. In Islam the black flag represents jihad. The black flag was a sign used in medieval European warfare to signify that there was "no quarter," that no prisoners would be taken and everyone would die. Pirates flew the black flag to signify the same meaning. Often frightening images such as swords were sewn to the buccaneers' black flag, the most familiar being the skull-and-crossbones emblem, the Jolly Roger (see fig. 9.1).

Later black was adopted by the anarchists for their black flag and was subsequently applied to shirt colors in 1920s Italy and Britain by the Fascists, who became known as the Blackshirts. Similarly brown was adopted by the German National Socialists, as worn by Hitler's Brownshirts. Other colored-shirt political parties of the era included the Social Credit Party of Britain, the Greenshirts (Ross and Bennett 2015, 106–7). Green later took on a different political meaning.

Fig. 9.1. The Jolly Roger, the mascot of pirates and buccaneers

Orange is the color of militant Protestantism in the north of Ireland and Scotland. It refers to the Dutch prince William of Orange, who seized power in Britain in 1688, driving out King James II, who was a Roman Catholic. Crowned as King William III, his followers founded the Masonic Orange Order, which long exercised great political power. On the other side of the Irish sectarian divide, green represented Irish nationalism, in allusion to the Emerald Isle, Ireland. Later, the nationalist political party Sínn Féin made green its color. In late nineteenth-century Scotland, sectarian football clubs adopted green if they were Roman Catholic and blue or claret if they were Protestant. So there were the green Hibernian and claret Hearts in Edinburgh, the green-and-white Celtic and blue Rangers in Glasgow, and the green Dundee United and blue Dundee Football Club* (Routledge and Wills 2018, 28).

In 1913 a French silk manufacturer had over-ordered some satin fabric dyed a brilliant orange-yellow color. It was not selling well, and he needed to shift the stock quickly. Then he had a brainwave. He called it satin-tango after the Argentine dance craze then at its height. It became a bestseller and sold out rapidly, making a good profit. Unfortunately, although demand was great, when stocks ran out he could not order any more because the dye formula had been forgotten. This color became known as *la veritable couleur tango*. Soon rivals had matched the shade, and the color went from strength to strength (Cooper 1994, 77).

---

*The sport known as football in Great Britain and other parts of the world is called soccer in the United States.

Psychologically this color will activate human physiological systems connected with aggression and sexuality (Papanek 1995, 77). In the 1920s tango was considered a lucky color, and orange amuletic jewelry was made. A century later there is still a popular orange drink called Tango that is sold in England and other countries.

In the 1930s activists of the Social Credit movement in the United Kingdom wore green shirts that did not reflect religious sectarianism. Subsequently, after the demise of that organization, the color and name were taken up by the political wing of the environmental movement as the Green Party. Green is also frequently used in Islamic contexts. In the 1970s, pink was adopted by breast cancer charities. In the previous decade the rainbow, formerly a religious symbol of God's covenant after Noah's Flood, was displayed as a symbol of peace. At a peace march in Perugia, Italy, in 1961, protestors carried a rainbow flag called the Peace Flag, designed by Aldo Capitani (1899–1968). Six years later rainbows appeared prominently in the psychedelic art on the cover of the Beatles recording *Magical Mystery Tour.* The rainbow Peace Flag appeared in the 1970 Jimi Hendrix movie *Rainbow Bridge,* on Campaign for Nuclear Disarmament badges along with the ubiquitous peace sign, and amuletically as small rainbows. Later the rainbow flag was adopted as the sign of the LGBTQ movement and other uses were abandoned. Until 2020, when, during the COVID crisis in the UK, the rainbow was adopted as the emblem of support for the National Health Service, and rainbow flags were displayed having this meaning.

Chapter 10

Knots, Knotwork, and Binding Charms

In the Northern Tradition existence is visualized as the Web of Wyrd. The interweavings of places, individuals, objects, and happenings within the flow of time can be likened to a fabric woven on a loom or a series of multistranded threads knitted together. This metaphor can be extended to the knots that catch and bind threads, which are sometimes useful and sometimes troublesome. Garments are knitted and held together by means of a series of carefully designed and executed knots. The net was an early human invention, woven and knotted from natural plant materials. It was a useful extension of the human hand, a catchall—trapping fish in the sea, beasts on land, and birds of the air.

An ancient Norse tale recounts how the trickster god Loki was trapped after he invented the net and then burned it lest his enemies should discover the secret of this new tool. But those who hunted him saw the pattern of the net in the ashes and, making one, ensnared its inventor and bound him. Knots bind up not only physical things but also bad luck and causes of bad luck. They trap and bind the harmful influences, blocking their effects. Knots are a method by which things can be tied physically, but they also operate on a magical level. Knots tied in string, rope, cord, and netting as well as hair when braided are of immediate use and hence are transitory, so there are few examples extant from ancient times. But some ancient knotwork patterns carved

Fig. 10.1. Celtic knotwork carved on the eleventh-century standing stone cross at Carew, Wales

on stone and wood, tooled onto leather, or drawn in manuscripts do exist today, often lumped under the rubric of Celtic art.

Binding spells are the magical equivalent of physical knots, making nonmaterial nets and ropes to entangle and capture the designated target. The string weavings called cat's cradles, although now considered no more than a children's game, are an important instance of traditional binding magic. In Scandinavia they are *troll-knutar* (troll knots). They are an element of string-magic traditions linked to shamanic practices. The photograph of a Swedish wise woman reproduced in figure 10.2 is a twentieth-century example of the tradition in Europe. Part of this binding tradition survives in the northern English and Scots word *warlock,* which means a cunning man or male practitioner of spellcraft. It is now a pejorative word, with connotations of deception and falsehood. But it derives from an earlier meaning, for the warlock has the power to shut in or enclose. He is a man who can make binding spells. The warlock's power is to ward off evil spirits and to lock up or bind their effects.

Fig. 10.2. Swedish wise woman making a troll knot, circa 1920.
Courtesy of the Library of the European Tradition

In English witchcraft the traditional magic cord has nine knots. It is made of red cord measuring an ell in length (one foot, six inches). Nine knots are tied in it at equal distances along the cord, while chanting this formula:

> *By knot of one, it is begun,*
> *By knot of two, the power comes through,*
> *By knot of three, so must it be,*
> *By knot of four, the power will store,*
> *By knot of five, the power's alive,*
> *By knot of six, the power to fix,*
> *By knot of seven, the power to leaven,*
> *By knot of eight, ties up the fate,*
> *By knot of nine, what's done is mine.*

An amulet against nosebleed, used in London in the early twentieth century, had nine strands of red purse silk with eight knots tied in it. It was tied around the neck of the sufferer by a ninth knot. A person of the opposite sex had to tie the knot (Wight and Lovett 1908, 299).

In folk tradition knots and interlacing patterns that resemble knots are believed to bind up bad luck and ward off the causes of bad luck (Pennick 1989, 180–88). European and Middle Eastern myths tell how destructive beings are captured and bound by the powers of righteousness and order. The Norse scripture *Gylfaginning* (*The deluding of Gylfi*, 34, 51) recounts the binding of both the monstrous Fenris-Wolf and the trickster god Loki. Similarly Saint John's Christian eschatology in the book of Revelations (20:1–3) tells of the devil being bound in chains for a thousand years. A carving of this image exists on a building in Stonegate, York (fig. 10.3).

Fig. 10.3. Image of the devil in chains, Stonegate, York (also see plate 7)

The complex rope-work knots of canal narrow boats from the eighteenth century to the present day are a notable feature of English folk art. The connection of knots with seagoing is not just from the necessity to tie them in rigging sails. There is an ancient magical connection of knots with the wind, and "sea witches" would sell seamen knotted ropes that they said contained wind. Ralph Higden's *Polychronicon*, written around 1350, tells how in the Isle of Man women sold shipmen three knots of thread that, when unloosed, would make the wind blow (Roud 2003, 522). Three knots were the standard form for many centuries. In 1880 William Jones reported that in Finland seamen used cord with three knots to raise the wind. When the first knot was untied, a good wind resulted; loosening the second produced a stronger wind, but the third generated a storm. He also noted the same tradition in Scotland (Jones 1880, 71). Cautionary tales of the sea tell how the seller warns the buyer not to untie the third one, but he does not take her advice and unties it, causing a gale that wrecks his ship.

Fig. 10.4. Shield-knot amulet (also see plate 8)

Interlacing patterns that resemble knots are part of the charm repertoire of ancient northern lands. The four-fold loop, which is the simplest interlaced knot, exists on a memorial stone in Habingo Parish on the Baltic island of Gotland (Havor II). It is dated between 400 and 600 CE (Nylén and Lamm 1981, 39). This sigil also is known from Danish bracteates around the same time (Wirth 1934, VIII, plate 424, fig. 1b; plate 427, 7b). A squared-off version exists on the Manx Andreas Cross. Column capitals, stone screens, and fonts of Lombardic and Romanesque churches in Germany, Italy, and Switzerland have the sign.

This simple sigil can be found in medieval graffiti all over Great Britain, for example, at Cowlinge in Suffolk (e.g., Pritchard 1967, 133). Although it is of pre-Christian origin, in Sweden this knot and its derivatives are called *sankt hans vapen* and in Finland and Estonia *hannunvaakuna* (Strygell 1974, 46). Here it is seen as a shield that wards off harm. Sankt Hans as in a name (may be a corruption of course).

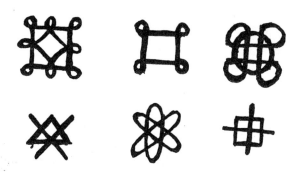

Fig. 10.5. Versions of sankt hans vapen (top row),
Saint Bengt's vapen (bottom row left), Saint Olaf's ros (center),
Saint Pehr's vapen (bottom row right)

Old English clog almanacs used a fourfold loop with a cross loop overlapping it to mark All Saints' Day, November 1 (Schnippel 1926, plates II and III). A variant of this pattern was found incised on a wooden vessel from Setesdal in Norway, and called *valknute* in its description (Weiser-Aal 1947, 126). The words *valknute, valnkútr,* or *valknut* usually mean three interlaced equilateral triangles. Literally "the knot of the slain," the words are connected with the Norse god Odin (Thorsson 1984, 107; 1992, 11; Aswynn 1988, 153–54). Such designs are widely available today from Northern Tradition–themed jewelers.

Fig. 10.6. The valknut

The center of this knot, the *triskele,* forms the basis of the heraldic "three legs" emblem of the Isle of Man, which was once part of a Norse maritime kingdom that included the Western Isles of Scotland. It is illustrated as a horse brass in figure 10.7.

Fig. 10.7. Manx three-legged triskelion horse brass

A different form of triangular knot, with a superimposed cross, is called Sankt Bengt's wapen (Strygell 1974, 46).

A simple open knot is the true lovers' knot, a charm in love-magic. It is the heraldic emblem of Staffordshire in the English Midlands.

Fig. 10.8. Staffordshire knot horse brass (also see plate 9)

Chapter 11

Witches' Ladders and Hangmen's Ropes

So-called witches' ladders are ropes with knots at intervals into which feathers are inserted. Apart from their similarity to other binding traditions, their function is uncertain. The first report of one was in 1887 by Abraham Colles, who described some items discovered in a sealed roof space in an old house in Wellington, Somerset. The workmen who discovered the "rope with feathers woven into it" told him that it was a ladder to enable witches to cross the roof. So Colles described it as a witches' ladder (Colles 1887, 2–3). Later that year, in a later issue of the same journal, Charles Godfrey Leland noted that in Florence, Italy, a girl had been killed by witchcraft and that one of the items used was a similar rope of feathers, called there a *guirlanda* (garland) (Leland 1887, 257). Shortly afterward, at a lecture given by folklorist Edward Burnett Tylor, the name and use was challenged because a device formerly used in hunting deer, the *sewel* or *sewell,* is identical. It was a device to scare deer and hem them in to a desired area. Native Americans in Newfoundland made sewells of narrow strips of birch bark attached to the end of sticks and stuck into the ground so that the strips would blow in the wind and herd the caribou where they wanted them (Story et. al, 1982, 463). In Britain feathers and string were used to make sewels. Contemporary British witches make witches' ladders based on those publicized by the British folklorists. Magically these objects hem in things just as the Newfoundlanders hemmed in the caribou.

But the witches' ladders caught the attention of noted folklorist and clergyman Sabine Baring-Gould (1834–1924), author of the famous Anglican hymn "Onward Christian Soldiers." In 1893 he published a novel titled *Mrs. Curgenven of Curgenven,* set in Cornwall. In it he talks of the Pixy World and describes the making of a witch ladder as a malicious item intended to bring ruin magically to a lawyer named Physic. Two of the protagonists, Justinian and Esther, enter her grandmother's cottage and see a line hanging by the fireplace. Esther goes up to the line: "It was composed of black wool, white-and-brown thread entwined, and at every two or three inches was looped about a bunch of cock's feathers, or pheasant's, or moorhen's feathers, set alternately," Esther says. "This be a witch-ladder," and she explains, "There be every kind o' pains and aches in they knots and they feathers; and when grandmother hev' done the ladder, her'll tie a stone to the end and sink it i' Dosmare Pool, and ivery wish will find a way, one after the other, to the jints and bones, and head and limbs, o' lawyer Physic. See if they don't" (Baring-Gould [1893] 1905, 132).

If it is disputed whether witches' ladders were used in cursing, it is certain that a rope spell existed in Scotland with that intention. It was used to remove the luck from a house, comparable to making a piece of land *álfreka.** Called *trailing the rape* (rope), it involved making a rope of straw by twisting it the wrong way, that is, from left to right. Then the rope was pulled round the house counterclockwise, thereby destroying its luck (Gregor 1881, 53).

The hangman's noose or knot, otherwise called the hemp collar or Jack Ketch's knot (named for an infamous English executioner), is reputed to have thirteen coils. However this is symbolic as between six and eight loops were normal, and from Victorian times, the rope ran through a metal eye and was not knotted at all. Hangmen's ropes were prized for their magical powers. Job Körnlein, executed at Nuremberg, Germany, in 1617 for theft and sorcery, had one in his collection of magical items (see page 179, chapter 29). Nineteenth-century English

---

*To render *álfreka* (an Icelandic term—the equivalent East Anglian term is *gast*) is literally to drive the elves away (i.e. to rid the land of all spiritual support, thereby rendering it barren).

gamblers used a piece for success at playing cards. In 1868 it was reported that one cost £8 and that they were difficult to obtain (Roud 2003, 239). In France *la corde de pendu,* the rope with which someone had been hanged, was sought after to bring good luck and combat many illnesses. Laisnel De La Salle quotes Charles Leopold Louandre, who wrote, "To be effective one must detach it from the gallows at midnight, on a moonless night" (De La Salle 1875, 165).

But hangmen frequently ran a lucrative trade in selling ropes and pieces of them, as they were a much sought-after commodity that fetched a good price. John Foxton (1769–1829), who hanged James Corder for the infamous killing in Suffolk in 1828 of Maria Martin, sensationalized as *The Murder in the Red Barn,* sold one-inch pieces of rope at one guinea (twenty-one shillings; £1.05) apiece (Evans 2009, 89–90). Hangmen were celebrities in nineteenth-century Britain. The public executioner James Berry (1852–1913) traveled the United Kingdom hanging the condemned wherever he was needed, hanging in all 130 people in his career. During his travels Berry stayed in public houses where he held "levees" to entranced audiences who plied him with free drinks and were a ready market for used ropes (Evans 2009, 89). Writing in 1880 William Jones reported a remedy against the evil eye by "giving in a drink the ashes of a rope with which a man has been hanged" (Jones 1880, 168). In France in 1916, during the wartime persecution of amulet sellers, Jean Talazac, owner of an occult shop in Paris, was prosecuted for selling talismans and *materia magica.* Along with wolves' teeth, moles' feet, and vultures' lungs, hangman's rope was on offer (Davies 2018, 107).

Chapter 12

Amuletic Stones

The shapes of natural objects in the world are not random: they are the result of natural processes and show them in visual form. Stones, especially ones that are notable in some way, feature large as amulets. Many are specific stones and especially gemstones, dealt with below. But there are other stones whose type did not seem important to their users. In Britain "Irish stones," that is any kind of stone brought from Ireland, were believed to have specific powers. Possession of an Irish stone was enough, the only stipulation being that it must never have touched British soil. According to William Henderson, Irish stones were believed to heal soreness and wounds and "were of high repute as a charm to keep frogs, snakes, and other vermin from entering the possessor's home" (Henderson 1879, 166). In this they contained the power of Saint Patrick, who is supposed to have expelled all snakes from Ireland. William Jones noted a stone of completely different origin that performed a similar function. He reported that in 1879 "a druggist in Texas paid $250 for a 'mad' stone found in the stomach of a deer reputed to possess the virtue of curing the bites of mad dogs, snakes, and all other venomous animals and reptiles" (Jones 1880, 161).

Ancient artifacts were frequently used as amulets. Prehistoric stone tools, especially arrowheads, were protective. "On opening a cromlech in Guernsey (1859) at L'Ancresse, Mr. Lukas found amulets of serpentine, clay-slate, and lapis ollaris" (Jones 1880, 157). When they found stone tools and arrowheads, people viewed them as a gift from otherworld beings such as pixies and fairies that would bring them protection. In an ancient chapel at Fladda Chuan in the Western Isles of Scotland was a blue stone fixed into the stone altar. It was always moist because fishermen needing a wind to sail would pour water over it (Jones 1880, 70).

The uncommon conglomerate stone formed of glacial gravel and pebbles cemented together naturally is called *breeding stone* in parts of Essex and was believed to be the source of smaller stones found in fields (Griffinhoofe 1894, 144). In 1881 J. W. Savill of Dunmow noted, "So far as Essex is concerned, not only the name but the fact implied is implicitly believed in, and that small stones increase in size and number" (*Notes & Queries*, 6th series, IV, 1881, 478).

Called *plum pudding stones* in Hertfordshire, they are much prized as charms against evil and placed in prominent locations, some with attached legends (Jones-Baker 1977, 95, 190). Other names for this notable conglomerate are *growing stone, oculatus lapis,* and *mother stone.*

Fossils are fascinating objects, clearly not ordinary stones but rather the petrified remains of former life. Because they were once living things, their nature is not entirely lost, so they serve as symbolic carriers of life energy. Fossil bones are still sold in Chinese communities for medicine. *Long gu,* fossil bones said to be "dragon bone," appear in lists of Chinese *materia medica.* They are ground up and used to treat heart and liver disorders. Various kinds of fossil teeth are *long chi,* "dragon teeth," and other fossils are also used in traditional Chinese medicine. Until the late twentieth century in the Ionian islands of Greece, bones of fossil pygmy hippopotami were dug from the cliffs. Said to be the bones of Saint Phanourios, a Syrian missionary who died on the cliffs in early Christian times, the hippopotamus bones were used in wedding rites. Soaked in a bucket of water, the bones of Saint Phanourios gave the power to newlyweds to produce children if they drank the bone water at the wedding and for forty days afterward (Van der Geer and Dermitzakis 2010, 326).

Belemnites, the cylindrical fossil remains of ancient squidlike cephalopods, because of their pointed, cylindrical structure, were believed to be the remnants of thunderbolts. So a person who carried one was protected against being struck by lightning. Other names for them indicate traditional beliefs: *thunderstones, elf bolts, devil's fingers,* and *Saint Peter's fingers.* In the Baltic, they were called Perkunas's stones, after the local thunder god (Van der Geer and Dermitzakis 2010, 325).

"Blessed be the spiral" was the motto of the Swiss sculptor Hermann Obrist (1862–1927), a significant figure in the Munich Jugendstil scene at the turn of the twentieth century. The most striking natural spirals in stone are fossil ammonites, the remains of ancient marine mollusks resembling the nautilus. In Roman times Pliny the Elder described them as *Ammonis cornua*—the horns of Ammon, after the Egyptian god (van der Geer and Dermitzakis 2010, 326). A Scottish name for them, *crampstone,* indicates one of their uses. Because of their resemblance to a coiled snake, they are used as *ophites* (remedies) against snakebite. In Whitby, on the coast of Yorkshire, ammonites were carved with snakes' heads and sold as Saint Hilda's stones. Ammonites are worn magically in Norfolk witchcraft to help the wearer find the next step in the path of life and provide the perseverance necessary to go along it once it has been found (Thomas 2019, 189). In Sussex some early nineteenth-century town houses were built using the Ammonite order, designed by architect George Dance (1741–1825). The volutes of buildings of the Ionic order are carvings of ammonites instead. The original buildings in London's Regent Street, designed by John Nash (1752–1835), also were of the Ammonite order. They have since been demolished. Real ammonites were frequently built into vernacular buildings, often beneath gable ends.

The curving fossilized shells of the extinct brachiopods called *Gryphaea* are the remains of one of the most ancient animals on Earth. Known as *lamp shells* or *devil's toenails,* they are carried as amulets of protection, for their form links them with claws and teeth. In Scotland they are *clach crubain,* "the crouching stone." As *shiy-yen, Gryphaea* fossils are used in traditional Chinese medicine. The fossil is crushed to a powder, boiled in water, and drunk to ward against rheumatism, skin diseases, anemia, digestive problems, and cataracts.

Fossil sea urchins of various species are the most notable amulets. They resemble a traditional form of bread made in England, so they

Fig. 12.1. Fairy loaves

are called *fairy loaves* and local dialect variants of the name. They were stood on shelves near ovens where bread was made or placed on kitchen windowsills to ensure that bread would never be lacking. In Jamaica their fivefold pattern and amuletic qualities gave them the name *lucky stars.* In southern counties of England, where they are called *shepherds' crowns,* they were placed outside a front door as a defense against evil and built into walls of buildings. A fossil sea urchin preserved in the Pitt-Rivers Museum in Oxford is labeled "Shepherd's Crown placed on windowsill outside to keep the Devil out."

Fossil echinoids have been found in human burials in Britain from the Neolithic, the Bronze Age, the Iron Age, the Romano-British era, and Anglo-Saxon times. The nineteenth-century church at Linkenholt, Hampshire, has two windows, one rectangular and the other a Gothic arch, with rows of fossil sea urchins embedded above them; the windows are said to have been taken from a thirteenth-century church that preceded the present one (McNamara 2007, 291). The local school, dating from 1870, also has embedded shepherds' crowns. Another name linking them with the "pixy world," as Sabine Baring-Gould called it, is *colepexies' heads,* recorded in the West Country of England (McNamara 2007, 287).

Shells of living species are also amuletic. The most common is the cowrie shell, although spiral shells are prized for their powers of confusing evil spirits and the evil eye. Rare shells with left-handed spirals occur occasionally and are considered extra special. Mother-of-pearl buttons derived from marine mollusk shells feature on the costumes of the

"Pearlies." This London Cockney tradition began around 1880 when costermongers, who sold fruit from handbarrows in the street, began to sew large numbers of pearl buttons onto their jackets and trousers. Various neighborhoods had their Pearly King and Queen, who appeared at events to raise money for charity. Emblems of good luck abound, although each design is different. Hearts and horseshoes are common (Lewery 1991, 108).

Chapter 13

Holed Stones and Rings

Naturally holed stones are called hagstones, mare stones, or holeystones. William Henderson called them "self-bored stones" (Henderson 1879, 166). In 1880 the National Museum of Antiquaries of Scotland was exhibiting a holystone from Roxburghshire that was "formerly a charm against witchcraft" (Jones 1880, 161). That actual holystone was "formerly a charm," but that did not mean that the belief in holystones was a thing of the past, as twenty-first-century examples attest. A holeystone tied by a piece of string—preferably of flax—to the key of a house, warehouse, stable, and so forth is an amuletic protection against the power of witchcraft over their contents (Gutch 1911, 62). The key is also an amulet in its own right (Bellucci 1889, 75).

Hung over a bed, a mare stone serves to protect the sleeper from becoming prey to nightmares produced either by ill-wishers' projections or evil spirits. Chrysolite is another protection against this. Hung in stables, hagstones prevented the horses being "hag ridden," that is, being ridden through the night by witches and worn out. Writing in 1910 at Clitheroe in Lancashire, W. Self Weeks recounted that it was not an uncommon thing to go to the stable in the morning and find the horses trembling in a state of fear and sweating as if they had been ridden hard. This was believed to be the work of witches. However this never happened again after hagstones were hung above the horses' stalls (Weeks 1910, 107–9). Chains of holystones strung on string are powerful amulets, as shown by the chain of them from Great Yarmouth, Norfolk, in figure 13.1. Holeystones were carried to defend the person to disempower "overlooking." Holed flints were used deliberately by the Arts and Crafts architect and university professor Edward Schroeder Prior at strategic points on the exterior walls of Henry Martyn Hall in Cambridge (Pennick 2006, 96).

Fig. 13.1. Holeystone chain, Great Yarmouth, Norfolk

Holeystones are a form of natural ring. All rings, as the belief in holeystones, mare stones, and hagstones shows, no matter how large or how small, are circles of power. A ring is symbolic of eternity, wholeness, the circle that has no beginning and no end. Rings of power featured in ancient Germanic culture. The key feature of the *Nibelungenlied* is a ring of power. Such rune-inscribed finger rings are from northern England. There are three in the British Museum with formulaic inscriptions in Northumbrian runes. The first, a golden ring, was discovered near Carlisle in 1817 on Greymoor Hill, Kingmoor, Cumbria. Its runes read on the outside ÆRÜRIUFLTÜRIURIThONgLÆSTÆPON and on the inside TOL. There is also a bronze ring with an identical inscription whose origin place is unknown. Made of agate, the third Northumbrian runic ring has the formulaic inscription: ERÜRIUFDOL ÜRIURIThOL WLESTEPOTENOL. In the twentieth century, J. R. R. Tolkien used these ancient rings as the exemplars of his fictional rings in *The Hobbit* and *The Lord of the Rings*.

Fig. 13.2. Runic ring found at Kingmoor, Cumbria, with cryptic runic inscription

An Icelandic ring talisman is called *Karlamagnus-hringar* (the Rings of Charlemagne). It represents the *nine rings of help* given to Pope Leo by an angel in the early ninth century to be sent to the emperor Charlemagne to protect him against his enemies. Charlemagne was the Holy Roman emperor who suppressed paganism in Saxony and defeated Islamic invaders in France, so he was considered one of the champions of Christendom. This talisman is threefold, three rings of three, and the accompanying spell is empowered by the three holy names. It is therefore a ninefold charm. The first ring protects against the wiles of the devil, attacks by enemies, and troubles of the mind. The second ring prevents collapse of the will, fear, and sudden death.

The third turns back the hatred of one's enemies onto themselves so that they are fearful and turn back. The fourth ring is against wounds from swords, the fifth against being disorientated by magic and getting lost, while the sixth defends one against persecution by powerful, evil men. The seventh circle brings success in legal disputes and general popularity, the eighth suppresses fear, and the ninth shields against all vices and debauchery. When expecting an enemy, these nine circles of Charlemagne are intended to be worn on the chest or on either side of the body.

Magic rings made from consecrated metal were being made in England centuries later. In a tradition that began with King Edward III in 1308, these "cramp rings," which protected against not only cramps but also epilepsy and palsy, were blessed in a ceremony held every Good Friday in the Chapel Royal at Westminster. A plateful of gold and silver rings was brought before the king, who rubbed them between his fingers. Then they were made talismanic by being dipped in consecrated holy water and distributed to worthy people. Because they had been touched by the hand of the monarch, they were infused with royal *main*. This royal custom of consecration was ended by the Tudor queen Mary I in 1558. But the custom did not die out. It only became unofficial, using transformed church offertory money.

Fig. 13.3. Medieval ring mottoes, England

The royal connection remained because each coin bore the numinous head of the monarch. There was a ritual involved. The person requiring a ring had to beg twelve or thirty different people to give him or her a penny. Some accounts tell how the people had to be of the opposite sex (Moss 1898, 166). When either a shilling (twelve pence) or half-a-crown (thirty pence) had been collected, the person went to the local vicar to exchange it for a silver shilling or half-crown piece that had been put in the offertory at a Sunday service. This was then taken to a silversmith and made into a cramp ring (Henderson 1879, 146). Although holy water was not used, this ceremony depended on the approval of the local vicar, which may not have been forthcoming. Other materials used in rheumatism rings include squirrel skin (Wright and Lovett 1908, 297). More transgressive rings are known, which may indicate church disapproval of the custom. In Yorkshire rings made from lead from coffins are recorded, and in Shropshire and Devon, coffin nails and metal fittings were fashioned into cramp rings (Burne and Jackson 1883, 193). Italian soldiers serving in World War I were known to wear amuletic rings made from coffin nails taken from patriots' graves (Davies 2018, 143).

Chapter 14

Amuletic Gems

Astrology is a very significant component of traditional magic. Although today it is marginalized even in magical practice, it played a significant role in determining when and how to implement a magical act. Gems played an important role in late Roman belief, as attested to by the Gnostic gems that still exist. Gems were considered powerful if they complemented the astrological horoscope of the individual, but could be detrimental if in conflict with the persons' signs. Wearing the zodiacal stone of one's birthday, the *birthstone,* is commonplace today, even if the deeper symbolic and magical meanings are rarely understood.

Traditional medicine is indistinguishable from magic, using sympathetic principles, the doctrine of signatures, and the planetary attributes of gemstones as a means of treating illness, disorders, and disease. Religious talismans used in traditional medicine include the Tau cross, which in northern Europe was conflated with the Hammer of Thor and the ax of Saint Olaf, and the Agnus Dei, a talisman bearing the Christian emblems of the Lamb and Flag. Traditionally gems are worn amuletically as remedies to stave off illness or as treatments for existing ones. They may remind the wearer of the beneficent power of his or her gods and exhort the wearer to live a life according to religious precepts. Gems may be used singly or in combination with other gems or amulets of a different kind. Gems engraved with particular sigils, words, or images act with a specific purpose.

Ancient gems were carved into religious talismans, bearing the images of gods and thereby accessing their particular powers. Serapis, the late Greco-Egyptian god, consort of Isis, was an important god in Ptolomaic Egypt and beyond. His image and name were carved on amuletic gems that bore the words in Greek characters ΕΙΣ ΘΕΟΣ ΣΑΡΑΠΙΣ: "There is but one God and he is Serapis." This or "The One Living God" were the parallel of the religious medallions made today in the Christian and Buddhist traditions. The short form of the first Serapian aphorism, ΕΘΣ, used for amuletic purposes, is perhaps the forerunner of the Christian IHS monogram. Some Serapian gems were for specific functions, bearing the inscription "baffle the Evil Eye, O Serapis" (Elworthy 1895, 303). In addition to Serapis, gems of the deity Abraxas, whose number is 365, were also powerful protective amulets.

Fig. 14.1. Ancient Abraxas gem

Almost every malady, disorder, and disease suffered by human beings has a stone said to alleviate or cure it. Stones as a "cure for madness" were formerly used in the days before any functional treatment was available for mentally ill people. They were much sought after and exchanged hands for considerable sums of money. Coral, red in color, was worn as a defense against coughs and cholera. Carved with an image of a man bearing a sword, a red coral amulet protected the home against epidemics and staunched bleeding (Christian [1870] 1972, 416). Those suffering from cramps carried fossil sharks' teeth, moles' feet, and cramp rings made from coffin fittings. For rheumatism the anklebone of a sheep, amber, malachite, and cornelian were deemed effective. To counter infections amber, carbuncle, a flint arrowhead, and an Agnus Dei medallion were deemed to be powerful safeguards. To avert the ague (malaria), lapis lazuli was recommended, and against asthma, cat's eye and topaz.

Stones carried against the gout included topaz, chrysolite, and lode-stone. Lodestones specifically used to suppress gout were carried in a flannel bag tied with a black ribbon (Jones 1880, 159). Lodestone is a common ingredient in the similar mojo hand made by hoodoo doctors (see "The Mojo Hand," chapter 39, page 272), although often as an attractor of luck and money. Paul Christian tells how it was used to detect whether a wife was unfaithful. Placed beneath her pillow, the lodestone would cause her either to turn in the night and embrace her husband, in which case she was faithful, or to awaken suddenly with a bad dream and cry out, which meant she was adulterous (Christian [1870] 1972, 417). The lodestone operated on the sleeping as does the mare stone, but in a selective, judgmental manner. The emerald was used against faintness, memory loss, weakness of the eyes, and to preserve chastity. A gem engraved with the image of a starling (*Sturnus vulgaris*) and worn in a gold setting will produce prophetic dreams (Christian [1870] 1972, 416).

It was thought that alcoholism could be treated with pink amethyst attached to the navel of the subject. The pink amethyst had to be set in a silver plaque with a bear engraved on it. The water in which such an amulet was dipped was said to cure sterility (Christian [1870] 1972, 416). Amethyst engraved with the ANANTIZAPTA formula in combination with a Tau cross was another preventative of drunkenness. Amethyst also countered neuralgia, and hysteria could be quelled using amethyst in combination with a lunar crescent of silver. The ANANTIZAPTA formula, in combination with jade, coral, jet, lapis lazuli, and a Tau cross was amuletic against epilepsy. Turquoise banished headaches, aquamarine alleviated toothache, and those with kidney problems wore jade. Aquamarine, beryl, and carbuncle were all used defensively against throat and stomach problems. Beryl was also worn to combat sea sickness; jacinth was effective as a contraceptive; jasper and emerald or onyx with a Tau cross were prophylactic against snakebite; and cornelian, jacinth, and jade were another preemptive of stomach problems. Sardonyx was worn as a general painkiller, but carved with an eagle and set in gold, it was a lucky charm. Finally wearing onyx brought one terrifying dreams if the gem was engraved with a camel's head (Christian [1870] 1972, 417).

AMBER

Brisingamen, the necklace of the Northern goddess Freya, was of amber, and traditional wedding necklaces in the Baltic region are made of amber. "People born under Leo should wear amber constantly, but it is absolutely unlucky for those of Taurus" (Villiers 1923, 15). Amber with inclusions that could be read as initials was sold at a high price (Kunz 1913, 58).

In his poem "The Passionate Shepherd to His Love" Christopher Marlowe (1564–1593) wrote:

A belt of straw with ivy buds
With coral clasps and amber studs.

That was a very magical combination. Medicinally amber was credited with numerous powers. It was supposed to suppress indigestion and stomach problems, treat goiter, mitigate against deafness, and assist teething in babies. Used with cyclamen and a Tau cross, amber was believed to disempower poisons.

AGATE

Agate is something of a universal amulet, promoting good fortune and deflecting many ills, especially those that generate fever. According to Elizabeth Villiers, the agate is a bringer of good fortune, especially to those who till the soil. Agates were attached to plows to bring a good harvest, and gardeners wore agates mounted on rings to promote bumper yields (Villiers 1923, 13). In Christian symbolism agate typified John the Baptist, who "pointed the way to the Pearl of Great Price, Jesus." Because of this, the agate was the amulet of pearl fishermen. It was believed that the means of finding oysters containing pearls was to attach an agate to a cord, and when it appeared to be attracted to a particular oyster, that one was picked because it contained a pearl (Evans 1896, 47). Agate was worn to combat eye problems, and when ground up, agate mixed with wine was drunk as an antidote to snakebite (Villiers 1923, 14). According to Paul Christian, whoever wears a black agate veined with white will be protected against all danger and will have victory over his or her enemies (Christian [1870], 415). Black-and-white agate bead amulets are worn in Tibet for general protection (Paine 2004, 101).

Glass marbles called agates also partake of the power of agate. Agate glass is made by blending two or more colors to simulate the gemstone. The best known are the *akro agates,* an American brand made in the early twentieth century by the first company to have a fully mechanized production method for glass marbles. *Cat's eye* glass marbles also embody the luck associated with cats. In 1891 among "the instruments of Obeah" exhibited in Kingston, Jamaica, was a glass marble (Thomas 1891, 10). Against general illnesses strings of blue glass beads are a universal amulet. The early-twentieth-century charm and amulet collector Edward Lovett had examples of necklaces of blue beads from all over London. These were worn to prevent or treat bronchitis (Lovett 1925, 81–84).

BLOODSTONES

Around three hundred of the known English charms dated between 1370 and 1540 were used against bleeding (Healy 2016, 1,213). The traditional gems used to neutralize wounds were bloodstone, agate, and carbuncle. Weapons buried with ancient Germanic warriors have been accompanied by large beads of glass and semiprecious stones that may have hung from scabbards as wound-staunching amulets. In Arthurian legend, according to Sir Thomas Malory in *Le Morte d'Arthur* (1472; book I, chapter XXIII), King Arthur's sword, Excalibur, had a scabbard even more valuable than the sword because so long as he had it, he could never die from wounds. Perhaps this was another woundproof warrior amulet, but it also related to the blood-staunching belief. Farm laborers in rural England certainly carried bloodstones. Those used by East

Anglian farmworkers were not natural gemstones but rather spherical beads of blood-red glass strung on a red thread or ribbon. These were last recorded around the middle of the nineteenth century as being made by a French glassmaker in King's Lynn, Norfolk. A bloodstone recorded in Cambridgeshire in 1911 was of dark-green glass containing white and orange twists like a cat's-eye marble (Porter 1969, 83). As with the Germanic warriors, East Anglian farm laborers attached their bloodstones to the handles of their scythes. As well as bloodstone, cornelian and red coral were also deemed to suppress bleeding.

EXCEPTIONAL ITEMS

In Luzern (Lucerne), Switzerland, a remarkable stone known as the Luzerner Drachenstein is preserved in an ancient velvet-lined box. In 1421, so the story goes, this spherical stone (about the size of a pool ball) fell from a dragon flying from the nearby Mount Pilatus. A local farmer, Stemflin, saw it fall and found a clot of blood with the stone inside. He took it to the authorities, who deemed it to be of use to the community. In 1509 it was legally declared a healing stone and used to forestall the plague, as a remedy against poisoning, to treat hemorrhage, diarrhea, and dysentery, and to stop nosebleeds. Today it is believed to be a meteorite.

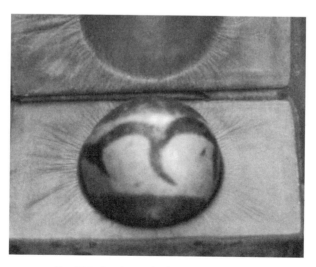

Fig. 14.2. Drachenstein, Luzern, Switzerland

The French emperor Napoléon III (1808–1873) possessed two exceptional amulets. One was the so-called Talisman of Charlemagne, found round the neck of the remains of the emperor Charlemagne when his tomb at Aachen was opened. It was a circular jewel of fine gold, set with gems with rough sapphires at the center and a fragment of the True Cross (Jones 1880, 191). Another of Napoléon III's charms was a carnelian seal with an Arabic inscription translated as "The slave Abraham relying on the merciful God"; it had been taken by Napoléon Bonaparte (1769–1821) from Egypt before he became emperor of France. He wore it when he proclaimed himself emperor, and after his death, it was passed on to his nephew, who took the title Napoléon III and wore it on his watch chain. It passed again to Louis Napoléon, the Prince Imperial (1856–1879), who wore it when he was with the British Army fighting in South Africa. "At the time of his lamentable death it must have been carried off in South Africa by the Zulus when they stripped his body, and it has never been recovered" (Kunz 1913, 64). The bad ends of these three leaders through lack of judgment show that the talisman was not a bringer of good luck to those who undertook foolhardy enterprises.

Chapter 15

Apotropaic and Magical Metal Items

IRON

When the smelting of iron for ore was invented, the resulting metal was so much harder and more durable than metals then in use. Iron axes could cut down trees far more effectively than copper or bronze ones. A man with an iron sword could overcome one armed with bronze, and chain mail made from iron rings was a far more effective armor than leather and bronze. Blacksmiths who forged iron were seen as possessing supernatural powers of transformation, taking seemingly useless ore and transforming it into hard, gleaming, useful metal.

The traditional function of the lord's smith was in the maintenance of power. It was the smith who crafted the weapons used by lords and kings to wage war. He forged the locks and bars of castles and prisons. He manufactured the chains that kept prisoners and slaves captive. The name of the ancient Irish smith god, Goban, is related to the word *govern* in reality if not in the science of linguistics. The craft of the armorer was also used to make prosthetic metal limbs for those mutilated in battle. In ancient Ireland the ceremonial Feast of Gobniu (Goban; also called the Feast of Immortality) was held "to ward off age and death from their high-kings."

Smith-wrought iron was literally the protector and maintainer of lords and kings, warding off death, so ascribing it magical powers against supernatural enemies was a natural extension of its uses. The chorus of a traditional song sung by English blacksmiths praising the biblical founder of smithcraft, Tubal Cain, emphasizes this:

> *So they sang hurrah to Tubal Cain,*
> *Hurrah to his spear and sword,*
> *Hurrah to the hand that would wield them well,*
> *For he shall be the king and lord.*

Vulcan, the Roman god of smithcraft, is an important mascot of iron- and steelworkers. From the early days of the Industrial Revolution, his image and name appeared on foundries and artifacts. In 1791 the iron master John Wilkinson issued a token depicting a seated Vulcan at an anvil, hammer in hand. In 1796 Birmingham industrialist

Fig. 15.1. The smith god Vulcan

Matthew Boulton ceremonially opened his new foundry, Soho Works at Smethwick. He walked ceremonially around the building and performed a rite recorded in the gatehouse mural frieze: "I come now as the father of Soho to consecrate this place as one of its branches. I also come to give it a name and my benediction. I will, therefore, proceed to purify the walls of it by the sprinkling of wine, and in the name of Vulcan and all the gods and goddesses of fire and water, pronounce the name of Soho Foundry. May that name endure for ever and ever and let all the people say, Amen."

In 1830 the Vulcan Foundry opened at Newton-le-Willows in Lancashire. On the front of the building was the Visage of Vulcan. Several railway locomotives built there over the year bore the name Vulcan. In the steel city of Sheffield, the town hall, designed by E. W. Mountford and built from 1891 to 1896, has a two-hundred-foot tower topped by an eight-feet-tall bronze image of Vulcan. His right foot rests on an anvil; in his right hand is a hammer and in his left a pair of pincers (M. Jones 2004, 143). The coat of arms of the city, granted in 1875, has two hammer gods: Vulcan as one bearer of the shield and Thor as the other.

Iron and steel swords feature in the rites and ceremonies of various currents of ritual magic and Wicca, where they serve to command spirits. The iron or steel knife has the power to cause immediate and drastic changes. Fishermen from King's Lynn in Norfolk, needing to sail northward to the North Sea fishing grounds, called up a south wind by sticking a knife in the south side of the mast and calling, "God, give us a south wind." In his book about Welsh folk customs and beliefs, *British Goblins*, Wirt Sykes noted the custom of "exorcism by knife" (Sykes 1880, 52). "Welsh ghosts and fairies are afraid of a knife," he wrote (Sykes 1880, 51). Knives were considered most effective against the Gwyllion, supernatural beings that "haunt lonely roads in the Welsh mountains and lead night wanderers astray" (Sykes 1880, 49). He recounts a Welshman, Evan Thomas, traveling at night across Bedwellty Mountain toward his home in the valley of Ebwy Fawr, when he saw the Gwyllion accompanying him on either side and the Wild Hunt riding by. "So he drew out his knife and the fairies vanished directly" (Sykes 1880, 53).

THE HAMMER

The essential tool of the blacksmith is the hammer, made, of course, from iron or steel. In the Northern Tradition the hammer itself is amuletic. Mjöllnir, the Hammer of Thor, whose name means "Crusher," is the most powerful tool of the Norse gods, defending them against destructive giants. The iconic form of Mjöllnir is close in form to Signum Thau, the Tau cross.

Fig. 15.2. Tau cross

The Tau cross was a very popular amulet in medieval Scandinavia, clearly a continuation of the pre-Christian amulet that was acceptable to the officials of the church. A metalworker's soapstone mold found at Trendgården in Denmark dated to the tenth century enabled the amulet maker to produce metal castings of both the Hammer of Thor and equal-armed crosses. Also in Denmark, in 2014 at Købelev on the island of Lolland, a metal Thor's Hammer was found with an inscription in runes transliterated as HAMR x IS (this is a hammer).

Fig. 15.3. Hammer of Thor amulet
(also see plate 10)

The smiths' motto, "By Hammer and Hand All Arts Do Stand," is used by the different Incorporations of Hammermen in Scotland, which are still operative in several cities in the early twenty-first century. These groups were associated as far back as 1372 with the Blacksmiths' Guild of London. The crowned hammer is the emblem of the Scottish Hammermen, showing smithcraft to be the king of all trades.

Fig. 15.4. Emblem of the Hammermen of Glasgow, nineteenth century

KEYS

Keys are a common lucky charm. Elizabeth Villiers writes, "As a modern mascot the key is given and accepted as a sign of love—symbolical of locking and unlocking the door to the heart" (Villiers 1923, 97). The lock and key were invented in the sixth century BCE by Theodore of Samos. The idea probably came from the interrelationship between the mold and the cast item. As a means both of entry and closure, the key symbolizes the way entry can be gained, but also a means of barring entry. Villiers states that in ancient Greece, it was the means by which the door was opened so prayers could reach the gods. "Silver keys attached to a ring were those of Hecate, goddess of the underworld, who had power over the spirits of the departed. Such a key formed the link between the living and the dead" (Villiers 1923, 97–98). In Catholic Italy the amuletic key is the Key of the Holy Spirit. It was worn to counter convulsions in children (Bellucci 1889, 75). Silver and

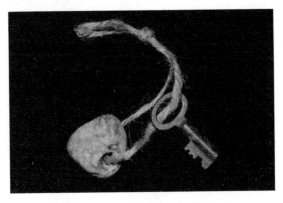

Fig. 15.5. Key and holeystone, England,
early twentieth century

bronze are the usual metals. Keys feature on charm bracelets and the lucky accoutrements of brides. Hanging a door key upside down is a means to deflect evil and have a good night's sleep.

Saint Hubert's Keys

Saint Hubert (656–727) is the patron saint of huntsmen, but his most important amuletic object is his key. His legendarium tells how when he was consecrated as the bishop of Liège, there was a miraculous visitation by Saint Peter, who presented him with a golden key that gave him power over evil spirits. An old medallion of Saint Hubert in the Wellcome Institute for the History of Medicine depicts on the obverse the iconic image of the saint kneeling before a stag that has a crucifix between its antlers. Around the circumference of the medallion is a hunting horn. The reverse has an image of a key, with lettering CLEF DE ST HUBERT. Le Clé de Saint Hubert is a particular relic preserved in the treasury of the Collégiale de Sainte-Croix at Liège, Belgium. Made of brass, it dates from between the thirteenth and fifteenth centuries (Martinot, Weber, and George, 1996, passim). The ornate upper part of the key contains a piece of metal reputed to be a fragment of the chains that bound Saint Peter.

A particular amulet of Saint Hubert is the *cornet de fer,* a tapering iron nail. In various parts of Europe, these nails, called Saint Hubert's keys, were hung on the walls of houses to ward off mad dogs and rabies.

Until the twentieth century the custom persisted that if someone was bitten, a Saint Hubert's key would be heated to cauterize the dog bite. As the *Encylopædia Londinensis* skeptically recorded in 1812, "There was a numerous set of men styling themselves 'Knights of Saint Hubert.'" They traveled around Catholic western Europe and "pretended to be able to cure that horrid malady, the hydrophobia [rabies]. . . . They used to brand dogs on the forehead with a hot iron in the shape of something like a horse shoe . . . and the country people had full confidence that any animal so stamped was not susceptible to imbibing the poison" (Wilkes 1812, vol. 11, 814). Medieval medallions inscribed ST HVMBER have been found at Bury St. Edmunds.

Fig. 15.6. Amulet of Saint Humber (Hubert),
late medieval period, Bury St. Edmunds, Suffolk

Chapter 16

Nails and Horseshoes

Amulets made from nails contain the inherent virtue of iron as well as the symbolic meaning of nailing down evil and bad luck. In Etruscan and Roman religions, nails sacred to the Roman goddess Necessitas (the Greek Atropos and the Etruscan Athrpa) were hammered into posts to mark the passage of time. The nail-driving rite of Clavum Figure was enacted annually at the Temple of Nortia. Nails are significant in Christian symbolism because Jesus was nailed to the cross. The supposed nails of Jesus were kept as venerable relics in a number of churches. Saint Hubert's cornet de fer is a form of nail, and in Santeria, railway spikes appear on altars of the deity Ogun, the patron of metalworking.

"A rather unpleasant mascot," Elizabeth Villiers wrote, "is a nail drawn from a coffin or from a door leading into a vault. Such a nail hung above a bed banished all evil dreams" (Villiers 1923, 114). Kriegsglückringe (war luck rings) fashioned from horseshoe nails were made in Austria during World War I for soldiers to wear at the front (Davies 2018, 141). Serving as a soldier in the Italian army in 1915, future Fascist leader Benito Mussolini noted in his diary that he wore a lucky ring made from a horseshoe nail on his little finger (Davies 2018, 143). Coffin nails, too, served World War I Italian soldiers as amulets when made into rings. These were nails found in the graves of soldiers who had fought in the Italian wars of independence between 1848 and 1859, which thereby had absorbed heroic virtue.

Fig. 16.1. Cross of nails bent and welded together, late twentieth century

The Coventry Cross of Nails came about in 1940 after the massive bombing attack by the German Air Force on that city in England at the November full moon. A large part of the city was destroyed, giving rise to the expression "coventrated," which was used for a while in German government propaganda to describe cities obliterated by aerial bombardment. Walking through the ruins of the cathedral, Arthur Wales, rector of the city's Saint Mark's Church, found a number of medieval nails in the rubble. He took three of them and bound them together with a piece of wire to make a cross. It was set up on a makeshift altar in the ruins and then took pride of place when a new cathedral was built near the old one, which remains today as a preserved ruin.

The Coventry nail cross became a celebrated artifact, and soon more were made. Eventually, the demand for them exhausted the supply of authentic medieval cathedral nails, and special new replica nails were forged by blacksmiths to satisfy the demand for Coventry crosses. This echoed exactly the proliferation of relics in the medieval period, of which there were never enough to meet the demand, and like Geoffrey Chaucer's Pardoner in *The Canterbury Tales,* religious people resorted to substitutes for the real thing. In 1982, during the Falklands War, the British Royal Navy destroyer HMS *Coventry* had one of the nail crosses on board when it was bombed and sunk by Argentine aircraft. Subsequently Royal Navy divers recovered the cross from the bottom of the South Atlantic Ocean, and it was returned to Coventry Cathedral.

It went to sea again in a new HMS *Coventry,* a frigate built in 1988 and scrapped in 2002, and finally in another new destroyer, the *Diamond.*

THE HORSESHOE

In his *Miscellanies upon Various Subjects,* John Aubrey wrote, "It is a very common thing to nail horseshoes on the thresholds of doors, which is to hinder the power of witches that enter into the house. Most houses of the West End of London have the horseshoe on the threshold" (Aubrey 1857, 148). In *The Magic of the Horse Shoe,* Robert Means Lawrence wrote, "It is the anti-witch charm par excellence, as well as the approved symbol of good luck, and, used for these purposes, it is to be seen throughout a large portion of the world" (Lawrence 1898, 88). Often it is said that such a horseshoe must be "cast," that is, been at one time attached to a horse, but fallen off. In 1834 John Graham Dalyell noted that in Scotland "finding a horseshoe is accounted fortunate by the vulgar" (Dalyell 1834, 200). On buildings it is generally nailed on doors or above them and above windows, also on the masts of sailing

Fig. 16.2. Horseshoes on traditional cottage at Heacham, Norfolk, 2018 (also see plate 11)

ships. "In Shrewsbury," Lawrence wrote, "horse-shoe talismans are to be seen not only above the house doors, but also on the barges that navigate the River Severn" (Lawrence 1898, 90). Stables, naturally, are a place where the preemptive powers of the horseshoe are applied. They are hung up above the horses' stalls and nailed to the walls of cowsheds "to keep off the pixies" (Elworthy 1895, 217). In Essex in 1894 George Day noted, "At Ilford I saw a horse-shoe nailed to the door of a cow-house, and on asking the lad the reason, he replied, 'Why, to keep the wild horse away, to be sure'" (Day 1894, 77).

Churches, too, have had horseshoes nailed on them "to keep away the witches" (Johnston 1912, 157). The impression of horseshoes in the plasterwork of houses applies the power of the horseshoe at one remove from the real thing. Among the real things a shoe cast from the left hind leg of a gray mare was deemed especially powerful (Thompson 1932, 142). In 1878 at Filey in Yorkshire, fishermen who went to attack Nanny Jones, a woman they thought was a witch, carried horseshoes in their pockets for protection. But during the religious persecutions in seventeenth-century Scotland, possessing a horseshoe in secret was deemed to be witchcraft, rather like "the instruments of Obeah" for the possession of which slaves were punished in the West Indies. In 1634 Elizabeth Bathcat was arraigned as a witch because she had a horseshoe kept in a secret place, allegedly for nefarious magical purposes (Dalyell 1834, 200).

The Witches' Memorial at Paisley in Scotland marks the place at a crossroads (currently the Maxwellton Cross, the intersection of Maxwellton and George Streets) where the ashes of people executed for witchcraft were buried. In 1696 seven people were convicted of witchcraft; one killed himself in prison, and the other six were garotted. The seven bodies were burned and the ashes buried at the Maxwellton Cross. On the scaffold one of the convicted, Agnes Naismith, cursed her persecutors and the town. So a horseshoe was set on the grave to suppress her dying curse. Eventually the horseshoe disappeared. In 2008 the point was marked again with a circular plaque with a bright steel horseshoe at its center.

"The traditionary power of the horseshoe to avert evil and

witchcraft," wrote C. J. S. Thompson, "probably had a twofold origin. First, on account of the metal of which it was composed, and second, because of its shape, which is roughly the shape of a crescent and therefore a lunar symbol of peculiar power" (Thompson 1932, 141). The crescent form of the horseshoe naturally connects it with the crescent moon and curved horns, fangs, and tusks. Any forked object has the power to drive witches away (Larwood and Hotten [1908] 1985, 117).

Fig. 16.3. Horseshoe amulet for luck, circa 1900
(also see plate 12)

According to Arnold Whittick a horseshoe on a mosque signifies the Islamic crescent symbol (Whittick 1971, 257). In 1898 Robert Means Lawrence noted, "Whether we regard the horse-shoe as a symbol of Wodan, the chief deity of the northern nations; as deriving magical power from the half-moon shape; as a product of supernatural skill in dealing with iron and fire; or as appertaining to the favorite sacrificial animal of antiquity, the pagan source of its superstitious use is equally evident" (Lawrence 1898, 111). In England it is a common belief that the horseshoe must be nailed up with the ends pointing upward. This sees the horseshoe as a container of luck. To put it with the ends downward would result in the luck running out (Villiers 1923, 92). With the horns downward it takes the form of the second rune called *ur* or *uruz* (Von Zaborsky 1936, 52–53), and it appears in this form in gamblers' lucky horseshoe charms, where an image of a horse's head is inside the curve.

Fig. 16.4. Horseshoe with horse's head, a typical
gambler's charm. This one is a horse brass.

Old horseshoes bound in fabric were used both in England and
Mexico. In England they were hung over beds, points downward in this
case, to ward off nightmares. The celebrated bound horseshoe amulet
of Mexico is called *el secreto de la virtuosa herradura* (the secret of the
virtuous horseshoe; see chapter 39, "Accretional Amulets"). Around
1910 the famous London department store A. W. Gamage, Ltd., commissioned Edward Lovett to design a mascot for motorists. It was a
composite of several lucky charms inside a horseshoe with seven "nail
holes." The horn buttons of the traditional Suffolk horsemen's suit
have seven-hole horseshoes engraved on them. In 1925 a silent Western
movie based on a story by Robert Lord and starring Tom Mix was titled
The Lucky Horseshoe, and the heavyweight boxing champion Jersey Joe
Walcott (1914–1994) carried a miniature horseshoe as his lucky charm.
The horseshoe-shaped magnet was a familiar toy in years gone by, and
because it attracts iron, it is a symbol of attraction—hence its use in
love, money, and gambling magic. The power of iron as a magnet is
another valuable attribute of the metal. As a natural lodestone, it is a
common component of the mojo hands made by hoodoo doctors.

Chapter 17

Bells

Terry Keegan notes the biblical reference to Zachariah's prophecy of the day of peace "when bells hung upon the necks of horses shall be inscribed Holiness unto the land" (Keegan 1973, 166). In ancient Egypt *sistra* and bells were used in the worship of the goddess Isis and were banned when the Christians took over. Legend tells how the Isian sacred bells were buried and, some time later, dug up again when the value of bells was recognized by the church. Iconically Saint Anthony of Egypt is depicted with a pig, which, according to tradition, was used to find the buried bells, just as in northern Europe pigs' acute sense of smell is used to find truffles.

Fig. 17.1. Serapis and Isis with a sistrum (from *The Pantheon* by Andrew Tooke, 1794)

Fig. 17.2. Fastnacht
(Shrove Tuesday)
carnival guiser with bells,
Rottweil-am-Neckar,
Germany, 1999 (also see
plate 13)

Small crotal bells are a significant part of the costume of English morris dancers, guisers in central European winter and Shrovetide festivities, and certain shamans in Asia. In Wales, "There was anciently a belief that the sound of brass would break enchantment" (Sykes 1880, 340). The shamans of the Altai, when attacked by evil spirits, ring bells to ward them off (Ivanov 1978, 136). Ivanov stated that the shamans' bells are not just there to make a sound, but the metal they are made of also is a significant repellent of harmful forces. Like the hanging brass plates called "shamanic shovels," they are symbolic plates of armor (Ivanov 1978, 138). Elsewhere, shamans wear the brass crotals known as "tiger bells," which are probably of Chinese origin, being widespread in Southeast Asia in various contexts. English morris dancers and masked German guisers in Fastnacht (Shrove Tuesday) carnival parades wear bells of the same form.

In her book *Old West Surrey,* Gertrude Jeckyll writes of "the Carter's Pride" and describes the harness bells worn by horses. Such bells were an integral part of traditional horse harness. There were two basic types of bell. The small round crotal or "rumbler" bells resembling those of

Fig. 17.3. Four sets of southern English tuned horse bells,
eighteenth to nineteenth century

morris dancers were worn by packhorses that walked in single file along
narrow cross-country trackways in gangs of up to forty horses (Keegan
1973, 167). Wagon team horses wore larger latten bells mounted on a
frame. There were up to eight bells in a set, although in Surrey, they were
in sets of four tuned bells (Jeckyll 1904, 163–65). (*Latten* is an old word
for "brass" or "bronze.") These "team bells" were in use until the 1930s
in the West Country of England (Keegan 1973, 166). In Surrey each
set was tuned to a chord that jingled in pleasant harmonies. These were
covered by a leather hood with a scalloped lower edge embroidered with
barleycorns from which hung a red woolen fringe (Jeckyll 1904, 163–65).
These bells were cast by specialist bell-founders, many at Walsall in the
West Midlands (Keegan 1973, 170). As with other traditional items,
they had utilitarian and magical functions. They served to warn other
road users of an oncoming wagon as well as to ward off evil spirits.

The English traditional song called "The Carters' Health" was sung
according to custom at the Harvest Supper that celebrated the successful conclusion of the harvest. It celebrates the "bob-tail mare" in the
greenwood carrying the bells away, which is a reference to the Wild
Stud, in which tame mares are let loose in a woodland to be served by
wild stallions living there. This version was sung in 1812 and 1813 at
Nuthurst, Sussex:

Of all the horses in the Merry Green Wood
'Twas the bob-tail mare car'd the bells away.
(Clark [ca. 1820] 1930, 796)

One one occasion in 2010 when I sang the Cambridgeshire version of this song at the Hardwicke Arms Inn at Arrington, a listener who kept horses told me that he knew a horse breeder in Scotland who still practiced the Wild Stud.

Handbells were part of the church's ceremony of exorcism, with "bell, book, and candle." There was a special handbell used by popes to curse and exorcise animals considered to be pests. Popes exorcised and cursed dolphins in the Mediterranean Sea, plagues of flies, and flocks of various species of birds that they wanted to kill off. The master goldsmith Benvenuto Cellini made a special exorcism bell for the pope, covered in dolphins, insects, and other "vermin."

PAPAL CURSING BELL FOR ANIMALS.

Fig. 17.4. Papal bell for exorcising and excommunicating animals considered "vermin," including dolphins, snakes, and insects.
Made by Benvenuto Cellini

Wirt Sykes asserted that "the Welsh were formerly strong in the belief that bells could perform miracles, detect thieves, heal the sick, and the like." Bells were believed to have the power of moving by themselves; they "would transport themselves from place to place when they had occasion, according to their own sweet will, and without human intervention. It is even recorded that certain handbells required to be tied with a double cord of an exorcism, or they would get up and walk off in the night" (Sykes 1880, 341). Sykes also noted that "the ghosts of bells are thought to haunt the earth in many parts of Wales" (Sykes 1880, 339).

In Scotland amuletic items were revered and used for various purposes, including blessing and cursing, taking oaths, validating kingship, and healing the sick. The *deòradh* was a hereditary official guardian of various relics that were kept as powerful amulets. The Dewar na Ferg branch of the Perthshire Clan Dewar were the designated keepers of the relics of the eighth-century Celtic saint Fillan. There were five relics; a crozier, a bell known as the *bearnane,* a manuscript, a stone, and an arm bone. All except the stone were encased in finely wrought bronze housings with gilding. The Dewar keeper of the crozier was the *coigerach,* meaning a "pilgrim or wanderer," indicating that the amulet was carried from place to place when requested, because these amulets were taken occasionally from their keeping places, being lent for specific purposes. In the early fourteenth century, King Robert Bruce borrowed the arm bone of Saint Fillan to carry it into battle to empower his forces against the king of England's army, culminating in Bruce's victory at Bannockburn. In 1488 the bearnane was taken to Scone to be carried in the coronation procession of King James IV.

HORSE HARNESS ORNAMENTS

Horse harness embellishments are what Gertrude Jeckyll called "the Carter's Trophy of horse ornaments" (Jeckyll 1904, 164). Before World War I collectors described them as horse amulets (e.g., Carter 1916). Today these are commonly called "horse brasses," and there are thousands of variations in designs.

Fig. 17.5. Horse brass of a beehive
symbolizing cooperative work
bringing abundance
(also see plate 14)

According to harness expert Terry Keegan, horse brasses had a twofold function: as an artistic wish for display, demonstrating the wealth and taste of the owner, and also as a charm or amulet, with the bright polished metal reflecting harmful influences (Keegan 1973, 124). In the early part of the twentieth century, Lina Eckenstein made a collection of old horse brasses and asserted that their designs were ancient ones that had been in continuous use until her day (Brears 1981, 43).

Chapter 18

Sun and Moon

SOLAR IMAGES

The sun and the moon appear in amuletic form in many parts of the world. Being our source of light and heat, the sun was worshipped in ancient times. Every time there was an eclipse, it was a reminder that the sun's existence could not be taken for granted. Early Greek religion did not give the sun god a major role, but Egyptian and Persian influence elevated Helios until by Hellenistic times he was viewed as the ruling deity, Helios Pantokrator. A Hellenistic prayer addresses him as "all-ruler, spirit of the world, power of the world, light of the world" (Cumont 1919, 322). The visible, physical sun was believed also to possess a spiritual dimension, known as the Intelligible Helios. This concept was transmitted to the Roman sun god, Sol. In the third century CE, the Roman emperor Heliogabalus (reigned 222–226 CE) instituted the worship at Rome of the Syrian solar deity El Gabel. In the year 274 CE, after his army had witnessed an epiphany of the god Sol, the emperor Aurelian proclaimed Sol Invictus, the "Unvanquished Sun," as the supreme god of the empire (Usener 1905, 465*ff.*).

Roman images of Sol Invictus show him with his right hand raised in benediction and carrying an orb, a whip, or a thunderbolt in his left (Usener 1905, 470*ff.*). When the Christian church overthrew traditional religion, it appropriated the pagan view of the sun god as the spiritual

Fig. 18.1. Sun over door in Heidelberg, Germany (also see plate 15)

light of the world. In place of the unconquered sun, Sol Invictus, Jesus was declared the Sun of Righteousness, Sol Iustitiae, the judge of mankind (Usener 1905, 480). He was given the role of cosmic judge that once was the possession of the Babylonian sun god Shamash, with a biblical justification taken from the prophet Malachi: "Unto you that fear my name shall the sun of righteousness arise" (Malachi 4:2). Biblical sun imagery became the new interpretation of the old supreme god, Sol Invictus. Now the birth of Jesus was celebrated on December 25, which in pagan times had been celebrated as the birthday of the son of Helios, Mithras (Usener 1905, 465).

Solar imagery appears as amulets all over the world. The sunwheel cross is an ancient northern symbol. The pioneer horse brass collector Lina Eckenstein noted that in Kent circular brasses were called sun brasses (Brears 1981, 43). "Perforated disks and brooches in the form of a circle are still worn by women in Scotland, in order to protect them against mischief" (Eckenstein 1906, 261).

Fig. 18.2. Sun with face, a very common horse brass

Fig. 18.3. South American ceramic sun amulet

LUNAR IMAGES

The crescent is a glyph common in English horse brasses, signifying the waxing moon. Some have a star inside the crescent, echoing the emblem of the goddess Aphrodite, later adopted as an Islamic sign. Ancient Cypriot coins have the crescent and star above a sacred propylon (Lethaby 1891, 183). Eckenstein viewed the crescent as a lunar symbol, which she traced back through Italian and Middle Eastern examples to ancient times. Another collector, Dr. Plowright, "has shown that many

of these ornaments, which are really amulets . . . are of Moorish origin"
(Webb 1907, 293). Although Eckstein, Plowright, and other collectors of the time are now castigated for appearing to have written of a
continuous unbroken link with antiquity, which cannot be proven, the
makers of horse brasses were not ignorant of ancient artifacts or those
from other countries, and it is likely that they reproduced them in their
Walsall brass foundries.

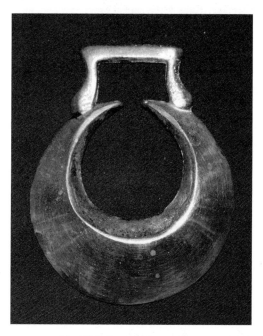

Fig. 18.4. Crescent horse brass

Chapter 19

Coins

Gold coins can be seen as symbolic of the sun. Holed coins that are suspended by chains or strings have been used as amulets since coins were invented. Roman coins with holes drilled in them were found in women's graves among other grave goods during excavations of the large Anglian cemetery under Saint John's College's cricket ground in Cambridge. They dated from the fifth to the seventh centuries (Taylor 1999, 41). Special coins were used in many countries to defend against bad luck, illness, and general evil. The *Benedictuspfennig* of German-speaking lands embodied the power of Saint Benedict. In England the angel, a gold coin with a hole drilled through it for suspension, was worn. Ordinary circulating coins were and are frequently perforated and

Fig. 19.1. Amuletic coin with image of Saint Paulus, Germany, 1760

hung round the neck to cure illnesses. Techniques of healing with coins also immersed them in water, which was then considered empowered by contact with the amulet. The water was then drunk by the patient. In Scotland the Lee penny was a famous amulet that was used to cure cattle by its immersion in water. Sir Walter Scott identified it as his *Talisman* in the book of the same name. Another was the black penny at Humebyers, which cured animals if dipped in water taken from a south-flowing stream (Henderson 1879, 163–64).

Elizabeth Villiers claimed that "the lucky coin, which gamblers toss, is a relic of those other coins with their symbolic designs" (Villiers 1923, 42) and that "pennies bearing the date of a leap year should be kept in the house. They will bring good fortune" (Villiers 1923, 142). But possessing a penny charm is not always enough. Folklorist Arthur Robinson Wright noted that a girl murdered near Hull in 1926 wore a perforated lucky penny (Wright 1928, 72). For centuries lucky coins have been carried by fighting men, whether soldiers, mercenaries, or brigands. In the early years of the Thirty Years' War in central Europe (1618–1648), coins bearing an image of Saint George killing the dragon, known as *Georgenthaler* (Saint George's dollars), were sought after by soldiers so much that they changed hands at up to thirty times their face value (Ahrens 1918, 53). These were considered the most powerful protection. The author's great-grandfather, Charles Robinson (1878–1947), from London, was a soldier in the Royal Fusiliers all through the First World War. He attached his lucky charm, a pierced-silver three-pence piece, to his personal identity tags and survived when most of his comrades were killed. It is illustrated in figure 19.2.

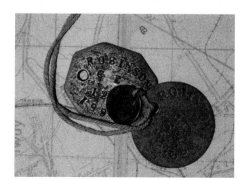

Fig. 19.2. Charles Robinson's identity tags with a lucky three-pence piece, World War I, 1914 (also see plate 16)

Coins carried by soldiers as charms in World War I are preserved in several museums. For example, the National Museum of Wales has a perforated one-cent coin suspended from a red ribbon that was bought by the collector Edward Lovett from an American sailor in 1918. Another item in that museum is a holed farthing (one-quarter of a penny) suspended from a red-and-blue string that was carried by a British soldier in 1916. In northeastern Brazil in the 1920s and 1930s, gangs of insurgent bandits known as *cangaceiros* were known for their flamboyant dress and accoutrements. They protected their ammunition bandoliers with amuletic silver and gold coins. The last notable cangaceiro leader, Lampião, who was shot in 1938, wore a remarkable amuletic hat. Made of deer leather, it had an upturned rim embellished visibly with seven gold and silver coins, the largest of which was from 1885, bearing the head of the emperor Pedro II. There were around seventy gold pieces inlaid in the leather, three gold rings, one with an emerald, gold plaques with sentiments, and two religious medallions with the inscription *Deus de guie* (God guide you) (Tribe 2001, 63–64). In World War II General Dwight D. Eisenhower carried seven lucky coins with him (Davies 2018, 228).

Baikonur Cosmodrome in Kazakhstan is the launching place for Russian spacecraft. Soyuz rockets are constructed in a facility that is linked by a special rail track to the launch pad. Rockets are carried along the tracks, and participants in spaceflights put coins on the rails to be flattened by the rocket-carrying vehicle as it passes. These flattened coins are kept as lucky charms. Launches at Baikonur may not take place on October 24 because two major rocket accidents occurred on that day in 1960 and 1963. Even in the most scientific form of travel, the rituals of luck are still observed.

Not a coin and neither a sacred medallion, but called a charm and later a talisman, is an item issued in 1916 by a major railway company that operated in England and Wales. On page 259 of *The Engineer,* dated September 22, 1916, we read, "A little medal is being sent by the Great Western Railway Company to its servants. Titled *Charm against Accidents,* it bore the legend 'is it safe?'" A leaflet that came with it asked employees to "always carry it with 'small change'" so that it would always remind them to be aware of the many dangers of working on the railway. An example of a later version, issued in 1922, is in the National Railway Museum at York. Renamed by then the Safety Talisman, on the obverse it read "The Safety Talisman. Look before you leap—ask 'is it safe?'" Beneath was a cartouche of olive leaves tied with a ribbon. The reverse read, "In every action ask yourself 'is it safe?' This will disclose unseen dangers, inspire forethought, induce care, and prevent accidents." In his *English Folklore,* Arthur Robinson Wright noted that the company had issued fifty thousand of these "pocket tokens" in 1922 (Wright 1928, 73).

Chapter 20

The Warding Mirror: Reflections of the Invisible

It is a widespread folk belief that mirrors reflect not only visible light but also intangible spirits and energies. Women's clothing in many cultures has reflective silver coins or small mirrors sewn to garments and headdresses. All over Europe there are traditions of straight spirit paths along which, at certain times, travel dangerous inhabitants of the otherworld. Like light, spirits travel in straight lines, and unless something is done to stop them, they will enter dwellings whose entrances (windows and doors) are approached by lines of sight. To prevent this from happening, various techniques are employed by those whose expertise it is to remedy bad places and ward off harm. Mirrors, often in the form of silvered glass balls (called witch balls), are placed at strategic points to reflect the perceived intrusion. Silvered glass vessels may also be placed at strategic points, such as mantel shelves. A parallel tradition exists in Chinese culture, where the *ba gua* geomantic mirror performs the same function. In recent years, with an increased interest in Chinese feng shui by people outside of Hong Kong, Singapore, and "Chinatowns" in Western countries, octagonal ba gua geomantic mirrors with an identical function have in some cases become popular (e.g., Lip 1979, 109–13).

Two different glass artifacts are used for good luck—the so-called *walking stick* and the *witch ball*. Walking sticks of glass were made mainly by the Nailsea factory near Bristol, which operated between

Fig. 20.1. Chinese ba gua geomantic mirror
(also see plate 17)

1788 and 1873. Nailsea was known for its high-quality crown window glass. Walking sticks are *friggers,* items said in glassmakers' folklore to be made by men in their spare time for fun. But a seventy-two-hour working week in the harsh conditions of the glasshouse hardly made for after-hours playfulness and creating exquisite *latticinio* swirls. These items were and are of value. They are made of clear glass with colored glass threads, often spirals, within. They are hung on the wall and dusted daily to keep away evil sprites and bad luck. Glass animals made at the seaside for summer visitors as they watch are the continuation of the tradition of friggers. Many of these are luck-bringers, such as pigs and elephants.

Witch balls are large silvered balls, frequently blue in color, but also old ones can be golden or silver. Some are made of clear glass. They were made by silvering the inside of a blown glass sphere using a mercury mixture and are hung in a window or the window above the door in Victorian and Edwardian houses without leaded glass.* Ill-wishers see their distorted reflection and are frightened off (Thomas 2019, 247–48). During summertime in German-speaking countries, similar silvered glass balls are set up on sticks in gardens. Clearly they have the same function but are explained away as enhancing the beauty of the roses.

Fig. 20.2. Witch ball (also see plate 18)

---

*They have to hang behind clear glass to be effective.

Chapter 21

Trees, Plants, and Seeds

Trees have been the objects of veneration in all tribal and traditional societies. The Tree of Life is an important motif in many different cultures. The ancient Romans had a sacred book dating from the sixth century BCE, the *Ostentarium Arborarium* of Lucinius Tarquinius Priscus (king of Rome, 616–579 BCE). This described numinous trees

Fig. 21.1. Tree of Life amulet

and how to recognize them; for example, an Arbor Felix was an auspicious tree under the protection of a god. Among these trees were poplars (*Populus* spp.), olive (*Olea europaea*), and laurel (*Laurus nobilis*). "Numen inest," which translates as "there is a spirit here," appeared in *Fasti* by the Roman poet Ovid; that there is a spirit within is the ruling principle of special trees. Wood taken from such trees naturally possessed the virtues inherent in the whole tree. But some trees were inviolate, and no wood could ever be taken from them. The custom of revering wood is still with us; "touch wood" ("knock on wood") is a saying that reflects the lucky or protective qualities of wood. Some British soldiers fighting on the Western Front in World War I carried small amulets called "touchwood" for good luck in a life-threatening situation (see chapter 32, "Little People: Small Humanoid Images").

The *arbor genialis* is the plane tree (*Platanus orientalis*), celebrated as the tutelary tree of London in 1603 on the ceremonial entry of King James I into London. The *ramus feralis* (the wild branch) is a straight branch of a tree that never bore leaves. It is a magical item, used in a ritual by the Dame of the Witches in Ben Jonson's *The Masque of Queens* (1609), which was performed before King James I. The Dame says:

> *Reach me a bough that ne'er bare leafe*
> *To strike the Ayre; and Aconite*
> *To hurl upon this glaring light:*
> *A rusty knife, to wound mine arm,*
> *And as it dropps, I'll speak a charm.*

In Northern Tradition legend the rowan or mountain ash (*Sorbus aucuparia*) was the tree that saved Thor from being washed away in an Underworld river. In Britain rowan is a protective wood. Twigs and branches pulled from a tree without the use of a knife (that is, without iron) were set over cowshed stalls or wreathed about the cows' horns. In Scotland farmers incanted the following formula while they arranged the rowan: "From Witches and Wizards, and long-tailed Buzzards, and creeping things that run in hedge bottoms, good Lord, deliver us" (Lawrence 1898, 297). Crosses made from twigs tied with red thread were a protection against witchcraft, as recalled in the old Scottish adage, "Rowan tree and red threid gar the witches tyne their speid" (Rowan tree and red thread make the witches lose their speed, that is, be disempowered). C. J. S Thompson notes the saying, "Witches have no power where there's row'n-tree wood" (Thompson 1927, 301). Rowan wood was used for the handles of Scottish cattle drovers' whips for this reason. Until 1938 a carpenter's shop in Whitby, Yorkshire, was known for selling rowan, known there as "witch wood," for luck.

A charm from Devon involves carrying five ash tree twigs in a bag as a safeguard against suffering fits. Runic amulets using wood from an ash recall the cosmic axial tree Yggdrassil of the Northern Tradition.

God's eye amulets are made from a cross of rowan twigs wrapped round with red wool. Occasionally other colors are used. To be effective the twigs must be taken from a tree one has never seen before. They are made at winter equinox, and a God's eye lasts for one year, when a new one should be made to replace it (Thomas 2019, 204). They are related to the Irish straw plaits called Saint Bridget's crosses, which are also hung up amuletically.

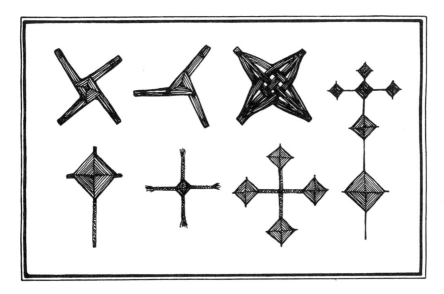

Fig. 21.2. Saint Bridget's crosses, various forms, Ireland

Fig. 21.3. God's eye of wool and rowan twigs, Norfolk, 1990s

A necklace made from rowan berries is worn as a protection from bodily illness, and strings of them on a linen thread, sometimes with a holystone, are hung round doorframes, windows, and mirrors to guard against evil (Thomas 2019, 205).

The elder (*Sambucus nigra*) is the archetypal magic tree. Its German name, *Hollunder*, has associations with the underworld goddess Frau Hölle. Branches of elder were hung in front of stables to ward off evil spirits and lightning. Elder was used in northern England in the magical test known as *bottry*, where elder *knots* (buds) were used to divine whether or not pigs or cattle were bewitched. Nine buds were picked and arranged in a straight line. A dish made of ash wood was inverted over them, and they were left overnight. The next morning, the dish was lifted and the buds examined. If they remained in a straight line, the animals were all right. But if the buds were "disordered," then that was a sign that the animals had a spell put on them (Gutch 1911, 63). Elder wood is rarely worn or carried as an amulet, but Norfolk witches' wands are made of an elder stick with a belemnite inserted in the end as a tip (Thomas 2019, 189). The Cornish surnames Scawn and Scown refer to the elder, called *scawen* in the Cornish language.

Albion knots are made to be worn openly. They are made from a twig of hawthorn (*Crataegus* spp.) tied round with red wool. The rune *thurisaz*, whose Anglo-Saxon name is *thorn*, signifies protection, defending against marauders who dare not risk the thorns. In this the thorns of hawthorn are the natural equivalent of pins, needles, and nails. In 1965 at Castle Rising in Norfolk, there was a witchcraft scare that included a sheep's heart pierced with hawthorn twigs openly nailed to the castle door along with two clay poppets (Hill and Williams 1965, 194–95). Related to the hawthorn is the rose (*Rosa* spp.), whose flower has a significant magical and heraldic lore (Pennick 2014, 88–94). In the Norfolk magical tradition, rose petals are chopped up and heated with a small amount of water to moisten them, then they are rolled into beads and strung as a rose rosary (Thomas 2019, 263–64).

The hazel (*Corylus avellana*) was the bardic tree of the ancient Celts. As charms, hazelnuts, also known as filbert nuts, are associated with the East Anglian medieval mystic Julian of Norwich. She had a vision in which God showed her "a little thing, the size of a hazelnut, round as a ball." When asked what it was, God told her, "It is all that I have made." She had a vision of the microcosm, filled with all potential. The hazelnut is an important amulet in the Norfolk spiritual tradition because of this. The Rosary of Mother Julian of Norwich consists of hazelnuts strung together and used in spiritual ritual or worn as a necklace. The number used is appropriate for whatever purpose is intended (Thomas 2019, 101). The Scots Clan Colquhoun has the hazel as its "plant badge," and the Cornish families Collick and Collett derive their names from the hazel.

In the European tradition the oak (*Quercus robur*) is the most powerful tree of them all, sacred to the sky god variously called Zeus, Jupiter, Taranis, Ziu, Thunor, Thor, Perun, and Perkunas. The sacred tree of the ancient druids of Gaul, Britain, and Ireland, the oak was ascribed the Ogham letter *duir* in the tree alphabet, with the phonetic value of *d*. Holy trees in pagan times in northern mainland Europe, sacred oaks were targeted by militant Christian missionaries such as Saint Martin of Tours in France and Saint Eligius in Flanders, who cut them down with Christian ceremonies. Centuries later the knights of the Teutonic Order fought a crusade against the pagans in Old Prussia and the Baltic lands, cutting down their sacred oaks and building churches on their sites. In Iceland the sigil called *dunfaxi*, carved on a piece of oak, was used to win in legal cases.

In the English Civil War, the fugitive future king Charles II fled from the Parliamentary New Model Army after losing the final battle of that war, fought at Worcester in September 1651. He hid among the leaves of an ancient oak tree at Boscobel, escaped the country, and subsequently returned to England to be crowned king in 1660. Then that oak became famous as the Royal Oak, inns were named after it, and wood from the oak was taken and sold as souvenirs that were treated as empowered amulets. Finally the tree was destroyed by people taking pieces away for themselves or to sell.

Fig. 21.4. Royal Oak Hotel sign in traditional form,
Welshpool, Powys, Wales

Some Irish and Scottish clans have a totemic "plant badge" or "crest badge," usually a tree. The oak is the plant badge of Clans Buchanan, Cameron, and Cameron of Lochiel, while the Andersons and Clan MacEwen display a crest badge in the form of a cut-off sprouting oak trunk. The Irish O'Connors also have the oak as a heraldic emblem. Welsh archers who fought with the English Army in France at the Battle of Agincourt in 1415 carried images of Merlin's Oak from Carmarthen. The British military unit called the Sherwood Foresters had oak leaves and acorns as their badge, and oak leaves appeared on the highest-ranking grade of the German military medal, the Knight's Cross of the Iron Cross.

Fig. 21.5. Acorn and oak leaves, Sherwood Foresters regiment, circa 1914, subsequently used as an amulet on a hat

Acorns were worn as protection against cholera and are carried in the pocket as a safeguard against lightning. Carvings of newel posts on stairs in Victorian houses frequently had an acorn carving for a finial, as were the ends of cords on window blinds. On page 39 of the spring 2020 edition of the catalog for the British jewelry company Pia, there was a picture of a pewter key ring with an acorn and a separate oak leaf of the same metal attached to it (see fig. 21.6). "Keep this pewter talisman of strength close," read the caption.

Fig. 21.6. Acorn and oak leaf
"talisman of strength,"
Pia Jewellery, spring 2020

Mistletoe (*Viscum album*) is an evergreen semiparasite that grows among the branches of trees. To the ancient Druids it was a holy plant, ritually cut with a golden sickle at certain times of year. Today it is a plant sold at Christmastime and hung up so people can "steal a kiss" beneath it. When it is taken down on Twelfth Night, twigs and berries can be kept and used as amulets.

Fig. 21.7. Wooden amulet with runes, Cambridge, 1970s

The yew (*Taxus baccata*) lives far longer than any other European tree. It is evergreen, appearing unchanged in summer and winter alike. Its exceptional longevity makes it a tree of everlasting life. But all parts of it are poisonous to humans and animals. European yew magic appraises the mysteries of life and death. In former times death-dealing longbows were made of yew, and rune-masters made yew sticks into talismanic bearers of magical power. In the Netherlands yew runestaffs dating from the seventh century have been recovered from waterlogged ground. Two found at Arum and Britsum in West Frisia bore runic inscriptions translated as "return, messenger" and "always carry this yew in the host of battle." A sliver of yew wood cut at an appropriate hour guards the holder against all harm. In his play *Macbeth*, William Shakespeare tells of the "slips of Yew sliver'd in the Moon's eclipse." But the yew rune *eihwaz* is sometimes called the "death rune." This is reinforced by its place in the Elder Futhark—number thirteen.

Pine (*Pinus sylvestris*) has a symbolic function: it signifies illumination in darkness, one of the meanings of the rune *kenaz*. This recalls the traditional form of lighting that used a burning chip of resinous pinewood in the days before candles and much later in poor households where candles were too expensive. The pine cone is an amulet that symbolizes fecundity and regeneration, healing and conviviality, and it is an embodiment of sacred number (Whittick 1971, 296). The pine was the tree of the gods Osiris and Attis, the latter of whom was personified as the pine spirit. The wand carried by the god Dionysos is the *thyrsus,* a stave tipped with the pine cone. The pine cone is also the emblem of the ancient Swabian goddess Zisa, and numerous large stone ones survive from Roman times at Augsburg in Bavaria, Germany. Zisa is the female counterpart of Ziu, a sky god of lightning and thunder, whose tree is the oak. The church of Saint Peter am Perlach stands on the site of her temple, and the *Stadtpyr,* a cone, is Augsburg's emblem (Pennick 2002: 107–9).

Fig. 21.8. Roman-era carving of pine cone Stadtpyr, Augsburg, Bavaria, Germany

As an emblem of healing, the pine is a minor attribute of Aesculapius, for the seed of the stone pine was an ingredient of ancient medicines. The Scottish Clans Ferguson, Fletcher, Grant, MacAlpine, MacAulay, MacGregor, and MacQuarne of Ulva have the pine cone as their plant badge.

PLANT MASCOTS

Mascots of clans and families, mainly Scottish, often have two separate heraldic components—a badge and a plant badge. For example, the Nesbitt badge is a boar passant and the plant badge the oak. Yew is the plant badge of Fraser of Lovat. As noted above, pine in the form of its cone is the badge of several Scottish clans. Another Celtic country, Cornwall, has its own tradition. Every large farm or *barton* there had its own heraldic device, mostly never authorized by the College of Arms in London. Some plant badges echoed family and clan names. Thus hazel in the form of filbert nuts is depicted as the badge of the Colquhoun clan and the Cornish Collett and Collick families (derived from hazel's genus name: *Corylus*). Oak is the badge of the Cornish family Penderill.

THE LUCKY BEAN

Writing in 1923 Elizabeth Villiers noted, "The 'Lucky Bean' is quite a common charm to find on watch chains and bangles." She explains that in the Western Highlands of Scotland, a certain kind of bean was believed to have the power to drive away evil spirits and to bring wealth. She does not state what kind of bean it was (Villiers 1923, 23). Large beans from the Caribbean floating in transatlantic currents sometimes reach the British Isles. Often called Molucca beans, they have been noted as lucky beans as far back as the seventeenth century. In 1602 Richard Carew wrote that in form they somewhat resembled a sheep's kidney and, although inedible, were valued, by those who believed it, in assisting women in childbirth (Carew [1602] 1969, 44).

Beans on charm bracelets are very uncommon a century after Villiers wrote about them. She also noted that beans appeared in sets of lucky charms sold before Christmastime to be stirred into Christmas puddings (Villiers 1923, 25). This was because in the old Christmas tradition, a bean was put in the Christmas cake, and whoever found it at the Christmas dinner was proclaimed as King of the Revels. Villiers notes that the threat, "'I'll give him the beans,' that is, punishment, may come from the power of the bean to exorcise ghosts and evil spirits" (Villiers 1923, 26).

The African mojo bean, used in hoodoo, is an ingredient of assemblages of amuletic and magic items in flannel bags known as mojo hands or nation sacks. The mojo bean is often the broad bean (*Vicia faba*), which along with the Molucca bean is also a lucky bean in British tradition. An "African bean" carried in 1916 as a good luck charm by a British soldier of the West Surrey regiment serving in World War I is preserved in the National Museum of Wales. Arthur Robinson Wright tells how a woman rescued from the Rive Avon at Bath, Somerset, refused to give her name to her rescuers but was identified by two lucky beans in her pocket (Wright 1928, 72).

Chapter 22

Roots

Traditionally roots are considered dangerous things. Many cultures view roots as powerful, not only for their medicinal qualities but also as amulets. Roots with gnarled humanoid forms are easily understood as harboring indwelling spirits. In Nuremberg in 1617 Job Körnlein was executed for theft and sorcery. Among his magical items was a chicory root (see page 179, chapter 29). The wild herb men of bygone England prized the humanoid root called *the root of life* or *the divine root,* better known as the mandrake (*Mandragora officinarum*). Because it resembles a human being, this root was considered to be an earth sprite whose magical pow-

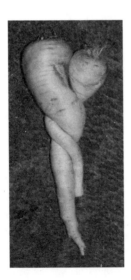

Fig. 22.1. Humanoid parsnip roots, 2018

116

ers could be used for amuletic, magical, and medical purposes. Until the twentieth century mandrake was important in English horse-doctoring (Grieve 1931, 510–12; Hennels 1972, 79–80).

Although the mandrake is alleged to scream as it is pulled out of the ground, proving fatal to the digger, the wild herb men did not die from digging out the root. The mandrake was supposed to take revenge on anyone who dragged it from the ground. So there was a cunning technique to pull it up without triggering the fatal response. The deed must be carried out on a Friday. A dog, which has not been fed for a while, must be tied to it, then attracted with a piece of meat. The dog will strain to get the food and pull the mandrake out of the ground. Then the mandrake's curse will fall on the dog, not the root digger.

> *Then on the still night air,*
> *The bark of dog is heard,*
> *A shriek! A groan!*
> *A human cry. A trumpet sound.*
> *The Mandrake root lies captive on the ground.*
> (Thompson 1934, 153)

However, once dug up, the mandrake was still a danger, for there was a belief that if one looked at one for too long one would go blind (Cielo 1918, 114). Another alleged power of the mandrake was that it is luminous at night, giving it a nickname, *the devil's candle* (Thompson 1927, 298).

In Germany a Franconian saying of someone who has unexpectedly had good fortune is that he or she must own an *Areile* (or *Alraun*) (Lecouteux 2013, 134). An Alraun is, like the mandrake, a natural humanoid root. It is considered to be an earth sprite possessing magical powers that can be used by magicians. Some owners dressed the Alraun in a white garment, held in place by a golden belt. The roots were kept in special boxes, and some were bathed or anointed every Friday. Possession of an Alraun could be troublesome. If someone wanted to be rid of one, throwing it away was ineffective, as it would be found back at home later. During the witch hunts it was a capital offense to possess an Alraun. Instigated by priests, bans were enacted on the *Homunculorum simulacra*. The witch-hunting bishop of Bamberg called them *der Teufeleiein der Hexenmeister* (the devils of the witch masters), and Duke Ulrich von Württemberg banned them in 1540. Three women were executed in Hamburg for possession, and there were many other prosecutions that resulted in the death penalty (Starck 1916, 45–46).

Although illegal in Germany at the time, they were imported and sold in Tudor England. After the witch craze they were bought and sold openly in the German states. A letter of 1675 by a citizen of Leipzig tells how he bought an Alraun for sixty-four Reichstaler and sent it to his brother in Riga (Starck 1916, 45). The Alraun is known by various other German names, including the diminutive *das Alraunerl, Baaras, Springwurz, Wurzelknecht* (servant root), and *Galgenmännchen* (little gallows man). In Holland it is the *pisdefje,* and in Iceland *Þjófarót.* Galgenmännchen recalls the tradition that the mandrake grows beneath gallows and is fed on the bodily fluids of those hanged there. Belladonna (deadly nightshade, *Atropa belladonna*) and white bryony (*Bryonia dioica*) have roots that resemble the mandrake. In Norfolk the local name for white bryony is mandrake.

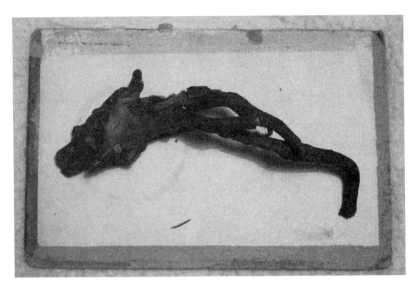

Fig. 22.2. Magic root, Cambridgeshire

Bryony roots grow very large. In former times charlatans faked them into human shapes so they could sell them for inflated prices as genuine mandrakes. A recipe, "To Make a Counterfeit Mandrake," was published in 1815. The faker dug up a large double root of bryony, carved it into the form of a man, then pricked it all over. Into the holes seeds were inserted. Millet, leek, and barley were recommended. Then it was buried again until the seeds had sprouted, producing a hairy effect on the hand-carved root (Lupton et. al., 1815, 19). Another technique produced more credible figures. It involved digging round the roots of a vigorous young bryony plant, taking care not to damage the lower part of the root. Then the faker fixed a human-shaped mold around the main part of the root. The earth was then packed around the mold and the bryony left to grow into the shape of the mold; this took one summer. Then the "mandrake" was dug up, ready to sell to a gullible customer.

Roots also feature large in the African American magical tradition of root doctors. High John the Conqueror root, the tuber of *Ipomoea jalappa*, is a spirit-embodying item used in African American luck- and power-bringing talismans, seen as a continuation of the Kongo tradition recorded from the seventeenth century, in which gnarled roots were revered as divine incarnations (Chireau 2003, 5). In his memoirs Frederick Douglass recalls that when he was a downtrodden slave, he was given a root by Sandy Jenkins that empowered him to stand up to his slave driver and rekindled his spirit and determination to be free (Douglass [1845] 1973, 72). There is a photograph of Bishop Charles Harrison (1864–1961), founder of the Church of God of Christ, surrounded by roots that he called "the wonders of God."

THE DEVIL'S PLANTS

Not only *weird plants* (like belladonna, also known as *the devil's herb*, and mandrake), as they are called in East Anglian tradition, were associated with the devil in popular imagination. High John the Conqueror root is related to the British plant bindweed (or *convolvulus*), which is also known as *the devil's garter* (Thompson 1927, 300). Asafetida (*Ferula foetida*) is called *the devil's dung;* yellow toadflax (*Linaria vulgaris*), *the devil's ribbon* (also *dead men's bones*); clematis, *the devil's thread,* and scandix (*Umbelliferaceae* spp.), *the devil's darning needles* (Thompson 1927, 298–300).

Chapter 23

Animals and Their Images

Charms in the form of animals are widespread throughout time and place. In his work on bear ceremonies, the American anthropologist A. Irving Hallowell categorized the worldview of tribal people toward animals. He asserted that their belief was that animals are seen as having the same animating agency as humans. Animals have their own language; they understand the actions of humans. They have their own social and tribal order, paralleling human society. Certain animals possess supernatural or

Fig. 23.1. Three lions of England heraldic amulet

magical powers. They can transform themselves into other species of animal or into human form. Some may use their powers to assist humans, while others may be hostile. Animals can serve as messengers of divine powers, they can be possessed by spirits and gods, and they can become deities in their own right (Hallowell 1926, 7–8).

In the early modern period, cats, hares, toads, and other animals were portrayed by witch hunters as *familiars,* a word that originally meant "a family or house animal" but that became the description of a supernatural animal or an evil spirit in animal form. Amulets in the form of animals or made from animal parts have been viewed by some as containing indwelling spirits. In the 1640s, during the English Civil War, Parliamentarians noted that their military adversary, Prince Rupert, fought in battle accompanied by a German white poodle dog called Boy. The dog had survived under fire and was believed by them to be "shot-free," that is, woundproof by bullets. Military leaders at that time were often said to carry amulets that made them invulnerable to gunfire, but Rupert's dog was condemned as being a familiar spirit, not a flesh-and-blood dog.

In 1644, at the Battle of Marston Moor, the Royalists' decisive defeat, Boy was shot and killed. A triumphant Parliamentary pamphlet was published in London that had the dog tell that he was not really a German dog but had originated in Lapland or Finland "where there none but Divells and Sorcerers live." The pamphlet claimed that the dog was shot with a silver bullet fired "by a valiant souldier, who had skill in Necromancy." Silver bullets, cast from melted-down religious medallions or coins from the church offertory, were an aggressive form of amulet used in counter-magic. Magic was a normal part of the arsenal of both sides in the conflict (Ashton 1896, 162–63).

Animal amulets and mascots take three forms. There are amulets made from part of the actual animal, like a rabbit's foot or a toad bone; there are amulets made in the shape of a lucky animal, such as a pig or cat; and there are live animals that serve as mascots, especially for military units. Animals considered to be dangerous or undesirable have specialized charms to repel or kill them, sometimes in the shape of the beast.

THE PIG

Although shunned as "unclean" by two of the three Abrahamic religions, the pig has been a significant image of fecundity and well-being in European tradition. In the Northern Tradition the golden-bristled boar Gullinbursti appears with the gods in Valhalla, and the god Freyr rides on the boar Hildisvini ("Battle Swine"). Some Viking-age helmets had a representation of a boar as a crest. Pork is the customary meat of the Norwegian Yule feast, signifying the spirit of prosperity and abundance. It is also traditional in the East Midlands of England to eat a pork pie for breakfast on Christmas Day, and "pigs in blankets"—pork sausages wrapped in rashers of bacon—are served with traditional Christmas dinners in Great Britain. The custom of bringing in the boar's head to the Yuletide feast is maintained at Queen's College in Oxford and at the Swan Hotel in Bedford.

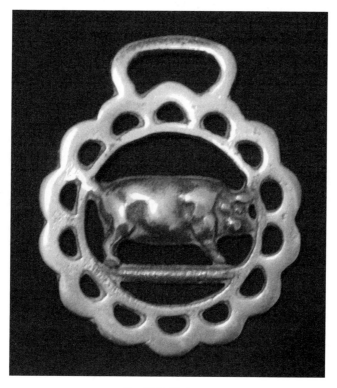

Fig. 23.2. Pig brass

In Scotland there is a record of a remnant of the tradition of slaughtering a pig for Yule in Sir John Sinclair's collection now called *The Old Statistical Account* (formally, it's *The Statistical Account of Scotland Drawn Up from the Communications of the Ministers of the Different Parishes*). For the town of Stromness in the Orkney Islands, volume 14, from 1795, records: "Superstitous observances—in a part of the parish of Sandwick, every family that has a herd of swine, kills a sow on the seventeenth day of December, and thence it is called Sow Day. There is no tradition as to the origin of this practice" (Sinclair 1795, 460). An old Irish description of the pig as "the gentleman who pays the rent" means that raising a pig for slaughter was a means of earning money for impoverished people. Irish pig mascots traditionally were made with one ear missing, as a pig image was said to be lucky only if broken in some way. In Ireland small black pigs were made from bog oak, a rock-hard ancient timber recovered from peat bogs. Pigs as lucky charms generally are intact figures. A black pig is especially lucky. The old rhyme "pig on the knee, safety at sea" tells how British sailors had a pig tattoo on the knee or foot to prevent drowning (Davies 2018, 156). French amulets with the inscription *"Porte Bonheur"* and showing a wild boar were popular during World War I.

Fig.23.3. Lucky pigs, black-and-white glass

In the early twentieth century, pigs appeared on luck-bringing post-cards, often along with other talismanic figures. A British card from 1912 shows a pig, a black cat, a horseshoe, and a swastika. The celebrated postcard artist Donald McGill, best remembered for his saucy seaside images, produced a lucky pig postcard in 1919. In 1920 another card showing a black cat near a crossroads signpost had a pig, a swastika, a wishbone, and a horseshoe hanging from its four arms, with this rhyme:

Whichever road that you may choose,
Good fortune ever meet you,
And as you journey on your way
Good luck be there to greet you.

In this combination the pig stands for health, the swastika for good luck, the wishbone for happiness, and the horseshoe for love. A lucky pig postcard on sale in England in the 1920s carried the following rhyme, a motto of one of the Sussex bonfire societies that parade through Lewes on Bonfire Night (November 5):

You may push
You may shove
But I'm hanged
If I'll be druv.

Fig. 23.4. War Pig, the mascot of the hard rock band Motörhead

Here the pig is an emblem of resistance. But although the pig is emblematic of luck and fecundity, there was also a demonic dimension. Pigs with crescent patterns on their forelegs were said to bear "the Devils marks" (Gregor 1881, 129). Another kind of pig that had no zoological existence was also feared and required the use of charms, amulets, or talismans to fend it off. In Scotland the *yird swine* was a feared beast that lived in graveyards, "burrowing among dead bodies and devouring them" (Gregor 1881, 130).

THE RAM

In ancient Egypt the ram was venerated. The ancient god Khnum, deity of the river Nile, was depicted with a ram's head, as was Amun, chief god of Thebes. The Temple of Amun at Thebes was approached by an avenue flanked by a series of giant stone rams. The Twenty-Seventh Dynasty temple at Hibis has hieroglyphs that record the hymns sung to the ram-headed god there. One hymn describes Amun-Re as with the face of a ram, with four heads on one neck. Another describes the god as "the ram of all rams" and "the most ram-formed of the rams" (Klotz 2006, 10).

Fig. 23.5. Stone carving of a ram's head on a nineteenth-century building in Derby

THE DERBY RAM AND HIS COLLEAGUES

"The Derby Ram" is a traditional English song that sings the praise of "the finest tup that ever was fed on hay." It is a song of exaggeration, the tup (ram) being one of impossible size whose horns stretched up to the sky and whose feet covered an acre of land each time he moved them. The ram is naturally the emblem of the city of Derby, in the Midlands of England. The local football team, Derby County, founded in 1884, has the ram as its mascot.

Fig. 23.6. Unofficial supporters' badge of the Derby County Football Club with ram's head

In 1838, when stationed in Ceylon (now Sri Lanka), Derbyshire's local military unit, the 95th Foot, was presented with a ram by a local ruler. This ram, called Rajah, later attacked the band during a ceremonial parade, was court-martialed, convicted of gross insubordination, and shot (Felix 1998, 54). After service in the Crimean War, the Derbies were sent to India to quell an uprising. After entering the city of Kotah, the colonel in command came across a sacred fighting ram tethered in a temple and took possession of it. It became the new regimental mascot, now known as Derby I. Subsequently the ram was present at six battles and was awarded the Indian Mutiny Medal for his service. As a fighting ram Derby I fought thirty-three other rams and retired undefeated. His death came in 1863 when he fell down a well. His head is preserved in Derby Heritage Centre. Over the years the regiment has had a succession of ram mascots (Felix 1998, 55).

Other regiments of the British Army also have living animal mascots. Like the ram, when one dies, its successor, if named, bears the same name, numbered, as happens with monarchs. The Parachute Regiment has a Shetland pony called Pegasus, named after the winged horse of Greek mythology; the Royal Irish Regiment an Irish wolfhound named Brian Boru, named for the famous Irish king who defeated the Norsemen in battle in 1014; and the Welsh Fusiliers have a billy goat. The goat tradition is said to have begun in 1775 at the Battle of Bunker Hill, when a wild goat strayed onto the battlefield and attached itself to the color party of the Welsh soldiers retreating from the fray.

THE CAT

The lore of cats associates them with both good and bad luck. Because this book is primarily concerned with good luck, I shall not detail the bad luck lore of cats, only to mention the trope that a black cat crossing one's path is considered to presage misfortune and the Scottish tradition that should a bride on the way to her wedding encounter a cat, it presaged bad luck (Gregor 1881, 124). Several well-known American blues songs detail this happening. In ancient Egypt the cat was a sacred animal, the living manifestation of the goddess Bastet. Temple cats were mummified and buried ceremonially when they died. English folklore tells that a three-colored cat protects the house where it lives from being destroyed by fire (Villiers 1923, 36).

Fig. 23.7. A bronze statue of an ancient Egyptian cat

Fig. 23.8. Black cat bone

In northern Scotland people moving house took their cat with them for an important ritual: "Before a member of the family entered the new abode, the cat was thrown into it. If a curse or disease had been left on the house, the cat became the victim and dies, to the saving of the family's lives" (Gregor 1881, 124). Black cats were lucky charms, supposed to have the power to cure epilepsy (Villiers 1923, 36), and in American hoodoo lore, a certain bone from a black cat obtained by a transgressive ritual is considered to bring good luck in love affairs and gambling (Hyatt 1978, vol. 1, 74–97; vol. 5, 3913–47). Its function is parallel with the toad bone used in British toadmanry (Pennick 2011a, passim).

From the late nineteenth century, Gablonz in Bohemia (now the Czech Republic) was a center of manufacture of glass charms, including black cats. From the 1890s to the 1930s, cats were manufactured in various forms, with gloss and frosted finishes. Large numbers were imported into the United Kingdom to be put into Christmas crackers (small gift-containing tubes that crack when opened, not baked goods), and some were sold with tags reading "The Lucky Black Cat Mascot," intended to be carried as a pocket charm or hung around the neck as a pendant. In 1919 the first airmen to fly the Atlantic nonstop were two British Royal Air Force aviators, Captain John Alcock (1892–1919) and Lieutenant Arthur Whitten Brown (1884–1948). Flying in a twin-engined Vickers Vimy biplane, they carried lucky charms with them. They each had a fabric black cat. Alcock's was called Twinkletoes and Brown's Lucky Jim. In addition, beneath Alcock's seat were some lucky white heather and a horseshoe. Tragically Alcock died in an air accident only a few months after the epic flight. Lucky Jim is preserved in the Royal Air Force Museum.

Lucky Black Cats in London

In British tradition, unlike in many other countries, the black cat is primarily a sign of luck. Where it is considered unlucky, it is through association with the belief in the witches' familiar. It appears that the once-popular Black Cat brand of British cigarettes got its name from this lucky context. The Carreras Tobacco Company, founded by Don Jose Joaquin Carreras, operated from a shop in London's Wardour Street, where his pet black cat is supposed to have dozed in the front window. Black Cat cigarettes were first produced in 1904, and the black cat was by then emblematic of the company. Craven "A," the first cork-tipped cigarettes, also carried the cat's head logo.

Frank Swinnerton, writing in 1954, says that the frontal image of a black cat, the company's trademark, was derived from the Doctor Nikola books of Guy Newell Boothby. According to Swinnerton Doctor Nikola's mesmeric image, accompanied by his golden-eyed black cat

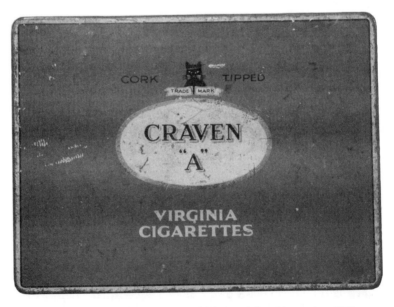

Fig. 23.9. Craven "A" cigarette tin with a cat's head logo, circa 1950

Apollyon, could be seen all over London, the cat's image was used on a popular brand of cigarettes (Swinnerton 1954, 13). The five Doctor Nikola books were published between 1895 and 1902, and Stanley L. Wood was the artist who produced the striking frontal image of Nikola and his cat (Quayle 1972, 75–77). The cat was named for the Angel of the Abyss, putting it squarely on the malevolent side. Yet, as a cigarette brand, it was placed on the side of luck, paralleling the name of the cigarette brand Lucky Strike in the United States. Black Cat cigarettes had a connection with gambling: packs contained coupons that could be collected and redeemed for prizes and, from 1907, the company promoted gambling on football pools, with coupons being issued from tobacconists selling the brand. In addition packs of playing cards bearing the black cat logo were produced.

In 1928 the company opened a new factory at Mornington Crescent. Built on a block fronted by Egyptian columns, it is now considered a masterpiece of London art deco. Along the front between the columns are black cat masks with metal whiskers, and two bronze Egyptian cats, each eight feet, six inches high (2.6 meters) flank the entrance. These cats are replicas of the originals, removed when the factory ceased making cigarettes in 1959.

Another London instance of the lucky black cat is at the Savoy Hotel. It has a mascot, an art-deco sculpture of a black cat. Named Kaspar, it was sculpted in 1927 by Basil Ionides. It came into being because of a superstition that culminated in a real tragedy. In 1898 South African diamond magnate Woolf Joel had a dinner at the Savoy at which a guest canceled at the last minute, leaving thirteen at the table. Afterward, a few weeks later, back in his office in Johannesburg, Joel was shot dead. Thirteen at the table is considered unlucky because it re-creates the Last Supper of Jesus and his disciples, after which Judas betrayed him. In 1927 the Savoy Hotel decided that a token fourteenth diner should be added whenever there were thirteen at the table. Ionides's cat was made for the hotel, and ever since it has been placed, with full settings, as the fourteenth diner at any dinner where thirteen guests are present. The cat subsequently became an icon of the hotel, and the private approach to the main entrance is flanked by a topiary image of Kaspar.

The author's song "Black Cat" expresses its apotropaic and luck-bringing aspect in the English tradition:

Black cat bring me good luck
Drive all harm away
Black cat bring good fortune
Bring it here today.

I own a ten-dot domino
Four-leaf clover from the lane
I have a stick of mistletoe
Good luck will come again.

A wishbone and a horseshoe
A hip-bone from a Toad
I got me a Saint Christopher
Protect me on the road.

Black cat bring me good luck
Be my lucky charm
Drive away misfortune
Keep me from all harm.

(LYRICS © 2018 NIGEL PENNICK,
MUSIC BY JON WARD)

Fig. 23.10. The mummified cat that hangs
as a mascot in the Nutshell public house
(the smallest pub in England),
Bury St. Edmunds, Suffolk

THE FOX

Fig. 23.11. Fox head horse brass

Although in the Old English animal classification the fox is seen as vermin, its agility and intelligence earned it respect, hence its replication in amuletic form. Amulets made in the likeness of a fox bring success in business. Elizabeth Villiers speculated that because the fox is a cunning animal, the charm may bring that quality to its owner (Villiers 1923, 82). The fox appears on horse brasses as a mask, and in this case it is ascribed to fox hunters' horse harnesses. In the 1980s the Badminton Horse Trials issued commemorative brasses with the fox mask emblem. The running fox titled Rénard appeared as a car mascot from the French glassmaker René Lalique in 1930. It also is the badge of the British Army unit the Queen's Own Yeomanry and, until the 1990s, was the badge of Carlisle United Football Club (Routledge and Wills 2018, 63). The fox mask is the badge of Leicester City Football Club, whose nickname is "the Foxes."

Fig. 23.12. The Queen's Own Yeomanry badge

Fig. 23.13. Fox mascot from the British steam locomotive Silver Fox

Also in Great Britain the running fox was used from 1932 as a mascot on a series of forty-two steam locomotives designated class D49 and designed by Sir Nigel Gresley for the London and North Eastern Railway Company. The engines were named after famous fox hunting groups, and a running fox made of hollow-cast brass appeared above the name of each hunt, facing forward on each side. Later the streamlined A4 class steam locomotive named Silver Fox, also designed by Gresley, was built in 1935 for the elite Silver Jubilee train. Painted silver, it had on each side a stainless steel mascot in the form of a running fox. These were made by the Sheffield steelmakers Samuel Fox and Company at Stocksbridge in the Upper Don Valley. Subsequently weather vanes were made in this form. This locomotive operated on the East Coast Main Line between 1935 and 1963.

THE DOG

"Black dogs are true mascots" (Villiers 1923, 70). A Russian belief is that the devil takes the form of a black dog, so a black dog will keep the devil away (Daniels and Stevens 1903, 1246). However, despite the power ascribed to them to combat evil, dog mascots are relatively uncommon.

The World War I German air ace Manfred von Richthofen carried a blue glass dog mascot. For many years porcelain dogs were a feature of homely mantel shelves in English houses. In Dorset they were considered to be protectors of the house against being "overlooked" by the evil eye (Roud 2003, 349). The skins of greyhounds were deemed ideal for the Irish frame drums known as bodhrans, although today goat skin is preferred.

Fig. 23.14. Dog horse brass

The British bulldog is a symbol of unfailing resolution and determination. Bulldogs were bred as fighting dogs and used to attack and kill bulls. The emblematic personification of Britishness is John Bull, a portly man in a Union Jack waistcoat who is accompanied by a bulldog, which is sometimes also wearing a similar waistcoat. During both world wars as a patriotic emblem, the British bulldog was depicted in propaganda on posters, in magazines, and on postcards. During the First World War, amulets of the British bulldog, called Bow Wow, were made and sold by Badcoe and Hanks, jewelers in London. Made in silver or gold, the bulldog's base was in the form of a German eagle. Thus the power of the British bulldog crushed the German emblem (Davies 2018, 157). For those with less money, fabric British bulldogs were also produced as wartime amulets. The Staffordshire bull terrier, very popular in the United Kingdom, was crossbred from bulldogs and terriers as a formidable fighting dog; it was recognized as a breed in the early twentieth century, and images are often worn or carried as amulets.

Fig. 23.15. Brass dog amulet

THE HORSE

Horses were protected with amulets and charms, among which horse brasses are the best known. These take many forms, several of which from the author's collection are illustrated in this book. Images of the horse are favored among gamblers who bet on horse racing. These are dealt with in chapter 36, "Amulets and Talismans for Gambling." However, in Northern paganism, horse heads and skulls were used to protect and attack. Saxo Grammaticus (circa 1200) noted the magical setting up of a horse's head: "He first put on a pole the severed head of a horse that had been sacrificed to the gods, and setting sticks beneath displayed the jaws grinning agape" (Saxo Grammaticus 1905, 209). A curse carved in runes was made on the pole. This was the *niðstong*, the "scorn post," erected by the magician to drive away the landvættir (land wights) and render *álfreka* the ground of his enemy, that is, to drive away the good elves, thereby destroying the luck and productivity of the land. According to Icelandic belief and a tradition in East Anglia recorded much later, it was known that places where helpful sprites of the land (e.g., the Icelandic landvættir) were driven out, the land is spiritually dead. In East Anglia this is *gast* land. Inevitably once these places are no longer tended by their spiritual guardians, they will become wastelands; the animals and people that live there will decline and die.

Traditional builders in Germany, Denmark, and Ireland laid horse skulls beneath the threshing floor in barns. A good threshing floor should "bend to meet the flail" and then the flails will "sing." Horse skulls had an acoustic property that assisted this, but also had an amuletic purpose. Acoustically horse skulls were found embedded in the pulpit of the Bristol Street Meeting House in Edinburgh, Scotland, and at Llandaff Cathedral in Wales, in the choir stalls. In 1897 a horse's head was buried as a foundation deposit beneath the Primitive Methodist Chapel at Black Horse Drove in the remote Cambridgeshire Fens. The builder poured a libation of beer over it as "an old heathen custom to drive evil and witchcraft away." It is the last record of the practice. A horse's head was used in Germany to prevent witches from entering a house (Bächtold-Stäubli 1927–1942, vol. 1, 143*ff*.).

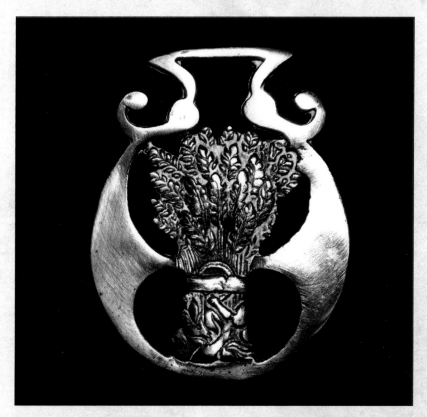

Plate 1. Wheat sheaf amulet of abundant harvest, horse brass

Plate 2. Vegvísir, pyrography on birch wood, Norfolk, 2019

Plate 3. Pentagram amulet with beads and bells

Plate 4. Hexagram with Hebrew texts on the gate of a Jewish graveyard, Middelburg, the Netherlands

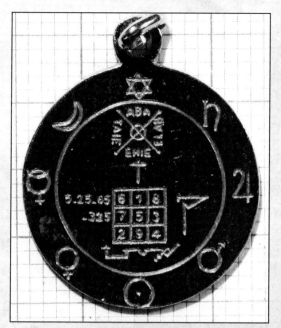

Plate 5. Talisman with magic square and planetary sigils

Plate 6.
Ex-Voto XI of Nigel Pennick's *Ex-Voto* series of amuletic artworks exhibited at the Walkers' Gallery, San Marcos, Texas, 2013

Plate 7. Image of the devil in chains, Stonegate, York

Plate 8. Shield-knot amulet

Plate 9. Staffordshire knot horse brass

Plate 10. Hammer of Thor amulet

Plate 11. Horseshoes on traditional cottage at Heacham, Norfolk, 2018

Plate 12. Horseshoe amulet for luck, circa 1900

Plate 13. Fastnacht (Shrove Tuesday) carnival guiser with bells, Rottweil-am-Neckar, Germany, 1999

Plate 14. Horse brass of a beehive symbolizing cooperative work bringing abundance

Plate 15. Sun over door in Heidelberg, Germany

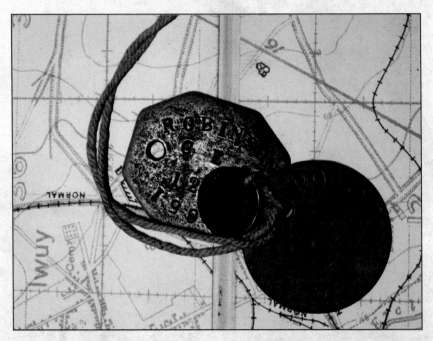

Plate 16. Charles Robinson's identity tags
with a lucky three-pence piece, World War I, 1914

Plate 17. Chinese ba gua geomantic mirror

Plate 18. Witch ball

Plate 19. British soldiers in bearskins.
Military parade in Cambridge, 2010

Plate 20. Belt buckle beast with horns, England, 1980s

Plate 21. Belt buckle with claw, red coral, lapis luzuli, and turquoise, Bavaria

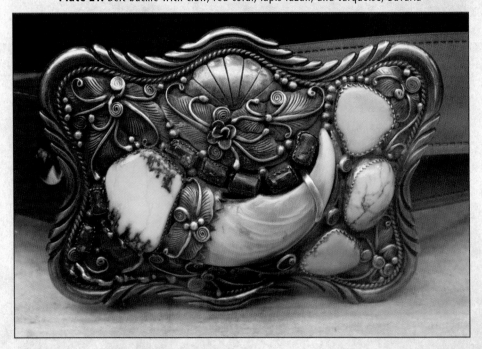

Plate 22. Bunzlau plates, dish, and teapot with pfauenaugen patterns

Plate 23. *Ex-Voto VIII* of Nigel Pennick's *Ex-Voto* series of amuletic artworks exhibited at the Walkers' Gallery, San Marcos, Texas, 2013

Plate 24. Wooden flaming heart covered with milagros, Mexico

Plate 25. Guatemalan "worry person" amulet, fabric

Plate 26. Pentagram mosaic on floor of the Basilica di San Marco, Venice, Italy

Plate 27. Horse's head terret, brass and horsehair, England, early twentieth century

Plate 28. Nineteenth-century house with brickwork runes, St. Ives, Cambridgeshire

Plate 29. Lion's head door knocker, made in 2019

Plate 30. String of blue beads with peacock feather amulet

Plate 31. Amuletic bottles, acorn, and fossil

Plate 32. IHS monogram marquetry work on the pulpit of Saint Margaret's church, eighteenth century

Plate 33. "Airn" (iron) warding sign against fairies and evil sprites, print by Nigel Pennick, 2020

This need not be an actual head, as gables of traditional buildings in lower Saxony, Germany, take the form of two carved horses' heads facing each other. They are the continuation of the *Windbretter* (bargeboards) beneath the roof at the gable end (Von Zaborsky 1936, 279–87).

THE BEAR

The bear, "the golden king of the forest," is a symbol of strength and watchfulness. Bear ceremonies in the far north of the Earth, performed by "the circumpolar bear cult," exist across Europe, Asia, and North America. From the Saami in Scandinavia across the Russian Siberian north to the Nivkh (Gilyak) of Sakhalin and the Ainu of northern Japan and Native American tribes, bear ceremonies were practiced. It was formerly more widespread even than this, existing in former times among the Thracians, Dacians, Geats, and Vikings. From hunting rituals to shamanic bear dance festivals, there are rites and ceremonies connected with the bear. In many traditions, ceremonies are conducted for the bear after it has been killed. In many traditions there are common features to the ceremonies. Food is offered to the dead bear (Hallowell 1926, 145); it is skinned in a ritual way (Hallowell 1926, 146), and its carcass is brought into the dwelling, not through the door but a window. Women are forbidden to see the dead bear, and men ritually eat the heart (Hallowell 1926, 147).

The bearskin cap is well known from the military uniforms of royal guards in England, Denmark, Belgium, and the Netherlands. However there is no apparent connection with the ancient use of bear imagery in European warrior cults. Bearskins, as they are commonly called, originated with the emergence of the specialist soldier called a grenadier. His function was to throw early versions of the hand grenade at the enemy. Naturally the tallest and strongest soldiers were chosen to perform the task. In order to make them appear even taller and more daunting to the enemy, tall hats of bearskin were added to the uniforms. The French grenadiers wore bearskins as early as 1761, and during the second half of the eighteenth century, other national armies adopted the headgear. The British Army Guard regiments wear real skins of the Canadian black bear, taken from the annual cull of bears by native hunters.

Fig. 23.16. British soldiers in bearskins. Military parade in Cambridge, 2010
(also see plate 19)

The teddy bear is clearly a luck-bringing charm and mascot for many. In 1923, when the teddy bear was quite new, Elizabeth Villiers wrote, "This is a modern invention, with no greater history behind it than the bright idea of a toy-maker in America who produced the well-jointed figure of a woolly bear and named it Teddy in honour of Theodore Roosevelt, then President of the Republic. Teddy was so fascinating that he became popular everywhere, and presently appeared on the fronts of motor cars, where he was given the dignity of a mascot. Perhaps he deserved his reputation, for in many parts of the world the bear has been a powerful totem, credited with the power of bestowing good fortune, and as a mascot is the outward sign of good wishes, this queer little creature does its part when given from one friend to another" (Villiers 1923, 160).

The teddy bear dates from 1902 when Morris Michtom made the first one in the United States and obtained Roosevelt's permission to call it "Teddy." Almost simultaneously Richard Steiff in Germany made a bear that he exhibited at a toy fair in Leipzig. Early Steiff bears are now prized collector's items that fetch premium prices at auction. As noted by Villiers, teddy bears became a runaway success and had an effect far beyond the toy market. Soon they became a subject for popular music. In 1907 John Walter Bratton wrote music titled "Teddy Bear March and Two-Step," which had words put to it in 1932 by Jimmy Kennedy as "The Teddy Bears' Picnic." Two decades later in the 1950s, Elvis Presley sang that he wanted to be a teddy bear. In the twenty-first century, each Christmas the upmarket London store Harrods has handmade teddy bears for sale, branded and marked on the left foot with the year. They are sought-after collector's items. Today, teddy bears appear frequently among floral tributes laid by people wherever there has been a well-publicized accident, murder, or terrorist incident. This reflects the protective function of the bear power. It is a pale reflection of "the circumpolar bear cult."

THE ELEPHANT AND THE TIGER

Bohemian glass elephants made in Gablonz were marketed in the United Kingdom as "The Lucky Elephant that brings you luck." The irresistible power of the Hindu elephant god Ganesh removes all obstacles. In Denmark the Elefantenorden is an order of chivalry whose badge is an elephant enameled in white, bearing a watchtower on its back and with a black man as its driver (Hieronymussen 1967, 145).

Fig. 23.17. Horse brass with elephant

Fig. 23.18. Brass Ganesh image, India

Claws reputed to be those of tigers or lions, mounted in gold, were collected in Paris by Lionel Bonnemère at the end of the nineteenth century (Boutellier 1966, 17–42). The tooth of a tiger was used by European gamblers at Monte Carlo in the early part of the twentieth century. It was believed to be a Chinese gambler's charm. Wearing a tooth or claw was believed to empower the wearer with the strength, courage, and cunning of the tiger (Villiers 1923, 163). An image of a "Royal Tiger" was the badge of the Royal Leicestershire Regiment between 1898 and 1964, when the infantry regiment was amalgamated with other British Army units and lost its identity. The tiger is the mascot of Bangladesh cricket supporters.

Fig. 23.19. Tiger of the Royal Leicestershire Regiment

Chapter 24

Dangerous and Unwanted Animals

ANIMALS CLASSIFIED AS VERMIN

In the hunting tradition of medieval Europe, there were three classes of animal: beasts of venery, beasts of the chase, and vermin. The old words for harmful dragons, *wyrm* and *orm,* are related to *vermin.* Rats are universally detested as vermin, and amulets and talismans involving rats are intended to disperse or destroy them. In Thuringia a whistle made from the hind leg bone of a rat was used to drive rats away (Lawrence 1898, 294). A monastery in the Ardennes, France, was reputed to be free of rats because it contained relics of Saint Ulrich, the erstwhile bishop of Augsburg (Lawrence 1898, 293).

To the Romans the wolf was a respected animal. The archaic bronze Capitoline Wolf that shows the she-wolf who suckled the twins Romulus and Remus—an emblem of the city of Rome—still exists. The wolf was sacred to the god Mars. In ninth-century England the East Anglian king Eadmund (Edmund) was shot to death by an execution squad of Danish archers after he was captured in battle. His arrow-riddled body was beheaded. Later (according to legend) his followers recovered his head, which they found guarded by a wolf. Around the year 915 his body was buried at Beodricsworth, now the city of Bury St. Edmunds, Suffolk.

In the churches and civic places of Bury St. Edmunds, the amuletic

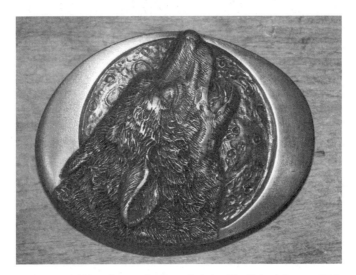

Fig. 24.1. Wolf howling at the Moon belt buckle, United States, 1994

emblem of the wolf and Saint Edmund's head can be seen. In the nineteenth century in Bury St. Edmunds, builders found twenty-one skulls beneath the medieval gatehouse of the Abbey. Twenty were wolves and one was a wolfhound. Wolf statues exist in the Abbey grounds and at Hunstanton, Norfolk, by the ruins of a chapel dedicated to the sainted king of East Anglia. In the medieval period the wolf was classified as vermin and hunted to extinction in many countries. In medieval England, when there were still wolves to be killed, the right forefoot of a wolf was deemed a remedy for "evil of the breast" (Reeves 1997, 110).

Fig. 24.2. Wolf with the head of Saint Edmund, Bury St. Edmund's Cathedral

TOADS AND FROGS

A dried frog worn round the neck in a silk bag was reputed to prevent epilepsy. Writing in 1932 C. J. S. Thompson stated, "In some parts of the country, within recent times, men called 'toad-doctors' used to visit the fairs selling toad's legs in little bags . . . as amulets to prevent sickness" (Thompson 1932, 236). Medieval bestiaries asserted that the toad was a dangerous venomous creature, fatal to humans and livestock. But its head contained a jewel, a powerful amulet with the intrinsic virtue to cure the bite of poisonous snakes and useful as a general antidote. The method of extracting the toadstone was by cutting it from the toad's head. It was illustrated in *Hortus Sanitatis* by Johannes de Cuba (published in Paris ca. 1490). Toadstones were highly valued as a remedy against poisoning, plague, and smallpox. An American compilation of superstitions and folklore from 1903 tells that it is believed that toothache can be cured by a toadstone (Daniels and Stevens 1903, 1668). They were supposed to be found in the heads of very old toads, from which they had to be taken as the toad was dying naturally. They varied in color from dark gray to light brown (Thompson 1932, 247). In *As You Like It*, William Shakespeare referred to the toadstone:

> *Sweet are the uses of adversity;*
> *Which like the toad, ugly and venomous,*
> *Wears yet a precious jewel in his head.*

Writing in the seventeenth century, the Norwich savant Sir Thomas Browne commented, "As for the stone commonly called the 'Toad Stone,' which is presumed to be found inn the head of that animal, we first conceive it not a thing impossible" (Browne [1635] 1927, xiii). In Scotland "the Witch of Aldie" is said to have possessed one that was described as about the size of a pigeon's egg. Despite its impossible size, it was said to have come from the head of a toad. It was credited with the power to heal all kinds of venomous bites and sores on the human body (Simpkins 1912, 357). The stone was boiled in water, which was then applied to the afflicted part. Sometimes a toadstone

Fig. 24.3. Medieval toadstone ring

was set in gold or silver and worn as a ring. In 1616, also in Scotland, John Nimok married Alisone Patersone and "consignit ane gold ring with ane toadstone thairin." Their gold wedding ring was set with a toadstone (Dalyell 1834, 408).

Clearly such stones did not come from the heads of toads. "In reality, they were artificially made of fused borax or other material" asserted C. J. S. Thompson, "and others were the fossilised tooth of the ray" (Thompson 1932, 247). Zoological taxonomy classifies the toadstone as a palatal tooth of the fossil fish lepidotus (Ettlinger 1939, 151), although the *Krotenstein,* in German-speaking countries, is a fossil echinoid. Clearly there is no consensus on what a toadstone actually is. At the Paris Exposition of 1889, toadstones were among the amulets exhibited by Giuseppe Bellucci. They were described as "three discoidal calcareous stones found in places frequented by toads" and hence believed to

Fig. 24.4. Toad and Moon amulets collected by
Giuseppe Bellucci, 1889

be toadstones by those from whom Bellucci obtained them (Bellucci 1889, 50). Bellucci also exhibited a toad made of silver that was used as an amulet against the evil eye (Bellucci 1889, 76).

East Anglian toadmanry depends on gaining and using a particular bone from a toad. The initiation into toadmanry involves throwing the defleshed bones of a toad into a river and choosing the bone that floats against the flow (Pennick 2011a, passim). This is a hook-shaped hip bone. Possession of the toad bone gives the owner (who must have performed the rite) the power to control animals, especially horses. It also gives the toadman power over women, and the toadwoman power over men. A person with the bone can open any door ("no door is ever closed to a Toadman") and can be somewhere and not be seen ("walking out of the sight of men"). African American hoodoo magic also uses the toad bone, as expressed in "Groundhog Blues" (1951), sung by John Lee Hooker (1917–2001), which tells of using "toad-frog's hips" to kill "that dirty groundhog." John Graham Dalyell reported a Scottish method that parallels the method of gaining the toad bone in East Anglia. It involved burying a toad in an anthill and extracting the stone when the ants have eaten away the toad's flesh (Dalyell 1834, 408). Traditionally toadmanry was seen as a dangerous profession, for many in the past were driven to insanity by the exercise of these powers.

Fig. 24.5. Toad bone locket, Cambridgeshire

Another tradition uses toad bones for men to have control over women. It tells of three bones that can be obtained from toads. During the month of March, two toads are caught and killed. Their carcasses are put in a box with holes in it, which is buried in a *pissmire bank* (anthill). Once the toads are defleshed, their disarticulated skeletons are thrown in running water: "You will see that one of the bones will go against the stream. Another will stand upright and another will sink. These three keep. Put that which swimmeth against the stream in a ring, and she that taketh it at your hands shall love thee. Put that that stood upright in a ring and give it to a woman and she shall obey thy wish. Grate that to powder that sinks and she that drinketh thereof shall hate thee" (Thompson 1927, 211). The technique of defleshing toads in "an earthen pot" in an anthill was recommended in 1815 as a means of obtaining the toadstone: "the bones of the toad and the stone will be left in the pot" (Jones 1877, 157).

Chapter 25

Birds and Their Images

THE DOVE

In Christian symbolism the white dove represents the Holy Spirit. "Seldom used as a charm or ornament" wrote Elizabeth Villers, "it is the symbol of peace, and anything made in its likeness should heal quarrels and unite parted friends" (Villiers 1923, 71). If used as an amulet, it represents a soul bird. Lancashire folklorists John Harland and T. T. Wilkinson noted, "A white dove . . . is an angel in that form ready to convey the soul of a dying person to heaven" (Harland and Wilkinson 1867, 143). A Lincolnshire folk song known either as "Betsy Wolton" or "Humber Banks" expresses this belief. It is sung in the persona of an abandoned pregnant woman who drowns herself in the River Humber estuary. The final verse says:

> *As signal that I died for love*
> *There shall be seen a milk-white dove*
> *Over my watery grave to fly*
> *And there you'll find my body lie.*

THE WREN

The wren is one of the smallest birds of Europe, where it is known as "the king of all birds" and is associated with the oak tree. In Celtic countries there was a *geis* (taboo) against killing wrens. The bird was the focus of traditions on Boxing Day, the day after Christmas Day, when the otherwise inviolable wren was hunted and killed by "the wren boys." The dead bird was then paraded around the locality to the accompaniment of the local "Wren Boys' Song." The song "The Cutty Wren" is sung in England, exaggerating the bird's size, as in other songs, including "The Derby Ram" and "The Herring Song." A Welsh wren song begins with the invocation:

> *Joy, health, love, and peace*
> *Be all here in this place.*

In the Cornish tradition the wren is the "bird badge" of the Pennick (Pen Knegh) family.

THE BLUEBIRD

The bluebird is a harbinger of joy. A folktale from eastern France recounts how, during the Flood, Noah sent a white dove out from the Ark, but it returned transformed into a blue bird by the rainbow that signified God's covenant—a kingfisher. Marie-Catherine Baronne d'Aulnoy's fairy-tale book *Les Contes des Fées,* published in 1697, contained the story "L'Oiseau bleu," which was one of the most popular stories in the compendium, giving rise to dramatized versions in the eighteenth and nineteenth centuries. The bluebird appears in Emanuel Swedenborg's *L'Arcana Cælesta* (1749–56). Despite the possible origin in the French tale, images of the bluebird certainly have not been kingfishers. The bluebird was popularized in 1909 by Maurice Maeterlinck through his play, *The Blue Bird,* which premiered in London in December 1909 and was a great sensation that captured the imagination of the public.

The bluebird had appeared in European art before Maeterlinck used it in the drama. A sailors' tattoo of a bird, blue, of course, signified completion of a voyage of five thousand miles (Binder 1973, 76). It appeared in jewelry: Charles de Soucy Ricketts's bluebird brooch, made in 1899 for the poet Katherine Bradley, being a famous piece (Munro 2006, 69). Ricketts made four alternative designs. The first one was lost in the street by Bradley, but another was exhibited at the Fitzwilliam Museum in Cambridge in 2018. The idea of it seems to have come from an earlier version made to the design of Edward Burne-Jones. In 2011 Frank Cadogan Cowper's 1918 painting, *The Blue Bird,* was sold at Christie's in London for £373,250. Blue Bird was also the brand name of a British toffee, widely available in the 1950s.

Fig. 25.1. Bluebird of Happiness brooch, 1970s

The Blue Bird play, revived in 1910, had an influence on British sportsmen. Motor racing speed ace Malcolm Campbell was known for his succession of ever-faster cars. In 1910 Campbell attended a performance of Maeterlinck's play in London and was so impressed that he went back home to Bromley and got his neighbor, who owned an auto body workshop, to paint his newly acquired "four-inch" Darracq racing car a particular shade of blue. It was painted overnight, and the next day Campbell took the car to Brooklands raceway and won two races. Subsequent cars, including ones that broke the world speed record, were all named Bluebird (Summers 1990, 14). Cardiff City Football Club adopted the sobriquet the Bluebirds after a performance of the play at the New Theatre, Cardiff, in November 1911. In 2012 the new Malaysian owner attempted to change the club's blue color to red and replace the bluebird badge with a red dragon. A campaign against this change, culminating in a supporters' march to the stadium to present a petition, resulted in 2015 with the reinstatement of the bluebird (Routledge and Wills 2018, 102).

Subsequent to Campbell naming his cars Bluebird, in London the name was given to more sedate forms of transport. The London General Omnibus Company was the largest independent bus operator in the capital before the corporate organization London Transport took over in 1933. The General was in the forefront of modern bus design and in 1931 produced a prototype double-decker of the LT class that had new seating far more comfortable than had hitherto been provided. The interior was predominantly blue, which led to the buses being known as Bluebirds (Glazier 1995, 75). The next year the London Country Council double-decker electric tram (streetcar) No.1, built in May 1932, was painted in a blue livery and, like other "one-off" experimental trams built by other London tram operators, was given an unofficial name. Following Bluebell, Poppy, and Cissie (Smeeton 1986, 366, 374, 397), inevitably it was called Bluebird. Even when it was painted in the later London Transport red, the tram was still known as Bluebird (Oakley 1991, 752). It ran subsequently in Leeds and is now preserved and rebuilt into its original form, again painted its original blue. From 1948 the Blue Bird Company built school buses in the United States. In 1957 the Nissan Company launched a car aimed at the female market, the Nissan Bluebird (Munro 2006, 25). Of course it was not intended to break speed records, but rather to bring happiness to its owners.

Sir Malcolm Campbell's son, Donald, was also an intrepid speed ace, piloting a series of powerful speedboats to set world water-speed records. Like his father's cars each boat was a Bluebird. The final one came to grief on Coniston Water in 1967 during an attempt on the speed record when it crashed and disintegrated, killing Campbell. Subsequently recovered from the bottom of the lake, the last Bluebird, a jet-powered hydrofoil, was rebuilt and returned to the water in 2018. Donald Campbell carried a teddy bear mascot called Whappet, manufactured by the Merrythought Company. Merrythought (who make the Harrods teddy bears mentioned in chapter 23) is another name for a wishbone, so these bears clearly were in the luck-bringing category. Originally called Woppet, the bear had been a cartoon character in the children's comic *Robin,* subsequently produced as merchandise. Campbell changed the name, and after his death, Whappet bears were made with a bluebird embroidered on each one and, latterly, with a Campbell tartan ribbon around the neck. Whappet is an interesting case of the conflation of charms and symbols.

The bluebird also appeared in popular song. In 1924 the American singer Eva Taylor, recording with Clarence Williams's Blue Five, sang that she was a little blackbird looking for a bluebird. Ten years later the popular song "Blue Bird of Happiness" by Sandor Harmati and Edward Heyman was a big hit in its day, being recorded by, among other stars, Jimmy Durante and Shirley Temple. In 1938 the bluebird was mentioned in the movie *The Wizard of Oz.* Vera Lynn's optimistic British World War II song looked forward to the postwar period when peace would reign and there would be bluebirds over the White Cliffs of Dover. In 1946, in the Walt Disney film *Song of the South,* the song "Zip-a-Dee-Doo-Dah" placed a bluebird on the singer's shoulder. Today in the United States, September 24 is designated "Bluebird of Happiness Day," and bluebird glass charms are produced by Terra Studios in Arizona.

THE LIVER BIRD

The city of Liverpool has a famous mascot—the liver bird. It is a heraldic form of the cormorant (*Phalacrocorax carbo*), holding a piece of seaweed in its beak. Anciently this large black seabird was known as *Corvus marinus,* the sea raven. Cormorants are notable birds because they stand still on rocks with their wings spread out. Their wings are seen as protective of the place where they stand, although if the bird is seen on top of a church tower, it is considered as a sign of bad luck (Daniels and Stevens 1903, 605). Norwegian legend tells how the spirits of those who die at sea return home in the shape of cormorants. In Liverpool various buildings, civic and otherwise, have carvings of the liver bird, as does Liverpool Football Club.

The Royal Liver Building at the Pier Head in Liverpool is an impressive landmark, said to be England's first skyscraper. Built between 1908 and 1910 to the designs of local architect Walter Aubrey Thomas (1864–1934), it is notable for having two equal-sized clock towers, each topped by a copper sculpture of a liver bird. Measuring eighteen feet high with a twenty-four-foot wingspan, these birds were designed by German sculptor Carl Bernard Bartels (1866–1955). They are the mascots of the city, visible from afar. One liver bird faces land and the other the sea. Local tradition is that one protects the city and the other protects those that go to sea. They remained unscathed during the massive aerial bombardment the city suffered in World War II.

ROOSTERS

Although it still goes on clandestinely in the twenty-first century, cockfighting was banned in the United Kingdom in 1849. Before that specially built cockpits existed where spectators could watch the fights and bet on the outcomes. One still exists, an octagonal building in New Street, Welshpool, Wales. On its conical apex is a metal mascot of a cockerel with spurs. Inside, in a niche in the wall of the top floor, is another one, painted in full color. Related in some way to this is the mascot of Tottenham Hotspur Football Club. Nicknamed the Spurs, Tottenham Hotspur is one of London's top football clubs. Founded in 1882 it was named for the famed fourteenth-century lord Harry Hotspur, an ancestor of the Duke of Northumberland, who owned the land on which the ground was built. His indefatigable fighting spirit was seen as a role model for the team (Routledge and Wills 2018, 59). The Spurs' mascot, however, is not a medieval knight, but rather a fighting cockerel fitted with artificial spurs to fight in the long-banned sport of cockfighting. In 1909 a gilded nine-feet-high bronze figure of the bird was set up on the top of the west stand at Tottenham Hotspur's ground, White Hart Lane. It was designed by William James Scott, a former player. The mascot was in the form of a fighting bird surmounting a sphere representing a football. It has been moved around the ground over the years, and when it was taken down in 1934, supporters saw the team's relegation the next year as a sign that it ought not to have been. Then it was restored to its position on the west stand, and in 1958 moved to the top of the east stand. When the cockerel was taken down yet again in 1989, the ball was opened and inside were found the "foundation deposits," a handbook for the season 1909–1910, and some coins. Subsequently a replica of fiberglass was made, and in 2018 this new one was reerected on the club's new stadium.

Chapter 26

Teeth, Claws, and Horns

In his comprehensive book *The Evil Eye,* published in 1895, Frederick Thomas Elworthy noted that the crescent is used as an amulet that distracts the eye of malevolent people, thereby deflecting its harmful influence away from the wearer (Elworthy 1895, 202). It is usually seen as a lunar sign, and as a heraldic symbol it is a notable form of traditional British horse harness ornament. But according to Elworthy and other commentators, any curving, crescent-shaped object can be worn as an amulet against the evil eye, including horns, teeth, and claws. The teeth, claws, and talons of dangerous predatory animals and raptors are particularly appropriate. Crescent-shaped wolves' teeth and boars' tusks

Fig. 26.1. Belt buckle beast with horns, England, 1980s (also see plate 20)

Fig. 26.2. Belt buckle with claw, red coral, lapis lazuli, and turquoise, Bavaria
(also see plate 21)

are known to have been used in ancient British burials. Wolves' teeth were sought-after amulets in nineteenth-century France. Bavarian traditional costume shops sell various items of clothing with horn buttons and buckles and silver chains called *Charivari* that contain traditional lucky charms and protective accoutrements, including tusks and teeth. The belt buckle illustrated in figure 26.1 has a bear's claw as its major feature, along with other reinforcing materials, including lapis lazuli, turquoise, and red coral.

Wearing a tooth as an amulet was formerly a remedy for teething pains in children. In 1898 Robert Means Lawrence wrote of the "alleged efficiency as amulets . . . horns and tusks of animals, the talons of birds, and the claws of wild beasts, lobsters, and crabs" (Lawrence 1898, 8–9). Tlingit shamans wore crowns made of mountain goats' horns (Anawalt 2014, 149), and their costumes were empowered with bears' claws and wooden spikes shaped like claws (Anawalt 2014, 145). Eagles' claws were notable in Yenesei shamans' regalia (Nioradze 1925, 72). "In southern Spain, particularly in Andalusia" wrote Lawrence, "the stag's horn is a very favourite talisman. The native children wear a silver-tipped horn suspended from the neck by a braided cord made from the hair of a black mare's tail. It is believed that an evil glance directed at the child is received by the horn, which thereupon breaks asunder, and the malevolent influence is thus dissipated" (Lawrence 1898, 10).

Under harsh and repressive regimes, such as what the slaves suffered in the West Indies, such items were classified as a form of malevolent witchcraft and possession of them was punished heavily. For example, in 1773, the trial of a slave called Sarah at Saint Andrew in Jamaica indicted her "for having in her possession cats' teeth, cats' claws, cats' jaws, hair, beads, knotted cords, and other materials, relative to the practice of Obeah" (Madden 1835, 92). Other lists of "the instruments of Obeah" included a large proportion of sharp organic materials as well as blood, feathers, ducks' skulls, dried fowls' heads, lizard bones, parrot beaks, the teeth of dogs and alligators, and egg shells, also broken bottles and grave dirt. Lists of these items appeared in official documents intended to suppress the practices of Obeah. "If there shall be found in the possession of slaves any poisonous drugs, pounded glass, parrots' beaks, dogs' teeth, alligator teeth, or other materials notoriously used in the profession of obeah or witchcraft, such slave upon conviction shall be liable to suffer transportation from this island, or such other punishment, not extending to life, as the court shall think proper to direct" (Williams 1932, 165).

Supposed "Griffins' claws" were shown as holy relics in former times. Edward Payson Evans noted in 1896 that certain churches in Cologne, Hildesheim, and Weimar, Germany, had these items, which had rites and ceremonies attached to them. He identified "Griffins' claws" as horns of the "Cafrarian Buffalo." He also noted that in medieval times, items made from material reputed to be unicorns' horns were made into "test spoons," salt cellars, and drinking cups. They were said to be a remedy against poison and epilepsy (Evans 1896, 106).

The impressive aurochs *(Bos primigenius)* was a species of powerful wild cattle with splendid horns that once ranged across northern and central Europe. It was impossible to herd or domesticate the aurochs, and so it was hunted to extinction. In England circa 1300, it was deliberately exterminated on the orders of King Edward I as part of his program of extirpating vermin and outlaws. In addition to the aurochs, all wolves and foxes were doomed by royal decree. The wolves were wiped out in England, but foxes remain today. There is a medieval legend in the West Midlands of England of the hero Guy of Warwick killing the dangerous and destructive Dun Cow, which was probably an aurochs. Gradually hunting reduced their range across Europe, until the final aurochs of all was shot in 1627 in Poland.

In addition to its forbidding size and power, the aurochs was noted for its long, sharp, curving horns. The *Old English Rune Poem* describes the beast as "bold with horns rising high, a fierce horn-fighter who stamps across the moors, a striking animal." This refers to the second rune, *ur,* which denotes primal strength. Because of the animal's immense length and capacity and fearsome reputation, aurochs' horns were used as ceremonial drinking vessels with amuletic power. At least one still exists in an old inn in Alsace. The traditional Scottish ceremonial drinking cup, the *corn,* was an aurochs horn with a lip of chased silver. A fine example was used until the early twentieth century at Dunvegan Castle in Scotland.

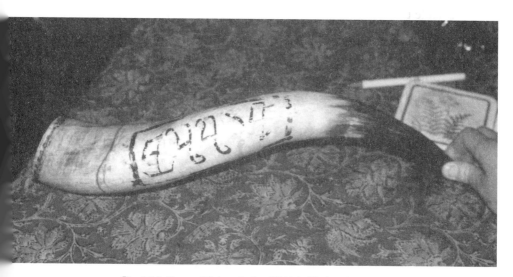

Fig. 26.3. Horn with inscription BAAL in Theban letters,
found in Norfolk barn

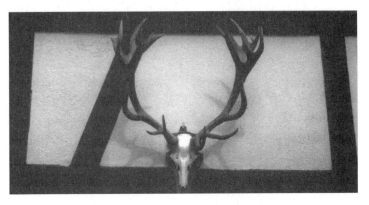

Fig. 26.4. Antlers and stag's head on building in Andlau, Alsace, France

Stag's antlers are often seen on buildings in the areas of central Europe where deer are shot by hunters. They are more than just a by-product of hunting or hunters' trophies. Set up on the outside of a building, antlers are amuletic shields against external harm, natural equivalents of gargoyles on churches. The Seaforth Highlanders, a Scottish regiment in the British Army, has an antlered stag's head seen face-on as their badge. In 1263 a member of Clan Mackenzie rescued the Scottish king Alexander II from a stag attack. The clan was awarded the stag's head as its badge, and from that came the regimental stag's head. The Gaelic motto means "help the king."

Fig. 26.5. Seaforth Highlanders' badge with stag

In Roman times a wolf's canine tooth from the right side was an esteemed amulet. In France they were worn by children as amulets against convulsions, and they were on sale as charms during World War I (Davies 2018, 107). In early-twentieth-century Britain and the United States, a badger's tooth was considered the gambler's luckiest charm, if carried in a waistcoat pocket (Villiers 1923, 21). In eastern England the jaw of a female hedgehog was carried as a remedy for rheumatism. Horses' teeth were worn on Lincolnshire countrymen's watch chains (Peacock 1908, 87–88), and boars' teeth were ground up and mixed with linseed oil to make a medicine to treat *squinancy* (sore throat) (Lupton et al. 1815, 44). Another sort of "tooth" is the pendant of United States Marine Scout marksmen. After completing training the sniper becomes an official HOG—"Hunter of Gunmen"—and is given a pierced sniper bullet, known as a *hog's tooth.*

Moles' feet have been used as amulets against various unrelated maladies and in money magic. Moles, which live underground in tunnels they dig, have prominent claws. The early-twentieth-century collector of amulets, Edward Lovett, wrote of the mole, "in the front feet, or digging feet, as they are called, which are selected, and it will be seen how strongly they are curved for this purpose" (Lovett 1928, 15). Moles' feet were prized as a cure for cramps, and Lovett saw the curvature as sympathetic magic for the curvature of cramped limbs. Lovett also collected dried moles' feet at King's Lynn in Norfolk, where they were used as a charm against rheumatism. In 1879 William Henderson had recorded the use of moles' feet as a remedy for toothache. "There is a ferocious character about the Staffordshire mode of cure. It consists of carrying about a paw cut off from a live mole" (Henderson 1879, 145). He tells that there were dealers in moles for this purpose. But an entirely different quality had been ascribed to mole claws nearly three hundred years earlier in seventeenth-century Scotland, for there they appeared as evidence in witch trials. John Graham Dalyell tells of John Feare, who was convicted of witchcraft for using moles' feet "given to him by Satan" that he kept in his purse "for this cause as long as he had them upon him, he should never want silver" [spelling modernized] (Dalyell 1834, 200). Another animal with powerful digging claws is the badger.

In the early twentieth century, badgers' paws were being imported to Spain for sale as amulets against the evil eye (Hildburgh 1906, 461).

THE RABBIT'S FOOT

As a lucky charm the left hind foot of a rabbit is deemed the proper one to have. President Theodore Roosevelt, who gave his name to another amuletic figure, the teddy bear, carried a gold-mounted rabbit's foot given to him by the champion boxer John L. Sullivan (1858–1918). The importance attached to this amulet was shown in 1905 in a legal action in New York. An attempt was made by the owner of a rabbit's foot to recover it after it had been borrowed by chorus girl Nan Patterson, who was acquitted of murdering an English bookmaker. It had been carried as an amulet in several murder trials. Later it was offered to another defendant, Harry Thaw, but he refused to use it (Wright and Lovett 1908, 296).

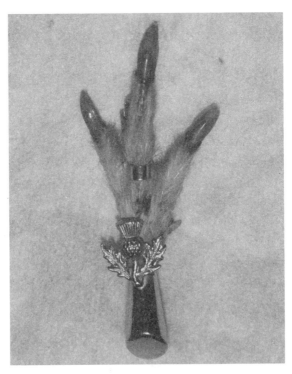

Fig. 26.6. Grouse claw amulet, Scotland

One of the most famous African American touring companies of the day was the Rabbit's Foot Minstrels, originally founded in 1899 by Henry "Pat" Chapelle (1869–1911). Later, after 1911, it was promoted as the Original Rabbit's Foot Company by Fred Swift Wolcott (1882–1967). The name came from an 1899 vaudeville review written for the company by Frank Dumont (1848–1919), titled *A Rabbit's Foot* (Abbott and Seroff 2009, 248–50). The popularity of the troupe certainly promoted a wide awareness of the rabbit's foot as a lucky charm. In 1908 a rabbit's foot was mentioned as an English amulet against the supposed bad luck of peacocks' feathers (Wright and Lovett, 1908, 296). In the United States in 1917, Koon Beck, "the Rabbit King of Kansas," offered a free rabbit's foot to every African American soldier who was going to Europe to fight in the war. They were by-products of Beck's industrial-scale farms supplying an order of 1,200,000 rabbits to the U.S. Army catering corps (Davies 2018, 145–46). However the tradition is old. English diarist Samuel Pepys wrote in his diary for Sunday, March 26, 1665, "my hare's foot, which is my preservative against wind." A Scottish amulet is the foot of a grouse, a common moorland game bird popular with shooters.

Chapter 27

Bones

Thomas Sternberg, writing in 1851 about Northamptonshire traditions (in the English Midlands), stated that "certain charms and amulets were (and still are) resorted to in order to procure immunity from the arts of the witch. Among the most common of these was the 'lucky bone'. . . . The *lucky-bone,* as its name indicates, is worn about the person to produce good-luck, and it is also reckoned an excellent protection against witchcraft. It is a bone taken from the head of a sheep, and its form, which is that of the T cross, may have, perhaps, originated the peculiar sanctity in which it is held" (Sternberg 1851, 150, 154). The Tau cross in the shape of the letter *T* is the emblem of Saint Anthony of Egypt. But the bone also resembles the hammer of Thor. In the National Museum of Wales is a T-bone that had been carried as a charm by a British sailor who served on a minesweeper in the North Sea during World War I. In 1928 it was noted that in London the gasworks stokers, men who shoveled coal into retorts to make coal gas, carried "the T bone from a sheep's head" as an amulet (Wright 1928, 72).

In northern England the kneecap of a sheep was carried as an amulet against cramps (Henderson 1879, 155). At the Paris Exposition in 1889, Giuseppe Bellucci exhibited a bone disc used against the evil eye and fascination (Bellucci 1889, 65). Other bone items in the exhibit were heart-shaped bone amulets and a fragment of human cranium shaped like a reliquary that was used against epilepsy (Bellucci 1889, 69).

The Portuguese version of the grimoire *Cyprianus* tells of a certain bone from a cat that will enable one "to walk out of the sight of men." This attribute is the same as that ascribed to the toad bone of the East Anglian toadmen. The black cat bone is an important element in the African American hoodoo and German Canadian traditions. It was obtained by ritually boiling a black cat in a pot at midnight until the carcass disintegrated and the bones were separate. Then the bones were taken out one by one and tasted by the practitioner. Unlike the toad bone of toadmanry, the bone containing the magic of the black cat was thought to be a different one in each cat. The one that tasted the most bitter was deemed to be "the bone." Another means was to hold bones in front of a mirror; the one that had no reflection was the right one. "Black cat bones" can be obtained from magic suppliers today, but most appear to be blackened chicken bones.

GOOSE BONE OSTEOMANCY

In northern Europe the furcula of a Saint Martin's goose was used as an oracle to predict whether the coming winter would be severe or mild. In Yorkshire the breastbone of a goose eaten in a Michaelmas (September 29) or Martinmas (November 11) feast was used. A tradition in the north of England was that if the bone was darker rather than light, it presaged a harsh, cold, winter. If it was mottled, the winter would be less harsh, but variable. The front part of the bone denoted the weather before Christmas, the inner part, the weather after Christmas (Gutch 1901, 70). A fifteenth-century comment by Johannes Hartleib (1410–1468) told that in their military crusades against eastern European pagans, the Teutonic knights waged all their wars by the goose bone, deciding their military strategy based on predictions of the weather using the bone. When members of the Teutonic Order were accused of practicing divination by reading bones, the bishop of Riga forbade it (Abulafia and Berend 2002, passim).

BONY RELICS OF THE CHURCH

Bones play a significant role in traditional Christian churches. Since the inception of the religion, relics of those who were revered for adherence to the faith in times of difficulty were held to possess exceptional holiness. Numerous skulls that are purported to be from major saints exist at major churches: Saint Peter at the Vatican, Rome; Saint Mark at Venice; Saint James at Santiago de Compostela, Spain; Saint Andrew at Patras, Greece; Saint Francis at Assisi and Saint Benedict at Montecassino, both in Italy; Saint Lambert in Liège Cathedral and Saint Hubert at the Abbey named after him, both in Belgium; Saint Willibrord at Echternach, Luxembourg; and Saint John at Ephesus, Turkey. There are a number of skulls attributed to Saint John the Baptist. Where they are displayed, they are the center of public veneration.

In 1625 the *baldacchino* over Saint Peter's tomb in his basilica in Rome was furnished with a remarkable set of relics. Loggias were constructed in the four pillars so that the relics within them could be displayed to the faithful at appropriate times. These were the most holy relics of all, directly connected with the crucifixion of Jesus. The northwest pillar contained a fragment of the True Cross, guarded by an image of its finder, Saint Helena, who held Christ's nails in her left hand. The southwest held the veil of Veronica, the southeast the head of Saint Andrew, and the northeast the lance with which Longinus pierced Christ's side. Inexplicably these key relics of the Christian faith were removed later. The head of Saint Andrew was sent to Patras in Greece, where it remains. This is the most extreme case of magical disempowerment of the central building of a religion anywhere. Many others have been destroyed down the years, but not by their own guardians.

Several Anglo-Saxon kings of England were revered, and their bones were used to effect healing and miraculous cures. The Anglo-Saxon cult of divine kingship that originated in pre-Christian times automatically made kings who died in battle or by assassination into saints of the church, without the necessity of the pope's blessing. King Ethelbert of Kent, who sponsored the building of Saint Andrew's Cathedral in Rochester, died in the year 616. His head was preserved as a relic at

Fig. 27.1. Carving of Saint Oswald on a building in Oswestry

Old Saint Paul's in London. It was destroyed in the reformation, and the building was destroyed in the Great Fire of London in 1666. King Oswald of Northumbria (604–642), a Christian king of Northumbria, fell in battle at Maserfeld (the modern Oswestry) fighting the forces of the kingdom of Mercia led by the devout pagan king Penda, who had his body dismembered and set on posts as a victory offering to the gods. His remains were later recovered by his followers, and a healing cult began.

The tenth-century king of England, Saint Edward, king and martyr (ca. 963–979), was a young man when he was murdered at Corfe Castle in Dorset at the instigation of his stepmother by the men-at-arms of his half-brother Ethelred, who succeeded him as king. It was said that a miraculous spring burst forth at Corfe where he was killed. His bones were recovered, and he was buried in a tomb-shrine. After his shrine was obliterated by Protestant reformationists, his bones were taken from place to place and even stored in a bank vault. At the present Edward's bones are enshrined in the Russian Orthodox church at Brookwood Cemetery in Surrey, southwest of London.

At Trier in Germany the brainpan of Saint Theodul, set in a silver mount, was used as a drinking cup for those believing it would cure them of the fever (Peacock 1896, 276). Similarly in a chapel built in 1670 at Ebersberg in Bavaria is a silver-gilt reliquary in the form of the head of Saint Sebastian with an amuletic necklace of real silver coins and medallions around its neck. The head wears a detachable silver cap that serves as a drinking cup once used in healing rituals. Inside the metal is the brainpan from a human skull, claimed as that of the saint. An oval-shaped flap can be opened to reveal a view of part of the skull.

PROFITABLE RELICS

In 1578 a catacomb was discovered in a vineyard by the Via Salaria in Rome. Inside were hundreds of skeletons. They were removed by the Vatican authorities and taken to churches, mainly in Bavaria, Austria, and Switzerland. Paul Koudounaris estimates that around two thousand skeletons were cleared out of that catacomb and dispatched to churches needing relics. When they arrived at their new resting places, the skeletons were dressed in fine clothes, bedecked with gold and jewels, and exhibited in glass cases in churches as objects of veneration. Those deemed to have been military saints such as Saint Gratian were decked in gilded armor and provided with weapons (Koudounaris 2013, passim).

Over the years numbers of these bedecked skeletons of invented saints have dwindled through fires, wars, and clear-outs. In his secularization decree of 1782, Emperor Josef II (1741–1790) closed and confiscated hundreds of monasteries and ordered that superstitious relics should also be removed from churches in Austria. Bones and skeletons for which no credible provenance could be established were destroyed and the jewels and gold that bedecked them used for other purposes. This did not happen in neighboring Bavaria, so, with ten embellished skeletons, the church of Waldsassen there remains as the outstanding example of this tradition.

Bone churches exist in several places in central Europe. The Kaplica Czaszek or Czermna Chapel at Kudowa in Lower Silesia, Poland, has

Fig. 27.2. Ossuary Schwäbisch Halle, Germany Hall

about three thousand human skulls lining the walls of the 1776 building. Beneath the church are the skeletons of thousands of people more. It is a mass tomb of victims of the devastating religious sectarian conflict of 1618 to 1648 known as the Thirty Years' War. In addition there are skeletons from the three Silesian Wars from between 1740 and 1763. Even more shocking to a modern sensibility is the Sedleč Ossuary near Kutna Hora in the Czech Republic. Here there are bones and skulls all over the walls, in addition to huge chandeliers hanging from the ceiling made from every bone of the human body. In Milan, Italy, the church of San Bernardino alle Ossa has walls covered with human bones and skulls. In the United Kingdom human bones can be privately owned legally, but only exhibited with a license.

BONESMEN OF EAST ANGLIA

The secret rural fraternity called the Ancient Order of Bonesmen operated in eastern England. Members of the order, who dealt with bones for various purposes, were suspected of practicing necromancy. Bonesmanry teaches that a certain residual part of the spirit of the dead person is still present in any fragment of his or her bones. The spirit can be summoned by various rituals using a bone; for example, ghosts can be summoned by playing a tune on a whistle or flute made from human bone. A whistle made from the hind-leg bone of a rat was used to drive rats away (Lawrence 1898, 294). In parallel with luck- and health-bringing beliefs elsewhere that used powdered bone, another East Anglian tradition states that if one drinks ale containing the ashes of burned human bones, it will induce visions in the drinker.

In the days before industrial manufacture produced everything in centralized factories, buildings were constructed with local, natural materials. The skills, techniques, and lore of these materials were lost when substitutes for them came from somewhere else, ready-made. That destroyed the need for them. Before this happened specialists were employed in laying skulls or bones in the foundations and walls of buildings, their having the proper knowledge of where best to put them. Bonesmen laid floors of animal leg bones, embedded bones in the chimney breast or the roof, and procured the bones needed, including horses' skulls, which were used beneath floors and in churches as sound enhancers. The last recorded horse-skull foundation deposit in England, under the new Primitive Methodist Chapel, took place in the Cambridgeshire Fens in 1897 at Black Horse Drove near Ely (Porter 1969, 181).

The mark of a Bonesman is to carry a knucklebone of a sheep or man as an amulet, ostensibly to prevent cramps. As with all such amulets in Europe and America, it is not something to be shown to others without good reason. In his 1851 study of Northamptonshire lore and language, Thomas Sternberg mentioned one instance he found of a human kneecap carried against cramps (Sternberg 1851, 24–25). The sign of Bonesmen's presence is three long bones laid side by side, one long, one medium, and one short, signifying "man, woman, and bairn": the leg bone of a man, that of a woman, and of a child.

Chapter 28

Bones and Other Parts of Human Bodies in Amuletic Medicine

Human bone was an ingredient of the first medicine to be patented in England. Jonathan Goddard (1617–1675) was physician to the Parliamentary Army in the English Civil War and after the restoration was a founder-member of the Royal Society and a professor of physick at Gresham College. His most famous concoction was Guttæ Goddardianæ (Goddard's Drops), also known as Guttæ Anglicanæ. King Charles II was so impressed with this medicine that he paid a large sum to Goddard for the recipe so that it could be used for the benefit of his subjects. The prescription called for five pounds of powdered human skull, taken from one who had been hanged or suffered other violent death, two pounds of dried vipers, two pounds of hartshorn, and two pounds of ivory. All were ground up and made into a decoction to be drunk by the patient. With this list of ingredients, Goddard's Drops were clearly magical and not pharmaceutical.

From the twelfth century in Europe, *mumia vera ægyptica* (Egyptian mummy) was a stock-in-trade of the apothecary. It was a medicine prescribed as late as the twentieth century, although as far back as the sixteenth century it had been challenged by the noted physician Ambrose Paré (1509–1590). Bitumen from the Dead Sea (a.k.a. Lake Asphaltites), a mineral pitch also sometimes called *mumia,* was used to staunch bleeding. It was believed that the mummification process of ancient

Egypt involved this material, but it was considered more effective when it came from a mummified human.

In 1564 Guy de la Fontaine, physician to the king of Navarre, visited Alexandria in Egypt on a mission to procure a supply of mummies for pharmaceutical use in Spain (Dawson 1927, 36). He visited a dealer in mummies, who had forty in his storehouse. They were fake mummies, recently made from the bodies of slaves, filled with bitumen, bandaged, and dried in the sun until they were indistinguishable from the real ones stolen from ancient tombs (Dawson 1927, 37). The lack of ancient Egyptian amulets and talismans in European Renaissance magic indicates that most, if not all, mummies were faked in Egypt for sale to European dealers. Genuine ancient Egyptian mummies were protected by numerous amulets and talismans set on the body at specific places and also wrapped in linen bandages. Fake or not, mummies were in demand by medical practitioners of the day. Paracelsus described "balsam of mummy" and "treacle of mummy" for various ailments, and Oswald Kroll, or "Krollius," (1580–1609) recommended fake mummy made from the body of a man, preferably of ruddy complexion, aged about twenty-four, who had been hanged (Dawson 1927, 37–38). In 1732 mumia was still in use, although Johann Heinrich Zedler in his *Universal-Lexikon* stated, "Let those believe in it who want to and can."

When the Saint Bartholomew's Day massacre of Protestant Huguenots took place in France on the night of August 23–24, 1572, the apothecaries of Lyon obtained six of the fattest corpses for extraction of the fat to make unguents (De La Salle 1875, 165). Not all medical procedures needed body parts as medicine, for the mere touch of a dead man's hand was also deemed to be curative. It seems that the preferred hand was of someone who had been hanged. In 1830 the *Stamford Mercury* reported one such event: "The execution at Lincoln of the three men who were condemned to death at the late assizes drew an immense concourse of people. . . . Two foolish women came forward to rub the dead men's hands over some wens or diseased parts of their bodies, and one of them brought a child for the same purpose" (*Stamford Mercury,* March 26, 1830, 3).

Another instance of the dead hand was recounted by a correspondent to *Lincolnshire Notes & Queries:* "Huttoft neighbourhood: A man, in this neighbourhood, was suffering from a swelling behind the ear, and it was suggested to his wife that medical advice should be sought. She replied that they had been much to blame, for they had been told that the touch of a dead hand would have effected a cure; there had recently been a death in the village, and they had neglected to try the supposed remedy" (*Lincolnshire Notes & Queries*, vol. iii, 59, 60).

In Germany bones of executed people were ground up to a powder and used as medicine or for magical purposes (Köhler 1867, 418). In nineteenth-century France men carried human bones as lucky charms in the hope that the bones would prevent them being drafted into the army (Peacock 1896, 268–69). In 1889 Mary Bateman, "the Yorkshire Witch," a professional fortune-teller, was convicted of murder. She was hanged at York and her body put on show to all who could pay the three-pence admission charge to see her. Then she was dissected. Three years later parts of her body were found to be on public sale at Ilkley as amulets (Gutch 1901, 143–44).

In former times human bones were not given the respect they would be given now, in the twenty-first century. The erstwhile Bone Mill at Narborough in Norfolk was set up to grind whales' bones, a by-product of the whaling industry carried on in the nearby port of King's Lynn. There was a bone-grinding mill on Boal Wharf in King's Lynn, which closed when the mill at Narborough was built. Then barges full of bones were brought from the port up the River Nar to the mill. Bone meal was used as an agricultural fertilizer. (In the United States the bones of buffalo were used for the same purpose once the systematic mass slaughter on the plains had made thousands of tons of bones available.) In the early nineteenth century, with the advent of gaslights, the use of whale oil in lamps was superseded, whaling became uneconomic, and it ceased at King's Lynn. The Narborough watermill continued to grind bones, some of which came from local slaughterhouses, but others were imported from mainland Europe. Human bones were among these imported bones. The medieval cemeteries of Hamburg in Germany were being cleared so the city could expand, and skeletons from them were bagged up and despatched to England to be turned into fertilizer.

Also, the majority of the slain of the Battle of Waterloo, fought in 1815, remained unburied, and many of their bones ended up being ground up at Narborough, too. The mill closed in 1864 when a sluice was built across the River Nar, blocking access by barges.

GRAVEYARD DUST OR GRAVE DIRT

Churchyards, graveyards, and cemeteries are places set aside for the dead. Many people dread them because they are an uncomfortable physical reminder that one day we will die. Many also fear graveyards because spirits of the departed are believed to be present there. In the Finnish tradition the *kalman väki,* the "death folk," the väki of the dead, resides in churchyards (Hukantaival 2015, 212). Graveyard spirits are not passive, and they may intervene in some terrible way if we do the wrong thing there or be present there at night or on certain days of the year. They must be placated by keeping the grave clean and making offerings of flowers and, in some cultures, food and drink. Graveyards are also a favorite place for magical activities. Many amuletic items have been discovered in graveyards, things that were not originally buried along with the dead but were put there later.

Unless they are collective graves, which have resulted from mass deaths through some disaster, graves hold the remains of individual people who led particular lives. The graves of famous and infamous people are noted features of graveyards. Some are visited by pilgrims, devotees, and tourists. There are also practitioners of magic who go to graveyards to contact the spirits or even to obtain graveyard earth, fragments of coffins, and even actual bones as materia magica. In traditional belief materials of the churchyard in general are deemed to possess magical and physical qualities. For example, coffin dust is said to be toxic.

Soil taken from places of execution or burial has a special significance. It is a direct link to the person killed or buried there and contains the otherworldly power of the dead. In the case of executions, the soil beneath the scaffold may be imbrued with the blood or semen of the executed, and hence be seen as magically empowered. If the person buried in the grave is an ancestor or an otherwise revered person, the grave dirt will have a special virtue for the user. If the executed person is viewed as a martyr, then its value will also be increased. In the American hoodoo tradition, practitioners believe that the soil must come from the grave of a person who died "before their time" and who "died badly," either through having been murdered or executed. The dust of these dead is said to be ideal for performing destructive magic. For protection one must use dust from the grave of a soldier, police officer, or firefighter. One must buy grave dirt by offering a silver dime to the spirit of the dead at the grave.

In London in 1196 the lawyer William Fitz Osbert (known as "Longbeard") incited a popular rebellion against the tyrannical rule of King John. Taken prisoner he was condemned and executed at Tyburn, the first recorded person to suffer judicial killing there. He died the hideous death of hanging and then drawing and quartering, and the parts of his body were taken away to be displayed on prominent landmarks. But Longbeard's death was seen by the people as martyrdom. In his *Historia Rerum Anglicanum* (ch. 5, 21.1) William of Newburgh records that the soil beneath the gallows was collected by hundreds of people to the point that a big hole was dug there. The soil "as if consecrated by the blood of the executed man" was used in healing. The authorities eventually sent men-at-arms to seal off the site and arrested the priest who was "head of the superstition."

Chapter 29

The Amuletic Body

Amulets of the human body take two forms: the actual body and its parts and representations of the body and body parts. Dead bodies may be preserved whole and serve as amuletic objects for devotees, but these, naturally, are relatively uncommon. The more or less intact remains of saints of religion and secular heroes of authoritarian regimes can be seen preserved visibly in churches and Communist pantheons. More common are the body parts of preachers and notable devotees preserved in certain Christian, Buddhist, and Islamic traditions. The skull, being the most characteristic human remain after death, features large in magic and symbolism. However the representation of parts of the body in various nonhuman materials is by far the most common element of this, with eye, hand, and heart images and the head having their own particular function.

Tattooing has been practiced for thousands of years, although its name—*tattoo*—was not used to describe this technique outside Polynesia until the eighteenth century, when it was described by European travelers returning from the islands of the Pacific. A predynastic mummy from Gebelein in Egypt that was radiocarbon dated to between 3349 and 3018 BCE had a tattoo of two horned animals. Many mummies from 3900 to 1069 BCE have various patterns tattooed on them. In this period Egypt and Nubia to the south had two distinct schools of tattooing (Krutak and Deter-Wolf 2017, 5).

There was a biblical prohibition on tattooing, that Israelites "should not make any cuttings in your flesh for the dead, nor print any marks upon you" (Leviticus 19:28), which meant that it was seen as unchristian by the later church. However it is uncertain what Saint Paul meant when he discounted the Jewish practice of circumcision as unimportant, writing "for I bear in my body the marks of the Lord Jesus" (Galatians 6:17). It is questionable whether he meant this literally in the form of tattoos. But Procopius of Gaza, writing in the fifth century, tells of branding or tattooing the body (Fleming 2000, 78).

When the British ship *Endeavour* visited Tahiti in July 1769, Captain Cook wrote in his journal, "Both sexes paint their body, *Tattow* as it is called in their language" (Price 1971, 37). This is the first known use of the word in English. When the intrepid Scottish traveler William Lithgow wrote of a visit to Jerusalem with pilgrim companions in 1612, he noted, "One Elias Areacheros, a Christian inhabitour at Bethleem . . . did ingrave upon our severall Armes upon Christ's Sepulcher the name of Jesus, and the Holy Cross . . . but I, deciphered and subjoined below mine, the four incorporate crowns of King James." Lithgow also had a patriotic poem tattooed there (Lithgow [1640] 1906, 253).

Fig. 29.1. William Lithgow's Jerusalem tattoo, 1612

Tattooing the body with talismanic religious signs was not the only sort of body-marking practices present in seventeenth-century Britain. Three years earlier, in London, the English medical astrologer

Simon Forman (1552–1611) had made the characters of Venus, Jupiter, and Cancer on his right breast and left arm. These were the rulers of Forman's horoscope. He used a special permanent ink made from *salarmoniack* (ammonium chloride) and gold, as he described in his *Of Apoticarie Drugs,* a manuscript written circa 1607 and now in the Bodleian Library, Oxford (Rosecrans 2000, 46–48). Forman applied the ink sigils at the correct astrological moment of his progressed chart to become the master of his fate. He intended that the sigils would remain and be visible even after he died, giving him the capacity to control his destiny in life and the hereafter.

Also in the early 1600s, Thomas Coryat had a Jerusalem cross tattooed on his left wrist and a cross, three nails, and the words *Via, Veritas, Vita* on his right (Fleming 2000, 79). In 1614 the Scottish pilgrim Fynes Morison was another notable for his Jerusalem tattoos (Anon. 1995, 17). In 1653 John Bulwer illustrated tattoos from various lands in his remarkable book *Anthropometamorphosis.* As early as the sixteenth century, pilgrims to the shrine of Our Lady of Loreto in Italy were being tattooed with religious emblems and sigils (Caplan 2000, xviii). Otto von Gröben from Hamburg was tattooed in Palestine in 1634 (Anon. 1995, 19). In nineteenth-century Bosnia Christian girls were tattooed with crosses and other cross-bearing sigils as signs of their religious identity to prevent them being converted to Islam as brides (Anon. 1995, 19).

In seventeenth- and eighteenth-century Britain, people convicted of various crimes were branded with a hot iron as a punishment and also to label them as criminals for the whole of their lives. The brands took the form of capital letters. To be branded with an *M* was to be a malefactor. False accusers were branded *FA,* those convicted of blasphemy bore a *B,* vagabonds (vagrants) a *V,* and coin clippers a *C.* "Sowers of sedition" were branded with *SS* on either side of the nose. Convicts were branded in France until 1832, and Russians exiled to Siberia until 1864 bore brands (Jones 2000, 14).

From the eighteenth century in Europe and America, tattoos became associated with sailors and criminals. Hence those early modernist architects who deplored ornament likened it to criminals with tattooed bodies, seeing it either as primitive or degenerate. "It is possible," wrote William Richard Lethaby in 1911, "that ornamentation arises in such arts as tattooing, belongs to the infancy of the world, and it may well disappear from our architecture as it has from our machinery" (Lethaby 1911, 244). Around the same time Alexander Lacassagne, military surgeon and professor of medical jurisprudence at Lyon University in France, stated that tattooing was "due to idleness and degeneration" (Miranda 2016, 31). He listed tattoos as patriotic, religious, military, occupational, written texts, and "metaphorical" (Miranda 2016, 32). These last were the charms and sigils that have a symbolic and magical function: anchors, stars, pierced hearts, birds, hands, and daggers. These were the most favored tattoos until the 1980s, when the contemporary styles of emblem became ubiquitous.

Simon Forman's story is a rare record of writing talismanic emblems on the body for occult purposes. But his actions in using a special ink are part of a larger tradition of charms intended to generate love in a desired man or woman. Charms from England are in the current of classical talismanic magic, such as that practiced by the English magus William Lilly (Lilly 1822, 32). His talismans were at the upmarket end of the practice, being individually crafted from gold and kept in fine red velvet bags. Charms written on the body were simple and temporary. One for a man to get a woman tells him to write these letters on his left hand before sunrise: *HLDPNAGU,* then to touch the woman "and she will follow." Another, written in the person's own blood in small squares before sunrise or after sunset, has the characters *NAPARABOCPLEA.* Again, touching the person will enchant him or her to follow the operant's will.

In the German lands, around the time Lithgow, Coryat, and Morison were tattooed, the body as amulet had developed other forms. A means of averting wounding by edged weapons and firearms or being taken prisoner was to write or print holy names on a piece of paper and swallow it. Saint Bernard was a popular saint for this technique. In 1611 the public executioner at Passau in Bavaria announced the "invulnerability pill," which soon was called *Passauer Kunst* (the Passau Art). This included both capsules and packets of parchment bearing protective magic texts and sigils (Bächtold-Stäubli 1927–1942, 1460–61). A defensive charm against cut and thrust (*für Hieb und Stich*) included formulaic crosses and numbers beginning † *A 3 6 ma 9 †††* (Elworthy 1895, 401). The Passauer Kunst came at the right time, for the Thirty Years' War broke out in 1618 and many soldiers and mercenaries used this form of protection. The technique spread across Europe, and great commanders were believed to use amuletic magic to be "shot-free" or "hard-shot," as invulnerability to bullets was called in English (Tlusty 2019, 14).

In Catholic Germany and Austria from the seventeenth century onward, a means of treating illness and of empowering the body against harm was the similar *Esszettel.* These papers were religious in content. Sheets with multiple images of saints were printed and sold, resembling a modern sheet of postage stamps. Individual images were cut out and eaten. They were empowered by saying a prayer appropriate to the image. The principle of these *Schluckbildchen* was adopted in the twentieth century by purveyors of LSD, who impregnated printed perforated sheets with the drug. Bearing smiley faces or cartoon figures, the individual detachable pieces were supposed to be a single dose.

Back in seventeenth-century central Europe, another means of making the body amuletic was the practice of *Einheilen.* This was the technique of "healing-in" an amuletic implant, sometimes a consecrated communion wafer smuggled out of a church, a parchment with sigils written on it, or a piece of moss that grew on an unburied human skull. The user would make an incision in himself (it was done by men, mainly soldiers), put the object in the wound, and allow it to heal, thereby imparting invulnerability (Tlusty 2019, 28). Skull moss was described in 1694 by Pierre Pornet, apothecary to King Louis XIV of France, as the "moss of an unburied cranium . . . like that on Oaks." It was not moss according to modern taxonomy but a type of lichen, possibly *Usnea,* a gray-green lichen of the order Parmeliaceae, known as "beard lichen" or "old man's beard." It was believed that those implanted with a communion host were not only woundproof but also that their bodies would not decompose after death (Tlusty 2019, 25). Unlike the pills of the Passauer Kunst and the Esszettel, which were only effective for twenty-four hours at most, the amuletic implant was permanent.

People who used this magic were subject to being tried as sorcerers or witches. In Nuremberg in 1617 Job Körnlein, a former mercenary, was convicted of theft and sorcery and executed. He possessed a finger and some strips of skin cut from a slain Turkish soldier on the battlefield, which he used in shooting spells. Also found in his possession were some other materia magica: a piece of fur, a chicory root, a piece of skull, a bullet from a dead man's head, a hangman's rope, and metal stamps to print papers for the Passauer Kunst (Staatsarchiv Nürnberg, *Achtsbuch,* 1615–18, 29, 6r–322r). The English clergyman William Watts wrote in 1632 in his *The Swedish Discipline* that this "devilish enchantment" was "common among Germans" (Tlusty 2019, 14–15).

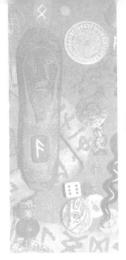

Chapter 30

Eye and Hand

Prescientific theory taught that sight was accomplished by the eye sending out a ray that alighted on a particular object, which the viewer then perceived. This disproved ray theory is still present without being recognized as such when people talk of someone "ogling" them or "the male gaze." During the Black Death in the fourteenth century, it was thought that the disease was transmitted by a glance from the eye of a sick person (Elworthy 1895, v). Belief in the evil eye was widespread in Europe, the Middle East, the Asian subcontinent, and East Asia, and amulets against it are common, as this book shows. In 1887 Lady Jane Francesca Wilde described the belief used in protective amulets in ancient Egypt. The *wadjet* or *ujat* is a left eye representing the restored eye of Horus. Corresponding amulets of a right eye are the Eye of Ra. These amulets were not made of a particular material. Examples are known from gold, silver, lapis lazuli, carnelian, faience, and wood. When made today as

Fig. 30.1. Eye amulet, Crete

Fig. 30.2. Ancient Egyptian
Eyes of Ra and Horus

jewelry, these eyes are frequently both referred to incorrectly as "the Eye of Horus." Roman gold rings bore the eye emblem in glass or semiprecious stones (Gerlach 1971, 219).

At the 1889 Exposition in Paris, Giuseppe Bellucci exhibited several Italian eye amulets among his exhibits. The Santa Lucia eye (eye of Saint Lucy) amulet was worn to keep the eyes seeing well, to prevent maladies of the eye, and to cure them of problems (Bellucci 1889, 59–60). A nineteenth-century use of the eye pattern in ceramics has become a well-known motif in the high-fired earthenware pottery of Bolesławiec in Poland, also known by its former German name, Bunzlau. The *pfauenauge* (peacock's eye) pattern was originated by a Lusatian craftsman from Bischofswerda, Paul Schreier (Snodgrass 2004, 771). It is clearly an apotropaic pattern, making the eye-bearing vessels and plates amuletic in function. Several items are illustrated in figure 30.3.

Fig. 30.3. Bunzlau plates, dish, and teapot with pfauenaugen patterns (also see plate 22)

Eye amulets exist today in various forms. When the author visited the eye clinic at Addenbrooke's Hospital, Cambridge, in January 2020, there was a painting of the Eye of Ra on the wall, a gift from a grandmother in thanks for the hospital saving her granddaughter's eyesight, a twenty-first century amulet and ex-voto in a secular setting. The *nazar* is a widespread Turkish eye amulet made of blue, white, and black glass. In the Nepalese Buddhist tradition, the "all-seeing eye" of the Buddha depicts an eye surrounded by sixteen "snail martyrs," recalling the image of the Buddha with his head covered with the 108 snails that died to keep him cool. This is the origin of the Amulet of Agamotto, which appeared first in 1963 in Steve Ditko's *Strange Tales* published by Marvel Comics and later on developed into its present form. The comic-book sorcerer Doctor Strange possessed an eye amulet that was his most potent magical tool. Soon, as stories developed in complexity in successive issues of comics, it became known as the *nazar* clock.

Fig. 30.4. A nazar Turkish clock

The human hand is such an important characteristic of the body that it has many symbolic connections. In chiromantic (palmistry) tradition, the fingers of the human hand are ascribed to different astrological planets. Ben Jonson, in his book *The Alchemist* (1610), explains, "The thumb in Chiromancy we give Venus; the fore-finger to Jove; the midst, to Saturn; the ring to Sol; the least, to Mercury." There is no finger corresponding with Mars or the moon. The open hand thus signifies these five astrological planets together. Lucky charms in the form of an open hand are associated with the Jewish and Islamic traditions. The *hamsa hand,* common in North Africa and the Middle East, is symmetrical, appearing to have a thumb on either side of the hand. It is made as jewelry and also as wall hangings. The name comes from the Hebrew *hamesh,* the number five. In Jewish tradition the number five represents the five books of the Torah, and in Islamic symbolism, the five pillars of Islam. Its function is to protect against harm, especially the evil eye. The symbolic use of the number five in these contexts probably comes from the five fingers of the human hand. In Islamic countries it is the *hand of Fatima,* and in Jewish tradition it is the *hand of Miriam.* Pendants of the hamsa hand exist with the hand inside a hexagram in a circle, in the apices of which are eyes. Two are illustrated in figure 30.5. Related to the hamsa hand is a hand with an eye in the

Fig. 30.5. Hamsa hand amulets
with hexagram eyes

Fig. 30.6. Ceramic hand amulets, Texas

palm. Sometimes it is indistinguishable from the hamsa hand except for the eye. Less stylized hands made in blue glass with an eye are common Turkish talismans, commonly suspended by a blue ribbon.

A hand and arm carved from red coral, mounted in silver, and used to avert the evil eye was exhibited in Paris in 1889 by Giuseppe Bellucci (Bellucci 1889, 53). A clenched hand with the thumb poking out between the first and second fingers is the *mano fica,* talismanic against the evil eye. It was known as far back as the Etruscan era, and in later times, it was customarily made of blue glass. C. J. S. Thompson noted its use in nineteenth-century England; he recorded that a Dean Ramsey remembered it from when he was a boy in Yorkshire, between 1800 and 1810. Ramsey stated, "The *mano fica* was not unknown in England. . . . To put the thumb between the first and second finger pointing downward, was believed to be an infallible protection against evil influence of one particularly malevolent and powerful witch" (Thompson 1932, 71).

The Roman Catholic image *mano poderosa,* the "hand of power," depicts a hand of Jesus with its stigma (nail wound). Above the four outstretched fingers is an image of a cloud on which stand four saintly figures. "Hands" made from plant stems were being made in Germany in the nineteenth century. Among various forms were the hand of fortune and the hand of Saint John (Lawrence 1898, 17). "The hand of

Fig. 30.7. Mexican milagros

fate" and "the hand of doom" are common expressions, as is "the hidden hand of destiny." In hoodoo an assemblage of magical items in a bag is called a mojo hand. Whether this relates to the hand proper, to the figurative hands of fate and destiny, or is analogous to a hand of cards is uncertain. A mojo hand can serve either purpose: as protection against evil-wishers and as a luck-bringer in gambling. Hands appear in the collection of charms known as *milagros,* popular in Mexico and parts of the United States formerly under Mexican rule.

In 1923 Elizabeth Villiers described the sign of "The Devil's Horn," in which "the hand is clenched with the first and fourth fingers outstretched." She attributes the sign as a representation of the horns of the Egyptian goddess Isis, and "in the Christian reaction against the older faith, the present uncomplimentary name was given" (Villiers 1923, 88). In a sheet music cover, illustrator Eugène Grasset had used this hand sign in 1892 for the musical composition "Enchantement" by Jules Massanet, a setting of a poem by Jules Ruelle. Grasset's drawing depicts an enchantress with upraised arms. In her right hand she wields a wand, while her left gives the sign with index and little fingers upright (Arwas 1978, 79). Grasset was a knowing user of esoteric material; on the title page of the French score of Wagner's *La Valkyrie,* Wotan's and Brünnhilde's weapons are depicted with correct runic inscriptions (Mota and Infiesta 1995, 266).

As the *mano cornuto* (horned hand), this amulet was widespread in nineteenth-century Naples, Italy, where it was either carved from coral or cast in silver. C. J. S. Thompson notes that "a large red glove filled with sand, with the thumb and the middle fingers sewn together so as to make the mano cornuto, is sometimes hung as a sign outside their houses by Neapolitan laundresses" (Thompson 1932, 71). In heavy metal music fandom, the identical characteristic "metal horns" hand sign is associated from the late 1970s onward with Ronnie James Dio (1942–2010), singer with the hard rock and heavy metal bands Rainbow, Black Sabbath, and his own eponymous band, Dio. However a photograph exists from 1969 showing Black Sabbath bassist Geezer Butler giving the sign, so it was already in circulation outside Italian heritage circles. In 2017 Gene Simmons from the heavy metal band Kiss attempted to copyright the sign, naturally without success.

Chapter 31

The Heart

The heart is primarily a symbol of love, life, and spiritual worth, emblematic as far back as ancient Egypt, where purity of heart was judged after death by weighing one's heart against the feather of truth. The Egyptian amulet for the protection of the heart was in the form of a scarab (Thompson 1932, 231). In ancient Crete heart amulets were sacred to Diana Virgo. But it is also a lucky sign (Von Zaborsky 1936, 120–28; Peesch 1983, 108–16;

Fig. 31.1. *Ex-Voto VIII* of Nigel Pennick's *Ex-Voto* series of amuletic artworks, exhibited at the Walkers' Gallery, San Marcos, Texas, 2013 (also see plate 23)

Fig. 31.2. Winged heart amulet, twenty-first century

Pennick 2014, 95–100). The medieval troubadours made a popular image of the *offrande du cœur,* the lover's heart as a gift to his beloved. In medieval France books of love songs bore the heart emblem on their covers. A heart brooch was found along with a cross and rings buried at Fishpool, Nottinghamshire, in 1464 (Reeves 1995, 66).

As a popular religious image in Europe and the Americas, the heart derives from the cult of the Most Sacred Heart of Jesus. This is a Roman Catholic emblem and devotional practice that arose in the mid-thirteenth century, popularized by the Norbertine religious figure Blessed Herman Joseph (died 1241). By the next century it had gone mainstream in the church. In 1353 Pope Innocent VI composed a mass honoring the Sacred Heart, and in 1675, Marguerite Marie Alacoque (1647–1690) was instrumental in the Most Sacred Heart of Jesus becoming a popular cult after she beheld the heart in a vision.

Fig. 31.3. Sacred Heart of Jesus medallion

The emblem, which became standardized, has the heart at the center surrounded by a garland of thorns. From its upper side emanate flames and a cross.

But this image was not original, for in the previous century emblematic engravings such as that of Jörg Bentz of Nuremberg (ca. 1529) had used the image, Bentz in a representation of the goddess of love, Venus. Alchemists, too, including Nicolas Flamel, employed the emblem. Flamel's shows a heart from which grows a plant surrounded by a garland of thorns. Of the forty Rosicrucian emblems of Daniel Cramer, thirty-three have the heart as a major motif (Cramer [1617] 1991).

The Miraculous Medal of Our Lady of the Graces, which originated in nineteenth-century France, is one of many talismanic items in Roman Catholic tradition. It is a double-sided image of Our Lady with rays emerging from her hands on the obverse and on the reverse side, a letter *M* surmounted by a cross, below which are two heart emblems. These are the Immaculate Heart of Mary, which is depicted run through with a dagger, and the Sacred Heart of Jesus, which is surrounded by a garland of thorns. Surrounding the composite sigil in contemporary medals are twelve five-pointed stars. However the engraving in M. Aladel's 1890 definitive book about the Miraculous Medal shows fourteen stars (Aladel 1890, 273). The medallion was created after a series of Marian apparitions and visions experienced by a French nun, Catherine Labouré (1806–1876), at the Vincentian church in Paris. The first medallion was commissioned from a goldsmith, Adrian Vochette, and soon mass production began. The Miraculous Medal of Our Lady of the Graces is readily available today from any seller of Catholic devotional paraphernalia, although it is identical in size and format to those of numerous saints.

The heart is an emblem in the jewelry of central and northern European traditional folk costumes. In France it was connected with the cross. The Jeannette cross, most closely associated with Brittany, is a gold or silver cross suspended on a black velvet ribbon, often itself bearing amuletic emblems, with a heart-shaped slide through which the ribbon ran. Lionel Bonnemère collected silver hearts that were slides for Normandy crosses (Boutellier 1966, 17–42). The heart is the most

Fig. 31.4. Wooden flaming heart covered with milagros, Mexico (also see plate 24)

common form of locket. Worn around the neck on a chain, a locket can be opened with a hinge and things can be put inside, which may be a lock of hair or a photograph of a loved one. In former times before photography, a miniature painting would be used. Lockets also contain other keepsakes and relics. Lockets are related in name to miniature padlocks, which often are shaped like hearts.

In former times English sailors favored heart charms. Pearl Binder notes that after completion of two voyages of five thousand miles, sailors got a heart tattoo in commemoration (Binder 1973, 76). There are two traditional forms of sailors' tattoos; the Marian religious heart stuck with a dagger and the heart of love pierced with a Cupid's arrow. At the beginning of a voyage, wives gave sailors a heart-shaped pincushion stuck full of pins as a luck-bringer (Lewery 1991, 104). The pins recall the thorns of the alchemical and religious heart images. "Anything in the shape of a heart," wrote C. J. S. Thompson, "was esteemed as a charm by sailors, as it was believed to avert the tempests and storms caused by demons" (Thompson 1932, 195).

In Thomas Middleton's play *The Witch: A Tragi-Comedie,* Heccat asks, "Is the heart of wax stuck full of magique needles?" And Stadlin answers, "'Tis done, Heccat" (quoted in Ashton 1896, 176). Hearts and heart-shaped items have been found as house deposits, objects deliber-

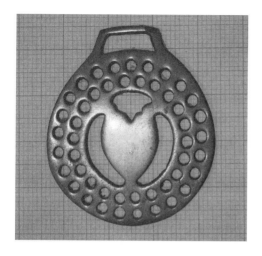

Fig. 31.5. Heart amulet horse brass

ately placed in the foundations, walls, and chimneys of old buildings for magical purposes (Elworthy 1895, 53–54; Rushen 1984, 35). These include hearts of cattle and pigs stuck with pins. In 1963 at Castle Rising, Norfolk, there was a "black magic" scare when a heart pierced with thorny hawthorn twigs was nailed to the castle door along with two pierced clay effigies. A black soot cross and circle were drawn nearby (Hill and Williams 1965, 194–95). The prophylactic function of the heart and pins or thorns also enters the lore of the witch bottle. A piece of fabric in the shape of a heart stuck with pins was discovered inside one found in a house in Ipswich, Suffolk (Bunn 1991, 4).

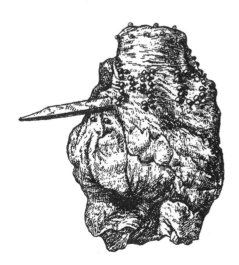

Fig. 31.6. Nailed heart, western England, nineteenth century

In the eighteenth century the heart appears in a military context. In 1782 George Washington issued a heart-shaped embroidered fabric patch, called "the Badge of Military Merit." It was awarded to men who had shown "unusual gallantry, extraordinary fidelity" during the War of Independence. In the United Kingdom during World War I, the Women's Branch of the National Service issued a heart-shaped charm suspended on a ribbon like a medal. Describing it as "the pendant of service and sacrifice," the advertising blurb read, "Is one dear to you fighting in the Great War? If so you are entitled to wear this badge. It is worn by women who have a relative or sweetheart serving."

Fig. 31.7. "Sacrifice" heart pendant, United Kingdom, World War I

In 1917, emulating Washington's Badge of Military Merit, the U.S. government instituted the Purple Heart medal, awarded to servicemen wounded or killed in action after April 5, 1917.

The Claddagh is an Irish ring depicting two hands holding a heart, above which is a crown. It symbolizes love, loyalty, and friendship, or "let love and friendship reign." Originating in the seventeenth century, it became widespread and popular in the nineteenth, when it acquired the name Claddagh after a fishing village of that name near Galway where it was believed to have originated. It is customary to wear it in certain ways that denote a man's marital state. If worn on the right hand with the heart pointing toward the fingertip, it signifies that the wearer is single and seeking a relationship. Wearing it on the right hand with the heart pointing toward the wrist denotes the wearer is in a relationship. When worn on the left hand with the heart pointing toward the fingertip, the wearer is engaged to be married, and on the left ring finger with the heart pointing toward the wrist, the wearer is married.

An Irish legend of the ring's origin ascribes it to Richard Joyce from Claddagh, who in 1675 was captured by North African corsairs and sold as a slave in Algiers. Purchased by a goldsmith the enslaved Joyce learned the craft of goldsmithing. When King William III bought the freedom of all British and Irish slaves from North Africa, Joyce returned home and brought a ring he had made in captivity. It was the prototype of all subsequent Claddagh rings (Quinn 1970, 9–13). However identical rings called *fede* (faith) rings were made and worn in Brittany in the eighteenth and nineteenth centuries. Breton married women who wore them frequently wore a red coral ring between the fede ring and their wedding band. By the late nineteenth century, the design had simplified. The hands were reduced to stylized lines and the heart enlarged and made more bulbous.

Another heart-related amulet, the Scottish luckenbooth, is strongly associated with the city of Edinburgh. It has many variant forms, but basically it is a crown above a heart or above two intertwined hearts. The crown above the heart is the central component of the Irish Claddagh form, but the crown above an emblem is an ancient Scottish motif most prominent in the emblem of the Incorporation of Hammermen, an ancient artificers' guild. The name Luckenbooth described the old Tolbooth of Edinburgh, the local prison in former times, but also has a more general meaning of a lockable booth (market stall) or workshop.

However, unlike the crowned hammer, it is not a craftsmen's emblem, but rather a charm in a wider sense that originated in the eighteenth century. It is a love token, a talisman to assist milk flow in nursing mothers, and a protector of babies against harmful spirits and the evil eye. Unlike the Claddagh, which has a very fixed form, the luckenbooth has many variations. In the nineteenth century, it developed into a version that looked like the letter *M,* the "Queen Mary *M*" form, which today is associated with Mary, Queen of Scots. An alternative form is "harp shaped," a distorted version of the heart.

Fig. 31.8. Luckenbooth, silver with agate

A silver brooch supposedly discovered by a Joseph Smith on a building site in Stratford-upon-Avon in 1828 is clearly a form of luckenbooth. Bearing the name 'W Shkespeare' on the back, it was the subject of a sworn declaration by Smith in 1864, and it became famous in 1883 when John Rabon published an article in *The Stratford Herald,* subsequently issued as a pamphlet. It is a heart-shaped brooch with stones set in the form of a crown above it. Whether or not it belonged to William Shakespeare is disputed.

Chapter 32

Little People: Small Humanoid Images

Small images of spiritual beings exist throughout the world. Some signify the spirits of departed humans, while others represent nonhuman spirits, angels, gods, and embodied principles. These images are frequently seen as ensouled in their own right. The art of endowing temporary life and intelligence on objects, especially images, statues, and other forms on inert matter, is called *theopeaea* (Rosen 1991, 382). Small images were universal in various ancient cultures. Ancient Egyptians buried *shabti* figures with the dead as well as images of gods

Fig. 32.1. Guatemalan "worry person" amulet, fabric (also see plate 25)

195

Fig. 32.2. Hlutr of Thor in "iron beard" posture,
England, 1980s

and goddesses, the most important of which was Osiris. The Romans had small household gods—often cast in bronze—that presided over their home shrines. Small portable images or icons of deities known as *hlutr* were made and carried in Viking times.

Shamans in Siberia had small humanoid figures on their costumes, signifying their spirit helpers (Anawalt 2014, 40). Christian images of saints, especially on medallions, are a present-day example. Saint Christopher as the spiritual guardian of travelers and, in modern times, motorists, is ubiquitous.

POPPETS AND INVULTUATION

Invultuation is making an image of a person whom the operative wishes to punish or kill. Such magic dolls, also known as poppets and voodoo dolls, are part of the magical traditions of many lands. They are stabbed with a knife or stuck with nails or pins, the act of "putting a pin in for someone" in English witchcraft. In 1603 the British king, James I, commented "at these times he [the devil—NP] teacheth how to make pictures of wax or clay: that by the roasting thereof, the persons that they beare the name of, may be continually melted or dried away by continuall sicknesse . . . they can bewitch and take away the life of man or woman, by roasting the pictures."

The Alder Child, otherwise called the Alder Boy and Alder Man, is a Finnish image used for various magical purposes. It can protect children against the "night-crying-maker," be used in healing- and love-magic, punish thieves, and act as a spirit-herdsman to protect cattle against wolves (Hukantaival 2015, 209).

These figures are closely related to religious images, and it is often a matter of semantics what they are called. The *nkondi* is an African figure made by Kongo people in the Congo Basin of central Africa. It is a carved wooden figure that contains *bilongo,* various items and substances with particular virtues, and is covered by mirrors fixed with resin. The nkondi is put in a graveyard and left until the ritual specialist detects that a spirit has entered it. Then it is taken away for use. The indwelling spirit can then be sent to hunt down people and punish or kill them. Each time this is done, a nail is hammered into the figure. Punishment of wrongdoers or unbelievers is an integral function of many deities, as many religious writings inform us.

CHARM DOLLS AND LITTLE GODS OF THE TWENTIETH CENTURY

Portable anthropoid representations of principles, personifications of luck, have existed for millennia. In the twentieth century several rose to fame through their use as mascots in wartime. Writing in 1908 Wright and Lovett noted that the Maori "lucky jade," or *hai tiki,* from New Zealand was an important mascot in sporting circles. They reported "stories that greenstone objects were carried by every member of the Victorious All Blacks Rugby team" [from New Zealand—NP]. Famous racehorse owners also carried the amulet: "Lord Rosebery when his horse Cicero won the Derby, and Lord Rothschild when St Amant won his race" (Wright and Lovett 1908, 293). Hai tikis, dwarf figures, and lucky six-pence pieces were the favorite mascots for bridge players (Wright and Lovett 1908, 293).

BILLIKEN

Billiken is perhaps the greatest success of all invented charms. Its origin is in a poem published in 1896 by Canadian poet Bliss Carman, "A Song of the Little People," in the book *More Songs from Vagabondia*. There is a "list of Little Men" that is reminiscent of the medieval Icelandic list-naming dwarfs in *Gylfaginning* in *The Edda* (*Gylfaginning* 14). "We're all here. Honey-Bug, Thistledrift, White Imp, Weird Wryface, Billiken, Quidnunc, Queered. We're all here, and the coast is clear. Moon, Mr. Moon, When you coming down?"

In 1908 Florence Pretz from Kansas City patented a small "charm doll" called Billiken as "god of things as they ought to be." The Billiken Company of Chicago held the patent, and the charm dolls were manufactured in the Craftsman Guild of Highland Park, Illinois. The mascot was described as "the smiling god of good fortune, the original divinity of optimism, whose cheerful countenance brings good luck and happy days to all who observe this rune of life: be cheerful and you will be rich in everything." The image, for so it was described, was treated as almost divine from the outset. The Craftsman Guild advertised it for "loyal worshippers of Billiken" in reverent language as "facsimiles of his August Presence," adding that as Billiken was the mascot of the guild, one could not be sold but only be lent to devotees for a period of ninety-nine years for seventy-five cents.

Billiken was an immediate success. In 1909 Angokwazuk, an Alaskan Inuit, carved a Billiken from walrus ivory, and subsequent images became known as Happy Jack. The image soon became part of the Alaskan carving tradition. In 1911 a Shriner Masonic group, the Royal Order of Jesters, adopted it as their mascot. Later Billiken also became the mascot of Saint Louis University. Billiken banks for children were manufactured by the A. C. Williams Company.

Writing in Britain in 1923 Elizabeth Villiers noted a similarity between this mascot and an ancient Egyptian god. She did not know Billiken's origin, but surmised that he was a recent invention that had "a purely commercial christening. Whoever first made Billiken and put him on the market to become a popular mascot, drew his idea from the

Egyptian deity, Bes" (Villiers 1923, 30). According to Villiers Bes is the god of laughter, merrymaking, and good luck. "In ancient Egypt," she writes, "little figures with his pot belly, his bat's ears, and quaint smile, were very popular, and were worn to dispel clouds of trouble and to bring joy into life" (Villiers 1923, 30). Billiken, as "a sure cure for the blues, that solemn feeling, the grouch, the hoodoo germ, hard-luck melancholia, the down-and-out-bacillus," clearly serves the same function.

NÉNETTE AND RINTINTIN

In France in 1913 a pair of porcelain charm dolls appeared. Designed by Francisque Poulbot (1879–1946), they were called Nénette and Rintintin. Nénette was the man and Rintintin his female companion. The onset of World War I in 1914 saw these figures become popular among French soldiers, who improvised them from yarn. Silver and Bakelite versions were produced by factories and ivory versions custom made for military clients. Allied aviators wore them for luck on wrist chains. In 1918, during the bombardment of Paris by the German siege artillery piece Dicke Bertha (Big Bertha) between March and August of that year, Nénette and Rintintin were considered amulets against being on the wrong end of Bertha's heavy ordnance. In 1919, in his *The Marines, and Other War Verse,* the American poet Adolphe E. Smylie wrote ironically about how he was bulletproof because of his amulets, Nénette and Rintintin:

> *Snipe on, you Boche! No bullet hole*
> *Can ventilate my hide*
> *Thanks to wee maid and man,*
> *Nénette and Rintintin!*
> (Smylie 1919, 55)

The French poet Guillaume Apollinaire called Nénette and Rintintin "the first gods born in the twentieth century." Clearly he had never come across Billiken. Rintintin gave her name to a famous dog that starred in many movies. In World War I an American soldier, Corporal

Lee Duncan, rescued an Alsatian (German Shepherd) dog that he came across in abandoned German military kennels near Metz. He named it Rintintin, and after the war, in 1922, it starred in a film that was so successful that it spawned numerous sequels starring a series of dogs with the same name. Duncan had Nénette and Rintintin figures made in gold and wore them for the rest of his life (Davies 2018, 173).

FUMSUP

Fumsup, that is, "thumbs-up," appeared during World War I as a lucky charm, a metal baby charm doll similar to Billiken. It is a standing figure with both hands giving the thumbs-up sign, marketed from 1916 by the leading British jewelry company J. C. Vickery, intended to be given to soldiers fighting at the front. Elizabeth Villiers explained its symbolism as originating in gladiatorial combat in the Roman arenas: "The saying comes from the Romans, with whom the position of the thumb was a matter of life and death. Only when a man had fought bravely and when he had been vanquished by extreme odds or by some influence beyond his control, was 'Thumbs Up' ever given. Hence while the sign means 'Live on—hope on,' it stands also for the reward of merit, and may be freely translated as 'Keep on trying, do your best, don't show fear, and you will come out all right in the end'" (Villiers 1923, 161).

In 1916 the postcard publisher Raphael Tuck produced a postcard titled *The Optimistic Child* with a figure in the same position. On the card, a version of Fumsup with a wooden head was combined with the image of another charm, Touchwood. "Touch wood" is an expression meaning "hopefully," and the Touchwood-Fumsup charm was marketed with the slogan "Behold in me the birth of luck, two charms combined, Touchwood-Fumsup." Touchwood is a charm composed of a small sphere of wood with metal arms and legs. The accompanying rhyme to Touchwood-Fumsup explained its symbolism and function, the last line clearly referring to soldiers and sailors serving in the current war:

My head is made of wood most rare
My thumbs turn up to touch me there

To speed my feet they're cupid's wings
They'll help true love 'mongst other things
Proverbial in my power to bring
Good luck to you in everything
I'll bring good luck to all away
Just send me to a friend today.

Touching wood is a far more ancient custom than the Touchwood mascot. Sacred trees are significant elements in ancient European paganism, and images made from certain kinds of trees are ascribed particular powers of healing, protecting against evil, and bringing good luck.

Fig. 32.3. Raphael Tuck postcard illustration of Fumsup, United Kingdom, 1916

PIXIES AND PISKIES

Twentieth-century charm dolls such as Billiken and Fumsup are related to lucky images localized in the west of England in the counties of Cornwall and Devon and are part of a wider Celtic belief in "the little people," the pixies of Devon, especially Dartmoor, and their Cornish counterpart, piskies. In his book *The Fairy Faith in Celtic Countries,* W. Y. Evans-Wentz stated, "The only true Cornish fairy is the Pisky, of the race which is the *Pobel Vean* or Little People" (Evans-Wentz 1911, 165). Anna Franklin notes that at one time "every cottage had

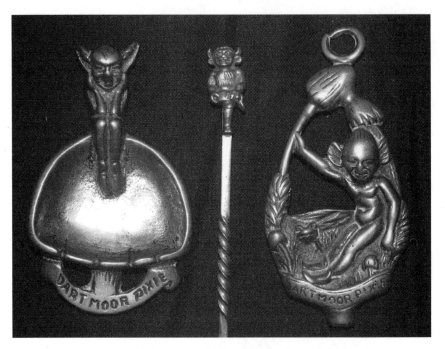

Fig. 32.4. Dartmoor pixies and Lincoln imp, brass,
late nineteenth and early twentieth centuries

a *pisky pow* on the roof ridge as a dancing-place for piskies" (Franklin 2002, 208). Pixies were not restricted to the far west of England, however. Evans-Wentz reported on a woman living on the Gower Peninsula, Wales, who described having seen them "like tiny men dancing on the mare's back." She thought they were spirits that appeared in the early morning, and "all mishaps to cows she attributed to them" (Evans-Wentz 1911, 158).

Generally pixies were considered to be equivocal in their dealings with humans. They could be helpful as house fairies (Franklin 2002, 208). But also they might be bringers of bad luck or, at the least, unwelcome mischief. Jack O'Lantern is an example of the equivocal character of these beings. As lucky charms their benevolent aspects are emphasized. A newspaper advertisement from the 1950s describes the piskies as the "cheery wonder workers of Cornwall." As lucky charms Cornish piskies take two forms: a female one called Joan the Wad and a male one, Jack O'Lantern. Joan the Wad is presented as queen of the piskies,

Fig. 32.5. Jack O'Lantern horse brasses

but Jack O'Lantern is not exclusively Cornish, as he is also presented as "king of the lucky Devon Pixies" in various forms including brass door knockers. Joan the Wad as the corresponding queen of the piskies is associated with Polperro, where there is a holy well. In the 1950s advertisement these charms were "guaranteed dipped in water from the saints' well" at Polperro. Advertisements of the period claimed that Joan the Wad brought health, wealth, and happiness, was a personal force for good luck, acted as a matchmaker, and won money in gambling. In recent years the sale of Cornish pisky images appears to have declined.

Jack O'Lantern is not considered a helpful sprite in many parts of Britain. Lady Camilla Gurdon noted that the Suffolk version, the Hobby Lantern, was a very desperate entity, for if one goes outside at night with a lantern in one's hand, the sprite will dash it out of his or her hand (Gurdon 1892, 559). In the Cambridgeshire Fens the equivalent sprite is Will o' the Wisp, a malevolent sprite that appears as a phantom light leading the nighttime wayfarer away from the path. Becoming lost one is disorientated, "will-led," and eventually will fall into a Fenland drain (canal) and drown. A Cambridgeshire vernacular description of a futile detour on a journey is "to go round Will's Mother's and back again," that is, going around and getting back to where one started, as if following the capricious leading of Will o' the Wisp.

IRISH LEPRECHAUNS

Cartoonlike representations of leprechauns appear frequently in advertising for betting shops, playing on the mythical "luck of the Irish." Leprechauns dressed in green, carrying four-leaf clovers, presiding over crocks of gold coins, and appearing with other images of luck and abundance entice the punters in to gamble. The kitsch representation of a red-bearded, pipe-smoking figure dressed in supposed Irish clothing elements—characteristically, an outsize green hat and suit with buckle and breeches, accompanied by a four-leaf clover and perhaps a shillelagh—puts these enticing images in the category of "Paddywhackery," comic stereotyping of Irish culture that appears in pubs and bars around Saint Patrick's Day. This image is derived from nineteenth-century xenophobic British derogatory portrayals of the Irishman in the theater and cartoons as an unfashionably dressed ignorant brute epitomized as "Paddy and his Pig." "The luck of the Irish could be yours when you bring the lucky leprechaun into your home" is typical of present-day advertisements for leprechaun charms. Hobbits as portrayed in the twenty-first century movies of J. R. R. Tolkien's books *The Hobbit* and *The Lord of the Rings* bear more than a passing resemblance to the received image of the leprechaun.

GREMLINS

From the 1920s Royal Air Force personnel half-jokingly blamed evil sprites they called "gremlins" when an aircraft failed to work properly despite the best efforts of the ground crews. The similarity of the name "gremlin" to Kremlin suggests that the malfunctions may have been seen by some airmen as the acts of communist saboteurs in the ranks carrying out the orders of the Boslsheviks from the Kremlin. Whatever their origin gremlins seem to have been noticed by Royal Air Force personnel serving in Malta and Iraq, and the trouble spread. A poem about them was published in the magazine *Aeroplane* in 1929. Gremlins were the bane of airmen, so some made small fabric gremlin figures to placate or counter the mechanical mischief-makers. The airmen's propensity to blame gremlins for mishaps soon spread to the factories, where industrial accidents also were half-jokingly blamed on them. In World War II propaganda posters warned factory workers to take care to avoid taking risks because "gremlins think it's fun to hurt you."

Just as Belgian and British soldiers and airmen in the First World War had made amulets out of German shell fragments, bullets, and shrapnel, the way Allied airmen of the next war chose to counter these evil sprites was to make amulets in their form. The Royal Air Force museum possesses two horned gremlin figures that were carried by British bomber crews in World War II. The United States Air Force museum has a fabric gremlin made for Staff Sergeant Theodore Carter of the 482nd Bomb Group, which was stationed in England at Alconbury, Huntingdonshire. Made for him by a local woman who lived near the base, the gremlin mascot flew on all of Carter's bombing missions on Germany from 1942 to 1945.

The poster gremlins were depicted in a similar form to pixies and piskies, but later more cartoonlike figures emerged. Some had the long bulbous noses of the Goons that appeared in the 1938 Popeye cartoon *Goonland,* directed by Dave Fleischer. The Goons attacked and tormented Popeye in the same way that gremlins were believed to act. Brass charms featuring gremlins and aircraft were manufactured during World War II, and from the mid-1940s, gremlins have appeared in numerous movies and television shows in the United States and the United Kingdom.

Chapter 33

Signs and Symbols

The twentieth-century British writers Rudyard Kipling and W. Somerset Maugham both used personal amulets on the covers of their books. Kipling, influenced by his time in India, used an elephant and a swastika. After World War I the increasing use of the swastika by extremist politicians led him to stop using the sign. Maugham used a Moroccan amulet on his books. He also had it as a hood ornament on his cars, and it was engraved on his cigarette case and in the glass of the windows of his house (Paine 2004, 58).

CADUCEUS AND ASKLEPIAN STAFF

In classical iconography gods and saints are depicted with their corresponding emblematic objects. Abundantia, the personification of abundance, carries a cornucopia of abundant fruits, while Fortuna has her wheel. Saint Anthony of Egypt has his pig and bell, and Saint James is signified by a scallop shell. Of all the many sacred attributes, the caduceus of Hermes (Mercury) is one of most striking emblems. Hermes is the swift messenger of the gods, depicted with a winged hat and wings on his heels. In his hand he holds a staff, the caduceus. This is sometimes depicted with a winged hat on top, or just a pair of wings and a pine cone or knob as the finial; around the staff twine two serpents (see fig. 33.1). Elizabeth Villiers asserted that the caduceus is "a very

Fig. 33.1. Caduceus amulet, brass, circa 1900

mystic talisman, and its influence was all for good" (Villiers 1923). Symbolizing communication, it was used widely on nineteenth- and early-twentieth-century buildings, such as telegraph and post offices.

The Hermetic caduceus is frequently misused as an emblem of the medical profession, which it is not. That is the staff of Asklepios (Aesculapius), which is a straight staff with a single snake twining around it. Unfortunately this elementary confusion is not recent, as might be imagined. Even in times when symbols were understood more widely, the mistake was being made. For example, a bookplate drawn in 1923 for a doctor by the noted British Arts and Crafts architect and designer Charles F. A. Voysey used the Hermetic staff (Livingstone 2011, 158–59). The Maitland Robinson Library at Downing College, Cambridge, designed by Quinlan Terry (built 1990–1992), is a neoclassical stone building that combines elements of classical temples with a version of the octagonal Tower of the Winds at Athens. On its facades are symbols representing various academic disciplines. The emblem he used for medicine is the caduceus of Hermes. Terry calls it "the brazen serpent," confusing classical and biblical symbolism (Terry 1993, 124).

THE SWASTIKA

Fig. 33.2. Swastika amulet, Scotland, 1920s

As a lucky charm the swastika had a relatively short life. In the 1870s Madame Helena Blavatsky, cofounder of the Theosophical Society, popularized Hindu and Buddhist spirituality in the West and adopted the swastika as a main emblem of her society. Prior to this the sigil had been known since antiquity, appearing in many traditional cultures, including medieval European heraldry, where it was called the cross potent rebated. Other pre-Theosophical names were gammadion, four-footed cross, tetraskelion, fylfot, and the German *Hakenkreuz*. Blavatsky called it by its Sanskrit name, *suvastika,* meaning "all is well." The Indian name caught on, the others were largely abandoned, and the swastika enjoyed a brief period of widespread use as a lucky charm as well as a logo of businesses and organizations (Pennick 2014, 105–13). Writer and poet Rudyard Kipling adopted the swastika as his personal emblem, using it on the covers of his books. In 1907, along with the fleur-de-lis, the Boy Scout movement adopted it as its main badge (Taylor 2006, 125), and around the same time, the Krit Motor Car Company of Detroit used it. Lucky swastikas were sold widely in the United States through the Sears, Roebuck mail-order catalog. During World War I it was the logo for British saving stamps (Taylor 2006, 126), and airmen on all sides painted swastikas on their aircraft for luck.

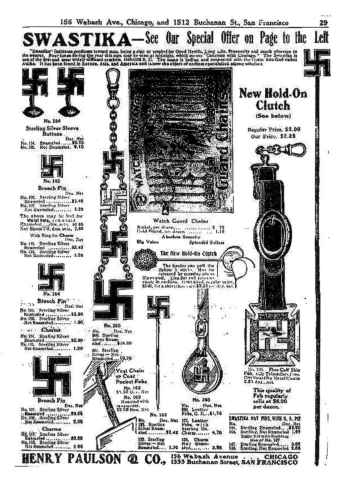

Fig. 33.3. Henry Paulson and Company catalog page
offering swastika jewelry, early twentieth century

In March 1920, during the German Civil War that followed the collapse of Germany after the armistice of 1918, a right-wing uprising in Berlin known as the Kapp Putsch was assisted by the Ehrhardt Brigade, a Freikorps unit founded by Hermann Ehrhardt with loyal war veterans to fight against armed communist revolutionaries in the city. For this incursion members of this unit painted swastikas on their helmets (N. Jones 2004, 181). Adolf Hitler, based in Munich, flew to Berlin during the Kapp Putsch and observed the sigil on the Ehrhardt Brigade members. Returning to Bavaria he adopted the swastika as the emblem of his National Socialist German Workers' Party (N. Jones 2004, 238).

Until the 1930s outside Germany, the swastika remained a lucky charm. As well as metal ones being warn as necklaces and on charm bracelets, it appeared on postcards, often along with other lucky emblems. As noted in chapter 23 (see page 125), a typical card of the period by artist Reg Maurice showed a lucky black cat at a crossroads where stands a four-way signpost from which hang a horseshoe, wishbone, pig, and swastika. In *The Mascot Book,* Elizabeth Villiers wrote that the swastika was a special mascot of those who have Jupiter as their ruling planet. She added, however, that as a general luck-bringer, the swastika could be worn by everyone (Villiers 1923, 158). Around 1931 the ascendance of the Nazis in Germany led to its rapid disuse in other contexts. Kipling stopped putting it on his book covers for this reason. As late as 1933 a lucky charm was issued at the World's Fair in Chicago. In the form of a metal medallion, it depicted a horseshoe, rabbit's foot, elephant, four-leaf clover, and swastika with the legend "good luck" at the top. Shortly afterward the swastika ceased to be regarded as a lucky charm and was never seen again in this context. Allied soldiers who had carried swastika charms in World War I did not carry them in World War II, for now it had become an enemy sign. It is even still banned in some Western countries today without any recognition of its sacred nature in ancient European paganism, Hinduism, and Buddhism.

THE PENTAGRAM

The five-pointed star called the pentagram has several names, of which the pentacle is most commonly used. Additionally it is known as the flaming star, pentamma, pantacle, Druid's foot, *Drudenfuss,* the remphan, and Solomon's seal. In the latter case it is often confused with the Star of David, which is six-pointed. Medieval and Renaissance magicians used the pentagram as a protective sigil, often to ward off evil from thresholds. Goethe's Dr. Faustus had a Drudenfuss traced on his threshold, but as it was drawn incomplete, the demon Mephistopheles could gain entry. The Basilica di San Marco in Venice has a pentagram mosaic in the floor just inside the entrance.

The pentagram appears in "jewels" of British Masonic and fraternal

Fig. 33.4. Pentagram mosaic on floor of the Basilica di San Marco, Venice, Italy
(also see plate 26)

organizations. It signifies the doctrine of "the five points of fellowship" (Cooper 2006, 120–21). A 1641 sigil of Sir Robert Moray, a Scottish Freemason, may be the first example of the pentagram in Masonic usage. The Orange Order and the Loyal United Friends were among the organizations that adopted it. For instance, the jewel of a past master of an Orange Lodge has an interlaced pentagram (Dennis 2005, 17). It is now the most common emblem of contemporary paganism and Wicca.

Fig. 33.5. Copper pentagram amulet, England 1970s

Chapter 34

Mascots

From the early days of the automobile, the makers of cars adopted mascots. Known in the United States as hood ornaments, they began as emblems on the radiator caps in the days when cars had exposed radiators. These may have been inspired by, or a continuation of, terret ornaments on horse harness (Kay and Springate 2018, 6). These can have bells and plumes or swiveling polished brass discs and other emblems known as "fly head terrets."

Fig. 34.1. Horse's head terret, brass and horsehair, England, early twentieth century (also see plate 27)

These horse ornaments had originated in the middle of the nineteenth century (Keegan 1973, 161–64). In 1908 Wright and Lovett commented on car mascots. They said they were "for fun," adding "the chauffeur, however, carries as a real charm a nail which has caused a puncture" (Wright and Lovett 108, 292). Carmakers adopted their own mascots, which may or may not have been also their trademark. The most famous is the Spirit of Ecstasy, the mascot of Rolls-Royce, designed around 1910 by Charles Sykes. Buick's mascots were goddesses. There was a standing figure with a scarf blowing behind her or just a goddess head wearing a winged helmet. The British carmaker Crossley had a lady riding on a winged wheel (Kay and Springate 2018, 30).

Birds were popular hood mascots. The British Swift brand of motorcycles and automobiles, made from 1900 to 1931, had the eponymous bird. Some were colored blue, recalling Maeterlinck's play, *The Blue Bird*. Alvis Motors had a silver eagle, Singer cars had a bantam hen, and the Vauxhall Velox the *speed bird*. Luxury brands Duesenberg and Hispano-Suiza both had flying bird mascots. Chevrolet had a *jet bird*, befitting the "jet age," and Oldsmobile, a futuristic chrome jet aircraft. But not all brands used birds, despite their symbolic qualities of speed and freedom. AC Cars, Delage, and Lincoln all had greyhound mascots, again emblematic of speed. Some mascots were more enigmatic, like the dancing elephant on some Bugattis. Pierce-Arrow had the image of an archer as its hood mascot.

Native Americans in war bonnets were mascots of Indian motorcycles, Pontiac cars, and the British Guy Motors trucks, buses, trolleybuses, and military vehicles. Incongruously Guy Arab buses, the company's most successful product, sported a Native American mascot with the inscription "Feathers in our cap." Rover had the head of a Viking warrior, and Armstrong Siddeley the head of a sphinx. Some manufacturers still produce cars with their particular mascots. An early one was the Mercedes-Benz three-pointed star, still familiar today. The British luxury cars Bentley have a *B* with wings, Jaguar has the Leaper, the eponymous big cat, and Rolls-Royces still sport the Spirit of Ecstacy. During the heyday of the mascot in the 1920s, companies independent of the motor manufacturers made various freelance designs. The influence of

Fig. 34.2. Rolls-Royce
Spirit of Ecstacy mascot

the movies meant that Charlie Chaplin and Mickey Mouse hood ornaments could be purchased (Kay and Springate 2019, 6). The Flying
Mascots Company of upmarket Piccadilly in London even made a bird
mascot with moving wings (Kay and Springate 2018, 8). The French
tire company Michelin also produced its own Monsieur Bibendum (the
Michelin Man) as a car mascot.

In the 1920s and 1930s, the French glassmaker René Lalique produced twenty-nine different art deco designs of hood mascots in frosted
glass. Like Pierce-Arrow and probably intended to be fitted to one,
Lalique also produced a glass mascot in the form of an archer. An early
Lalique mascot from 1921, Cinq Chevaux, depicted five stylized horses;
others depicted a fox, a rooster, a falcon, a wild boar, and the head of
a ram. In 1928 appeared Saint Christopher, the patron saint of travelers, and in the same year Lalique produced his most celebrated design,
a head with swept-back winglike hair titled Victoire, usually called the
Spirit of the Wind. In 1929 horse racing in England and France was
celebrated by three different designs of a horse's head: one called Epsom
and two Longchamp, named for two of the most famous racetracks in
the respective countries.

But any found object can also be tied on the front of a vehicle as a
mascot. In the 1980s the author's local garbage collectors' truck, which
came every week, had a bendy rubber Pink Panther attached to the
front by wire. Clearly it had been rescued from the trash and became
their mascot. Also in England one often sees large red plastic poppies

attached to the front grilles of cars. Sold before every Remembrance Day each November to raise money for veterans, these poppies remain all year round and take on an amuletic function.

NAMES AS MASCOTS

Naming vehicles makes them into more than mere utilitarian things: they become mascots. Ships have had names since antiquity, and in the late eighteenth century, the stagecoach operators in Great Britain began to name individual coaches. This practice was taken up by the railways that superseded the stagecoaches. At first locomotives had individual names, not numbers. Catch-Me-Who-Can of 1808 and Puffing Billy of 1813 were among the originals. In 1829 Robert Stephenson's locomotive Rocket won fame by winning the Rainhill Trials contest for the best design. Vulcan was the first locomotive to run on the Great Western Railway in 1837. In the 1830s in the United States, Tom Thumb, John Bull, and Lafayette were among the most notable early locomotives. Only with the appearance of Pullman cars late in the nineteenth century were passenger vehicles named. Once locomotives began to carry numbers, names became less "personal." In Britain names ranged from kings and princesses to Greek gods, knights of the Round Table, castles, army regiments, warships, cities and counties, football teams, Battle of Britain aircraft, military bases, racehorses, antelopes, national worthies, and directors of railway companies. There were even several that served as war memorial locomotives after World War I, among them Valour and Remembrance.

Most of these locomotives had elegant cast-metal nameplates, many of which also had other images, such as military regimental badges, air force unit badges, and coats of arms appropriate to their names. To many onlookers the names and emblems must have appeared random and largely meaningless. To veterans of the named military units, they had meaning, as did those named after horses that won the Saint Leger at Doncaster to the racing fraternity. Royal Lancer, named for the 1922 Saint Leger winner, is seen during its final days in 1962 in figure 34.3. Although the names were specialized, the name plates were nurtured by

Fig. 34.3. Class A3 Pacific locomotive Royal Lancer at King's Cross Station, London, 1962

their crews, who often polished them to a bright finish even when the rest of the locomotive was dirty and neglected during the last days of steam traction on British railways.

In the same class as Silver Fox (from chapter 23, see page 134) was Mallard, named for the species of wild duck common in Britain. It is notable because in 1938 it achieved the fastest speed a steam locomotive ever reached, 126 miles per hour. It is now preserved in the National Railway Museum in York (Burridge 1975, 130–35). Two experimental diesel locomotives built in 1961 and 1968 both followed on. Falcon, which carried the number D0280, had a large modernistic aluminum bird on its side above its name in metal letters. The name recalled a recently scrapped streamliner of the same A4 class as Mallard and Silver Fox. The later experimental diesel Kestrel, numbered HS4000, was, at the time, the most powerful diesel locomotive in existence. Its name had been carried by another A4, the next in numerical sequence from Falcon (Jones 2018, 79–81). Neither locomotives exist now, although a Falcon mascot is kept in the storehouse at the National Railway Museum. Locomotive nameplates and emblems are much sought after by collectors. In 2016 a nameplate of the A4 locomotive Golden Eagle was sold at auction for £31,000.

PERSONS AS MASCOTS

In 1925 the African American harmonica player DeFord Bailey featured on the WSM radio station's country music *Barn Dance* show, the forerunner of the *Grand Old Opry*. For sixteen years, until 1941, he was introduced on air as "our little mascot" (Davis 2003, 88–89). Most British football clubs (and many sports teams in the United States) have a living mascot to encourage the home team supporters and bring good luck. It is a person dressed in some particular costume related, often humorously, to the club's name or iconography. Some are directly related, such as the wolf of the Wolverhampton Wanderers (nicknamed the Wolves) and the swan of Swansea City. Angus the Bull represents Aberdeen, recalling the Aberdeen Angus cattle breed.

Others, like Gunnersaurus Rex, the dinosaur of Arsenal football club, whose nickname is the Gunners, and Marvin the Moose of Cambridge United, are more abstruse. Pottermus, the mascot of Stoke City, comically recalls the main industry of the city of Stoke-on-Trent—pottery. The noted potter Lorna Bailey has made ceramic figurines of him, a female version called Miss Pottermus, and K9 Boomer the Dog, the mascot of Stoke City Football Club. Some important matches played by Derby County Football Club see the local British Army unit bring their mascot, a live ram, onto the pitch. This animal is the living embodiment of the legendary Derby Ram, the subject of a local traditional song and a character in a mummers' play (see chapter 23, page 127).

Football's World Cup has had a range of mascots since the lion World Cup Willie emerged in England in 1966 wearing football equipment and a Union Jack shirt, clearly derived from the symbolic patriotic figure John Bull. In 1982 in Spain, Narangito, a humanoid orange, no less, was the mascot; in 2008 in Russia, Zabivaka the Wolf; in 2010, the South African Zakumi the Leopard; and in 2014 in Brazil, Fuelco the Armadillo. American football teams also have the full gamut of mascots, ranging from the inevitable Billy Buffalo of the Buffalo Bills to the jaguar Jaxson de Ville of the Jacksonville Jaguars, the Atlanta Falcons' Freddie Falcon, and the Detroit Lions' Roary. Every U.S. professional football team has a mascot, as do the college football teams. Bangladeshi cricket supporters carry "cuddly toy" tigers and brandish them at matches, as the nickname of the Bangladesh cricket team is the Tigers.

Olympic Games have also taken to mascots, which have proliferated, to cover the summer Olympics and Paralympics and their winter counterparts. The 1980 Olympics in Russia had a bear cub called Misha. In 2010 in Vancouver, there were four mascots, *Miga, Quatchi, Sumi,* and *Mukmuk,* two for each of the winter Olympic and Paralympic games. The London Olympics of 2012 had cyclops mascots called Wenlock and Mandeville. They were named after Much Wenlock, a village that staged the Olympic Games in 1850, and Stoke Mandeville Hospital, which staged the precursor of the Paralympics in 1948. The Mandeville mascot had one leg to emphasize disabilities.

Chapter 35

Military Mascots and Amulets

Baron Manfred von Richthofen (1892–1918) was Germany's most successful fighter pilot of World War I. Before he was finally shot down, "the Red Baron" destroyed eighty Allied aircraft in combat. When his remains were recovered, his mascot, a small dog made of blue glass, was discovered. Such mascots, carried by many pilots, were taken as trophies by those who killed them. Writing in 1920 about the Great War, which had ended recently, amulet collector Giuseppe Bellucci noted that the amulets carried by military men for luck and protection ranged from ancient items to things that had never existed before 1914. Ideas, concepts, and beliefs that had "primordial beginnings" coexisted with "beliefs formulated in the present" (Bellucci 1920, 14).

The range of amulets and charms from World War I that still exist in many collections attest to this.

Fig. 35.1. Joan of Arc medallion, France, 1915

These amulets and charms could be from any appropriate source. In World War I Jewish soldiers carried *mezuzot* taken from the doorposts of their homes (Davies 2018, 214). In World War II officers in the British Army fighting in North Africa carried the bull's pestle swagger stick, made from the penis of a bull (Binder 1973, 76). Many individuals and units serving in the First World War also had live animals that were considered to be lucky mascots. They included ponies, kangaroos, and baboons, but were more commonly dogs. Figure 35.2 shows the dog mascot of the unit in which the writer's great-grandfather was serving in Belgium in 1917.

Fig. 35.2. World War I British soldiers with their mascot dog, Belgium, 1917
(Pennick family archives)

In both world wars air force pilots painted personal mascots on their aircraft. In the First World War, Italy's greatest fighter pilot, Count Francesco Baracca, had his mascot, the Cavallino Rampante, a rampant black horse, painted on the side of his Spad fighter aircraft. This famous horse later became the emblem of Ferrari automobiles. In the Second World War, the German air ace Adolf Galland had a Mickey Mouse mascot on his Messerschmitt fighter plane (Gunston 1982, 140). World War II United States Army Air Corps bombers were famous for their "pin-up" mascots of scantily clad women painted on their noses. They were always accompanied by the woman's name in cursive script, such as Honey Bunny, Sally B, Glamorous Glennis, A Bit O'Lace, Sweet Lola, Sunshine, and Cherry Mac (Gunston 1982, 25, 31, 47, 165). Some were designs of noted graphic artists. Walt Disney designed numerous squadron mascot patches for the United States military. His "war insignia" featured his famous cartoon characters, including Donald Duck, Goofy, Pluto, and the Big Bad Wolf.

AMULETIC MILITARY FRAGMENTS

Soldiers' amulets made from bullets, fragments of shrapnel, and pieces of shot-down aircraft exist today in several military and nonmilitary museums. Giuseppe Bellucci noted in 1920 that amulets "formed from the copper rings of gas grenades" were carried by Italian soldiers along with traditional amulets of all kinds (Bellucci 1920, 14). The National Museum of Wales has a number of World War I British and Belgian soldiers' amulets made from fragments of enemy projectiles. There is a bullet mounted with an enameled metal Belgian flag soldered to it with a loop to hang it from, an anchor made by a Belgian soldier of metal from a German projectile, a copper horseshoe amulet with seven holes made by a Belgian soldier from an enemy shell, and an airplane mascot made from fragments of German munitions worn by an Allied airman in 1917 and 1918. The Wellcome Collection in London has a small lucky horseshoe made by a Belgian soldier from a piece of shell that bombarded Ieper (Ypres) and also a wooden horseshoe with seven bosses made from shell metal. Sometimes fragments of munitions were engraved with the names of places and the dates they had fallen.

Bellucci noted that in World War I projectiles taken from wounded soldiers were often made into amulets (Bellucci 1920, 106). Bullets and pieces of shrapnel taken from the bodies of the fallen were also used.

These projectiles had already killed a fellow soldier, and now that they could harm no one else, they became amulets against being wounded or killed. The tradition was continued in the Second World War twenty years later. The author's father, Rupert Pennick (1924–1999), who served in the Royal Air Force in World War II, had a small plexiglass mascot model of a British Supermarine Spitfire fighter plane about one inch long (now lost). It had been made by a fellow airman from a piece of the acrylic bubble canopy of a Spitfire that had been shot down.

"WOUNDPROOF" AND BULLETPROOF SHIRTS

The imagined power of amulets to obstruct weapons is an ancient one. Scottish folklore tells of the *warlock fecket,* a jacket woven from the skins of certain water snakes that protected the magician against all harm (Warrack [1911] 1988, 656). In medieval Scandinavia it was believed that wearing a magic reindeer-skin coat would render one "woundproof." *The Saga of St. Olav* in Snorri Sturluson's *Heimskringla* recounts how Þórir hundr (Thorir Hund), one of the leaders of the pagan peasants' and artisans' rebellion against the militant Christian king of Norway, Olav, possessed an amuletic reindeer coat obtained from Finnish magicians. Thorir wore it at the Battle of Stiklestad in 1031, where he and his companions fought through the royal body-guards to attack the king. The king struck Thorir with Hneitir, "the sharpest of swords, the handle of which was bound with gold," but "it would not bite when it hit the reindeer-skin coat." Thorir, Thorstein the Shipwright, and Kalv then cut the king down. Thus symbolically three wounds brought about the doom of Olav (*Heimskringla,* ch. 228). After his death the church elevated Olav to sainthood. He is depicted with an ax, with which Thorstein the Shipwright struck him, but his image in churches was taken by those who remained pagan for the hammer god Thor.

Five centuries later Ottoman talismanic shirts called *tilsimli gömlek* served the same purpose as Þórir hundr's woundproof reindeer coat. Ottoman coats were inscribed with verses from the Qur'an, the name of God, prophets, numbers, magic squares, formulae of conjuration, prayers, and astrological signs and sigils. The protective power of religious names, texts, and numbers was believed to protect the wearer from harm, even deflecting bullets. Sigils and figures were calculated by the Munajjim-bashi, Ottoman court astrologers. A number of sultans, including Suleiman the Magnificent, commissioned elaborate talismanic shirts. The Grand Vizier Kora Mustafa, commander of the Ottoman army that was defeated by Austrian and Polish forces at the siege of Vienna in 1683, wore a very fine tilsimli gōmlek, which was captured and exhibited in the city (Ahrens 1918, 53). An Ottoman tilsimli gōmlek dated 991 AH (1583) was auctioned by Sotheby's in 2015 for £185,000. William Jones remarked in 1880 of an amulet containing a Qur'anic text as a preventative against wounds that was then in the museum of Sir Ashton Lever. It was a multicolored "chaplet for the head" containing the text, "It had belonged to a king of Brak in Senegal, who, however, had the misfortune to be killed in battle with the charm upon him" (Jones 1880, 162).

In the late 1880s Lakota Sioux followers of the prophet Wovoka (Jack Wilson) donned special white muslin shirts and dresses embellished with eagle feathers. Painted in yellow and blue with an eagle on the back, these "ghost shirts" were worn in dance rituals of the new messianic religion that took elements of traditional Lakota beliefs syncretized with apocalyptic themes from the Christian religion (Mooney 1896, 798). Ghost dancers believed that soon nonnative settlers would be miraculously obliterated and the exterminated buffalo would return again to a new, cleansed, regenerated land. Wovoka preached that this supernatural prodigy would happen as a matter of course, without violence. A faction led by Kicking Bear believed that violence was necessary and claimed that those who wore the shirts were invulnerable to the bullets from the guns of the United States Army (Keyhoe 2006, 13–14). As ever, this claim proved to be false, and those who wore the Ghost Shirts died, along with those who did not, in the massacre at Wounded Knee on December 29, 1890.

James Mooney suggested that the ghost shirts had been inspired by Mormon "endowment robes" of white muslin. These were embroidered with four enigmatic marks—a *V* on the left breast, a reversed *L* on the right, a line over the navel, and another mark over the right knee. The breast marks were said to stand for the compasses and square, as in the Freemasons' symbolism. Many Mormons believed at the time that their garments protected then generally and against bullets in particular (Mooney 1896, 13).

A few years after Wounded Knee, Spanish soldiers in the Spanish-American War (1898) wore amulets with the text *Détente Balla* (stop bullet), hopefully protecting their wearers on the battlefield. Almost thirty years earlier German soldiers had used amuletic charms to protect themselves. Writing in 1880 William Jones noted a charm "taken from a German soldier in the late war [probably the Franco-Prussian War of 1870–1871—NP] by an English surgeon." This charm was believed in "by a large number of German soldiers" and was believed to have originated in a vision seen "over an image of the baptism of Saint Mary Magdalene." The letters on it, *LTLKHBKNK,* had to be pronounced "in the Name of the Father, Son, and Holy Ghost." The text with the amulet stated, "Whoever wears this charm need have no fear of thieves and murderers, swords or fire-arms of any sort, neither will he receive injury from storm, fire, water or any assault of the Evil One, nor will be taken prisoner. No bullet will strike him, be it gold, silver or lead" (Jones 1880, 154–255).

AMULETIC BULLETS

The latter reference to the composition of bullets refers to the belief that a silver bullet can be used against someone carrying or wearing am amulet of invincibility. There was a claim that a silver bullet was used to kill Prince Rupert's supposed "familiar" in 1644 at the Battle of Marston Moor during the English Civil War (see chapter 23, page 122). It was fired "by a valiant souldier, who had skill in Necromancy" (Ashton 1896, 162–63). Magic bullets made of metal from sacred medallions were believed to have intrinsic power, especially if they had been made ritually. There was a tradition that lead bullets could be made that were guaranteed to hit the target. The material religious connection was that the lead should be stolen from a church roof.

The unfailing bullet is the theme of Carl Maria von Weber's 1821 opera, *Der Freischütz* (*The Magic Marksman*), which has a scene involving the ritual casting of magic bullets at a crossroads. As with all crossroads magic on both sides of the Atlantic, the aid of a supernatural being identified usually as the devil is required, hence the valiant soldier's "skill in Necromancy" in shooting Prince Rupert's dog. Weber's theme came from a 1730 story by Otto vom Graben zum Stein that recalled a trial held in Bohemia in 1710. To cast magic bullets eighteen-year-old Georg Schmid had sat naked at a crossroads inside a magic circle scribed with a knife and surrounded by magical sigils. Graben zum Stein set the bullet-casting scene at the traditional crossroads, but Weber set it in a doom-laden *Wolfsschlucht* (Wolf's Glen). The demon Samiel is invoked with numerological principles: "Now the blessing of the bullets!" This included bowing to the earth in each of three pauses. "Protect us, you who watch in darkness! Samiel, Samiel! Give ear! Stand by me in this night until the spell is complete! Bless for me the herb and lead. Bless them by seven, nine and three. That the bullet be obedient! Samiel, Samiel, to me!" Samiel, often identified with the devil, is the demon of violent hot sandstorms in the Saharan and Arabian deserts and may reflect the use of sand in metal casting.

A nontextual amulet that is usually associated with preventing seafarers from drowning is the caul; it was also used by soldiers who believed one would avert gunfire. In 1834 John Graham Dalyell wrote, "Many virtues were believed inherent in that portion of the *amnios* accompanying children at birth, named the *Caul,* and in Scotland the *haly* or *sely how*. Elsewhere it was obtained to render soldiers invulnerable, and advocates eloquent; it was acquired at a high premium, and viewed with such superstitious confidence as to incur the censure of the pious [my italics] (Dalyell 1834, 200).

But there are also other items that actually did stop bullets unintentionally and save the lives of their owners. From the English Civil War in the seventeenth century to modern times, items such as Bibles, diaries, and cigarette cases have been kept as lucky charms, showing the place where the would-be-fatal bullet was stopped. Several from twentieth-century wars reside in museums.

THE BLOOD-STAINED
GARMENTS OF HEROES AND MARTYRS

In 1649 Charles Stuart—King Charles I of Great Britain—who had lost the English Civil War, was tried and executed in public. He was beheaded with an ax by a disguised executioner who took two blows to sever his head. Security was poor, and people rushed forward to steep their handkerchiefs in the royal blood. These blood-soaked handkerchiefs became amulets reputed to heal illnesses. Even in the twenty-first century, these relics of the king's execution are revered. In 2008 the *Mirror* newspaper reported that a handkerchief steeped in the blood of King Charles I had been sold at auction at South Cerney, Gloucestershire, for £3,700 (*Mirror,* May 20, 2008). The blue silk vest he is reputed to have worn on the scaffold is also preserved. After the republic was overthrown and King Charles II became king, his executed father became a popular martyr, and the day of his execution was celebrated as a religious festival.

Fig. 35.3. The vest King Charles I wore when
he was beheaded, nineteenth-century photograph

Uniforms of heroes who died in battle have been preserved as national amulets. The British admiral Horatio Lord Nelson (1758–1805) was the revered hero of naval battles against French and Spanish fleets, culminating in the victory at Trafalgar in 1805. At the culmination of the victory, Nelson was shot by a sniper and died. As a national hero he was awarded a state funeral the like of which had rarely been seen before and buried in a magnificent tomb in Saint Paul's Cathedral in London. His uniform, complete with bullet hole, was treated as a relic and now takes pride of place in the National Maritime Museum at Greenwich. The bullet that killed Nelson is displayed in Windsor Castle and a lock of his hair at the Edashima Naval Academy in Japan. Similarly the Irish rebel and national hero Michael Collins (1890–1922) was shot by a sniper. In 1922, during the Irish Civil War, his Free State convoy was ambushed by a unit of the Irish Republican Army. After his state funeral his bloodstained and bullet-holed uniform was taken and exhibited in the National Museum. His cap, which had been buried by an aide, was later dug up and also put in the museum.

Chapter 36

Amulets and Talismans for Gambling

If it wasn't for bad luck, I wouldn't have no luck at all.
"Born under a Bad Sign" by Albert King

Ancient worldviews ascribed every event to the agency of supernatural beings. So nothing happened by chance, for chance did not exist. Everything was determinate. Consequently gambling with, for example, dice did not exist as just a pleasant pastime but was a form of divination where the will of the gods was expressed. Casting lots for something, such as who would be allocated a piece of land, was a means of determining which person the gods favored. It was not seen as a random event, as we would now, subject to the inherent statistical probability inherent in whatever form of divination was used. *Chance* is defined as the happening of events and the way in which things fall out; a happening or occurrence of things in a particular way, perceived as a casual or fortuitous circumstance without conscious manipulation or a deterministic end. Gambling is by nature a matter of statistics. Odds can be calculated, and the probability is that the gambler will lose, but the actual outcome to an individual gambler at any particular time may be a win. Wearing or carrying amulets that change the odds in favor of the punter—"odds tippers"—will bring the gambler luck, for as in hunting, "better lucky than good."

An Icelandic tradition tells that Odin, god of consciousness and insight, was the inventor of dice. Dice are a metaphor of the unpredictability of life. Rolling the dice, although random and only predictable in the long run through the principles of statistical probability, produces a real and immediate outcome. As the dice are rolling, before they come to a halt, a state of temporary liminality exists. The outcome is imminent, but the process is still in play, so it is not yet determined. Once the dice come to rest, the outcome is present and cannot be altered. The uncertain becomes certain immediately as the dice come to a halt. Whatever the result, it has an immediate incontrovertible presence. Fortune or ruin becomes apparent. Such is the nature of gambling and a metaphor for the nature of presence.

Astrology's influence in gambling is significant. Yet many gamblers are so addicted that they fail to use it to determine when they should play. They want to play at any time and every time. But tradition teaches that there are times to do things and times to desist from doing them. Astrology can assist in finding these proper times. A most notable success in astrology in modern times was the work of William Hall Walker (1856–1933), who in 1900 decided to breed and race horses according to their horoscopes. He set up a stud (a stable of horses used specifically for breeding) at Tully, County Kildare, Ireland, where he applied astrological principles to horse breeding. He designed stalls for the horses so that the sun, moon, stars, and planets could be seen from them. Guided by astrology Walker raced his horses in major races. In 1906 his horse Minoru won the Epsom Derby, and in 1911 Prince Palatine won the Saint Leger race at Doncaster. By the beginning of the First World War in 1914, his horses had won all of Europe's major races. In 1943 the stud was moved to Newmarket, where it became and remains the National Stud. His stud in County Kildare became the Irish National Stud in 1945.

The use of amulets and talismans with or without the aid of astrology is an attempt to turn the outcome of gambling to the advantage of the gambler. There are three different magical approaches to winning. The first seeks to solely influence the outcome of the game to the gambler's advantage. The second seeks to disempower one's opponents'

Fig. 36.1. Libra amulet with signs of the zodiac, 1960s

luck so that they lose. The third is counter-magic, defensive and pre-emptive techniques employed against any magic one's opponents might use. Various kinds of amulets and talismans can achieve one or more of these objectives. To crap games players dice are themselves luck-bringers, for instance, a pair of dice showing the lucky number seven, which may be actual dice, fabric fuzzy dice hung in a car, or dice of precious metal carried in a pocket or worn on a charm bracelet. It is considered lucky to carry a coin bearing the year date of the gambler's birth. Writing in 1903 Daniels and Stevens note, "When playing poker, keep a copper penny lying on the table, and they can never 'break' you" (Daniels and Stevens 1903, 1478). In nineteenth-century England card-playing gamblers paid a premium price for pieces of a hangman's rope (Roud 2003, 239). Hoodoo and conjure traditions have much to say about gambling magic. The gambler should carry a mojo hand or conjure bag that contains various significant charms, amulets, and talismans deemed effective in bringing luck and intended to empower the gambler.

In early twentieth-century England, a badger's tooth was considered the gambler's luckiest charm. It was sewn in the right-hand pocket of the waistcoat to ensure good fortune when playing cards (Villiers 1923, 21). Other animal parts deemed beneficial to gamblers include rattlesnakes' rattles, tigers' and bears' teeth, and the feet of rabbits or alligators. The Atlantic City gambling pouch contains special "good-luck salt," a royal flush of diamonds, and two $100 chips. In Poland, the Czech Republic, and Slovakia, fish scales from a carp eaten in the Christmas meal are gamblers' amulets. The Chinese *jin chan* or *jan chu* three-legged toad amulet with a coin in its mouth also assists the gambler; lottery players

Fig. 36.2. Ten-dot domino, ebony and ivory, nineteenth century

place their tickets beneath it. From the plant kingdom, nutmegs and buckeye nuts may be carried in a pocket or purse, and carrying a cat's-eye gem is believed to guard wealth and reduce gambling losses. The ten-dot domino is a powerful amulet. Viewed with four dots at the top and six at the bottom, it has spaces that, seen from a distance, look like the Christian cross.

The author's grandfather, who played drums and xylophone in various American and British jazz bands in the 1920s and 1930s, like many musicians of the era, was an avid gambler. He owned a dog called Tranquil, named after the winner of the 1923 Saint Leger horse race at Doncaster. He carried a number of mascots, including a fabric Felix the Cat (black, of course), an ivory skull wearing an ebony top hat, and a machine-engraved metal cigarette case bearing a gamblers' emblem. In it he carried the Black Cat cigarettes he smoked.

Fig. 36.3. Ivory skull, gambling amulet of Charles Pennick (1900–1960)

Fig. 36.4. Black Felix the Cat mascot of Charles Pennick, 1920s

The cigarette case has an enamel image of a horse in a horseshoe with the name Rudiobus, a Gallo-Roman deity who rules horses. In that era he was invoked for good luck in betting on horse racing.

The god Rudiobus is known from a first-century BCE hoard discovered in 1861 in France at Neuvy-en-Sullias. A meter-high bronze horse was among the votive images. It bore a dedication to the god Rudiobus, otherwise unknown. Toward the end of the nineteenth century, match cases and pin badges were manufactured in Birmingham. A rearing piebald horse, set in a horseshoe with the legend "Rudiobus" is the standard image. The manufacturer of Buckley's Cough-Cold Syrup, founded in 1919 in Toronto, Canada, issued base metal medallions with the image of Rudiobus. They had the legend "RU-DIO-BUS" and the standard horseshoe–rearing horse image on one side and "Carry this for

Fig. 36.5. Charles Pennick's Rudiobus cigarette case

GOOD LUCK and use BUCKLEY'S mixture for cough and colds" on the other side.

Current gamblers' amulets of Lady Luck, which is the secularized name of the goddess Fortuna, have a complex, cumulative imagery. Sometimes she is portrayed as a green-clad, auburn-haired Irish woman, carrying "the luck of the Irish." She wears dice earrings showing seven dots, she has two black pool-game eight balls over her breasts, and she holds a four-leaf clover and a horseshoe, and sometimes a monkey wrench.

GAMBLING AMULETS OF THAILAND

Amulets of all kinds are big business in Thailand. A brass war elephant or a lizard with two tails are common charms, also amulets depicting Jujaka the Fortuitous Beggar. In Italy in 1889 Giuseppe Bellucci had a two-tailed lizard among his amulet collection (Bellucci 1889, 80). The common amulet with an image of the Buddhist monk Luang Pu Thuat (1582–1682) is a general luck-bringer that also works for gamblers. The current version of the amulet was created in 1962.

Fig. 36.6. Thai Buddhist monk amulets

Considered the most effective amulets for success in gambling are images of Er Ger Fong, otherwise known as Yee Gor Hong (1851–1935). He was a Chinese businessman and a member of the secret society Hong Meng Tian Di, which pursued activities against the Qing Dynasty. Er Ger Fong emigrated to Thailand, where King Rama V gave him a franchise to establish gambling houses and casinos, which profited the state immensely. There is a Buddhist temple dedicated to Er Ger Fong, where devotees make offerings in the hope of acquiring wealth through gambling. He was known as the King of Gamblers, and on his amulets, the golden image of Er Ger Fong is enshrined between four elephant tusks mounted in gold. Gold-embossed amulet medallions are sold to hopeful punters. Technically in Buddhism it is not permitted to buy and sell amulets, so the euphemistic practice of *chao pra,* "borrowing an amulet," is what takes place. These Buddhist amulets are empowered by the owner chanting a specific mantra, the text of which is usually supplied with the item. Followers of Er Ger Fong are warned not to be too greedy and try to get even more if they win—the old gambler's adage of "quit while you're ahead."

Fig. 36.7. Buddha's head amulet, twenty-first century

THE ACE OF SPADES

Of the four suits of the "poker deck" of playing cards, the card carrying the most significance is the Ace of Spades, which has a bad reputation among card players. This card was given prominence in the United Kingdom when, in 1711, the government imposed a "stamp duty" tax on decks of cards. From 1712 the Ace of Spades of each deck was marked with a handstamp showing that tax had been paid. It was illegal to sell cards without the stamp. From 1765 the Ace of Spades in each deck was required to have the royal coat of arms, denoting that tax was paid. Ornate forms of this card were developed by various card makers, emphasizing its difference for the other cards in the deck. In 1828 the Duty Ace of Spades design, known as Old Frizzle, showed that tax of one shilling per deck had been paid. The necessity for the ornate design was removed in 1862, when the duty was reduced to three pence and a "duty wrapper" replaced the tax notification in the Ace of Spades. However the ornate ace had become so well established by then that it was not simplified, and the Ace of Spades remains the most embellished card in the deck until the present day.

The tarot equivalent of the Ace of Spades is the Ace of Swords, signifying the theoretical force that lies at the root of the element of air. The Ace of Swords embodies the power of attacking its objective with full force. During the Vietnam War C Company of the 2nd Battalion of the 25th Infantry Division obtained thousands of Aces of Spades from the U.S. Playing Card Company for distribution among American soldiers fighting against the communist insurgents of the Viet Cong. They were left on the ground during raids into enemy territory. The justification for this was psychological warfare; although the beliefs of the enemy concerning the Ace of Spades were uncertain, if it were interpreted as the Ace of Swords by the Viet Cong, then its symbolism as the embodiment of the power of attack may have had some amuletic purpose.

The Ace of Spades is a notorious card, associated with death and the devil. Some playing-card readers say the Ace of Spades represents death, although the Queen of Spades is an alternative. If one is dealt a long sequence of black cards, it is unlucky, and some believe it foretells the death of the player or a family member. The Four of Clubs is another bad card and is associated with the devil. A Worcestershire farmer was quoted in 1879: "There never was a good hand at cards if the four of clubs was in it . . . because the four of clubs is an unlucky card; it's the Devil's own card . . . the Devil's four-post bedstead" (*Notes & Queries* 5th Series 12, 426). The gamblers' reverse luck principle means that any of these cards can be used as an amulet for good luck in gambling. Silver amulets of the Ace of Spades and the four aces are common gamblers' charms.

Fig. 36.8. Ace of Spades button badge, twenty-first century

THE DEAD MAN'S HAND

This hand of cards is the subject of much speculation. Some gamblers carry hands made of enameled metal as amulets, while others have the card sequence tattooed on an arm. Currently *the dead man's hand* is considered to be "aces and eights": the Ace of Spades, the Ace of Clubs, the Eight of Spades, and the Eight of Clubs. Folklore ascribes the name of dead man's hand to a famous event on August 2, 1876, when Jack McCall shot and killed James Butler Hickok, better known as "Wild Bill" Hickok, the gambling gunslinger lawman. When McCall attacked him, Hickok was playing five-card draw in Nuttal and Mann's saloon in

Deadwood, Dakota Territory. It is said that in his hand he held an ace of diamonds, ace of clubs, eight of hearts, eight of spades, and perhaps a queen of hearts. This story was first published half a century after the event by Frank J. Wilstach in his book *Wild Bill Hickok: The Prince of Pistoleers*. McCall was hanged six months later for Hickok's murder.

However, less than ten years after Hickok's death, the Washington correspondent of the *New York Mail and Times* published a piece in a Saturday morning edition of the *St. Paul Daily Globe*. His piece, titled "Draw. Big Game of Poker at Washington—$600 Won on One Hand," told readers, "I was present at a game in a senator's house one night and saw him win $600 on one hand. It was the Dead Man's Hand. What is the Dead Man's Hand? It is called the Dead Man's Hand because about forty years ago, in a town of Illinois, a celebrated judge bet his house and lot on three jacks and a pair of tens. It was the last piece of property he held in the world. When his opponent showed up he had three queens and a pair of tens. Upon seeing the queens, the judge fell back dead, clutching the jacks and tens in his hand; and that's why a jack-full on tens is called the Dead Man's Hand" (*St. Paul Daily Globe,* April 17, 1886, 11).

So the dead man's hand is disputed both in origin and composition. Daniels and Stevens stated in 1903 in their *Encyclopedia of Superstitions,* "Jacks and sevens are called the 'dead man's hand.' In a poker game it is very unlucky to hold them and win the pot" (Daniels and Stevens 1903, 1478). But also, on the same page, "When playing poker, should you hold a jack full on red sevens, it means death and is called a 'dead man's hand'" (Daniels and Stevens 1903, 1478). Aces and eights, jacks and tens, or jacks and sevens may all be a bad deal except when carried for "reverse luck," as gamblers do.

Chapter 37

Sacred Objects

Religions that permit the use of sacred sculptures, paintings, and prints have conservative images that are the real meaning of the much-misused word *iconic*. An icon has a specific set of attributes and forms, made so that every new one follows the appearance of the older ones. Icons, which are made according to formulaic principles, are the pictorial equivalent of the unchanging sacred words that appear in holy texts, spoken prayers, and incantations. There are also secular and political icons, such as that of Che Guevara. But these are not made devotionally according to the principles of the spiritual arts and crafts. Iconic images are standardized forms that appear in mass-produced religious items, such as the medallions reproduced in figure 37.1.

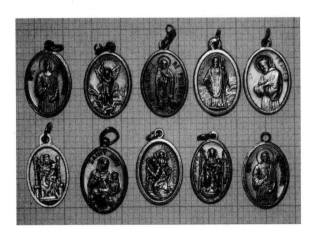

Fig. 37.1. Iconic Catholic saints' amulets

THE CRUX ANSATA

Also known as the Ankh, the Crux Ansata is worn today as an amulet. Originating in ancient Egypt it is a sacred artifact symbolizing life. In 1922 Pavitt and Pavitt gave a detailed explanation of the complex meanings of the structure of this sign. "The loop at the top of the cross, consisting of the hieroglyphic *ru* (*o*) set in an upright form, meaning gateway or mouth, the creative power being signified by the loop, which represents a fish's mouth giving birth to water as the life of the country, bringing inundations and renewal of the fruitfulness of the earth to those who depended upon its increase to maintain life. It was regarded as the key of the Nile, which overflowed periodically and so fertilized the land" (Pavitt and Pavitt 1922, 60–61).

AGNUS DEI—THE LAMB AND FLAG

The Lamb and Flag is a Christian emblem that found its way to be a badge in the British Army and of an English professional football club. It originates in ancient Israelite religion, as the lamb sacrificed in the Temple at Jerusalem in the Jewish festival of Passover. According to religious prescription, it had to be a young ram, an unblemished male lamb one year old (Exodus 12:3–11). It entered Christian tradition when Saint Paul referred to Jesus "sacrificed for me" as the spotless Lamb of God who by his death redeemed humankind (1 Corinthians 5:7). Because the death of Jesus was interpreted as a sacrifice for humankind, Saint John's Gospel refers to him as "the Paschal Lamb who takes away the sins of the world" (John 1:29). The lamb representing Jesus came to be depicted in a formal way as an Agnus Dei, a haloed lamb facing left, holding a flag bearing a cross emblem.

Talismans called Agnus Deis bearing the Agnus Dei image are produced today as sacred objects by the Roman Catholic Church. They are wax discs bearing the image of the lamb that are blessed on special occasions by the pope. The ritual was first recorded under Pope Gregory XI in 1370. The wax is the leftover from the previous year's Paschal Candle, the consecrated ritual candle burned at Easter, which is made new each year. As early as the sixth century, Magnus Felix Ennodius (474–521) noted that wax from Paschal Candles was used as amulets against storms and blight. Agnus Deis made of Paschal Candle wax mixed with dust from the bones of martyrs are special versions of the talisman. They are called Paste de' SS Martiri. Unlike the ordinary Agnus Deis, they require no special consecration, as the martyrs' dust automatically makes them holy relics. Technically the consecrated Agnus Deis are talismans, while the Paste de' SS Martiri are amulets.

Fig. 37.2. Papal Agnus Deis collected by Giuseppe Bellucci

The Lamb and Flag was once a common inn sign in England. It was also the British Army badge of the Queen's Royal West Surrey Regiment, originating in the 2nd Regiment of Foot at Tangiers in 1661. It is the classic lamb and flag with a standing lamb. The lamb and flag military badge illustrated in figure 37.3 is the 1920s pattern, with a straight-edged flag, the common form. Earlier examples had a two-tailed pennant. The football club for Preston North End has the emblem as its badge (Preston North End is the name of the club). It is taken from the Preston town seal of 1415, which has a kneeling lamb with a cross bearing a pennant. The club badge has a topped staff, not a cross, but otherwise it is the same (Routledge and Wills 2018, 110–11). Despite these secular uses being associated with the Papal Agnus Dei wax talismans, the use of the lamb and flag as an amulet is uncommon outside that context.

Fig. 37.3. The Queen's Royal West Surrey Regiment lamb and flag

The Miraculous Medal of Our Lady of the Graces is one of many talismanic items in Roman Catholic tradition (see page 189). It is a double-sided image of Our Lady with rays emerging from her hands on the obverse and on the reverse a letter *M* surmounted by a cross, below which are two heart emblems on the reverse side. The hearts represent the Immaculate Heart of Mary and the Sacred Heart of Jesus. Surrounding the composite sigil in contemporary medals are twelve five-pointed stars. However the engraving in M. Aladel's 1890 definitive book about the Miraculous Medal shows fourteen stars (Aladel 1890, 273). The medal originated in a series of Marian apparitions and visions experienced by a French nun, Catherine Labouré (1806–1876) at the Vincentian church in Paris. The first medallion was commissioned from a goldsmith, Adrian Vochette, and soon mass production began. The Miraculous Medal of Our Lady of the Graces is readily available today from any seller of Catholic devotional paraphernalia, although it is identical in size and format to those of numerous saints.

In addition to the Miraculous Medal, consecrated talismans bearing images of Christian saints and emblems have always been popular in the Roman Catholic tradition. Saints' attributes, perhaps related to the mode of death of martyrs, give each saint a particular area of reference against certain disasters, disorders, and diseases. Every trade, craft, and profession also has its own patron saint. Thus there is Saint Christopher for travelers, Saint James for pilgrims, Saint Florian for firefighters, Saint Anthony of Padua for finding lost items, Saint Benedict for cave explorers, the Quatuor Cornonati, or Four Crowned Matryrs, for stonemasons, Saint Barbara for architects, and even Saint Sebaldus, the patron saint of heating systems. The powerful Tau cross of Saint Anthony is used in traditional healing and is protective also of pigs.

Fig. 37.4. "Pelican in Her Piety" belt buckle, nineteenth century*

---

*In medieval belief the pelican was supposed to shed her own blood to feed her young, and this was seen as being emblematic of the blood shed by Jesus.

Chapter 38

Amuletic Protection of Buildings

FOUNDATION SACRIFICES AND DEPOSITS

The horse-skull foundation deposit under a chapel at Black Horse Drove in 1897, mentioned in chapter 23 (see page 136), is an instance of a tradition that originated thousands of years ago and was conducted in every continent. According to belief a living thing had to be sacrificed when the foundations of a building were laid. This had the function of placating the local land spirit whose ground was disrupted by the building and also of providing a ghostly guardian for the new structure. In 1894 G. W. Speth explained a historical progression in which our ancestors "buried a living human sacrifice . . . to ensure the stability of the structure; their sons substituted an animal; their sons again a mere effigy or other symbol; and we, their children, still immure a substitute, coins bearing the effigy . . . of our Gracious Queen" (Speth 1894, 22). Coins have been used as foundation offerings for many centuries. Alexander Laurie, writing in 1859, noted that at the laying of the foundation stone for the Wet Docks at Leith, Edinburgh, the Freemasons "deposited a jar containing several medals and coins of the present reign" (Laurie 1859, 164).

Five years after Speth, George Tyack wrote, "According to one tradition it was the rule at one time to provide each church and churchyard with a ghostly defender against the spells of witches or their diabolic

Fig. 38.1. Mummified cat from the roof of a farm building, Newport, Essex

practices. In order to do this a dog or a boar was buried alive under one of the corner stones of the building, and its apparition kept off all profane intruders. In case any person buried in the churchyard is unable to rest, but haunts the place at night, the ghost may be laid (so at any rate it was supposed in Staffordshire not very long ago) by cutting a turf, at least four inches square, from his grave and laying it under the altar for four days" (Tyack 1899, 59).

Tyack also notes a double burial of man and dog that was found in 1849 during excavations inside the Collegiate Church of Staindrop, Durham, when a human skeleton was exhumed, with a dog skeleton at his feet. "The man was supposed to have been a Neville, of Raby Castle, and the hound was probably in this case some special favourite with its master, killed and buried with him" (Tyack 1899, 80–81).

Precious metal was laid in the ground as an offering beneath ritual centers in pagan Scandinavia. It took the form of pieces of gold foil embossed with images. In Norway at Maere the postholes of a building that existed on the site before a Christian church was built there contained nineteen gold pieces (Lidén 1969, 23*ff.*). At Helgö in Sweden twenty-six pieces were uncovered. Similar embossed gold foil images, probably of Wotan, are known in Germany as far south as Konstanz. They were sacred offerings placed in the earth during the rites and ceremonies of foundation to give the building spiritual protection. A

Fig. 38.2. Alemannic gold foil image, Konstanz, Germany

German custom is to lay sprigs of the juniper tree (savin, *Juniperus communis*) in the foundations. This will protect against disharmony among the people who will live there.

Although a large number of artifacts have been found embedded in the fabric of old buildings in Britain and northern Europe, they have all been discovered randomly and few have been reported. Perhaps the largest number of found objects is shoes. There is a very large collection in Northampton of old shoes taken from buildings. Unusual and even unique artifacts are in the possession of private individuals and not publicized either widely or through academia. Some are kept in situ and considered guardians of the building. Around 1940 in Cambridge a clay or putty humanoid figure was noticed lying on top of a beam in the University Anatomy School, a building that had been completed in 1938. M. Hume, who had worked in the Anatomy School, told the local folklorist Enid Porter that the senior laboratory men knew of the figure and were protective toward it as a safeguard. It was still there in 1962, but subsequently disappeared (Porter 1969, 397–98). The ceramic church illustrated in figure 38.3 was discovered up a chimney in an old house in Histon, Cambridgeshire.

Items discovered in old buildings—shoes, mummified cats, bottles, skulls, and bones—are of perennial interest to the media, although unfortunately they provide an opportunity for journalists to indulge in sensationalist hyperbole. On December 18, 1981, the *Southend Evening Echo* carried the shock headline "Devil Dolls Uncovered at Hospital." The journalist who wrote the lurid piece tells how in Billericay, Essex, "horrified workmen" had discovered what he called "a black magic

Fig. 38.3. Ceramic church found in the chimney of a house in Histon, Cambridgeshire

shrine" at St. Andrew's Hospital, containing what were described as "bones, voodoo-type dolls, and a pin box." Police were called in to investigate this cache of Victorian amulets, although why they were we can only imagine. The cache included two human poppets, four inches in length, made of rag, a slightly shorter notched wooden tine, a piece of coal, and ruminant bones including part of a jaw with teeth and the head of a thigh bone. The items appeared to date from the 1850s, when the hospital was a workhouse.

INDOOR SHRINES

In central and eastern Europe and Scandinavia, the traditional living room of farmhouses is orientated on a diagonal axis. The corner diagonally opposite the stove has built-in benches and the family table. Russian folklore warns that one must not sleep in the path used by the *domovoj*, the house spirit, which travels diagonally across the room (Ivanits 1989, 54). Archaeological evidence from Poland shows this to be a pre-Christian room division (Pokropek 1988, 46). In Roman Catholic Austria and Bavaria, the diagonal tradition includes the house shrine known as *Herrgottswinkel, Herrgottseck* (Lord God's corner) or *heilge Hinterecke* (holy back corner). This is located in the corner of the living room. In it are kept sacred images, religious texts, crosses, amulets, and offerings. Salt and pepper are stored in a cupboard beneath the niche for protection against evil magic.

Fig. 38.4. Tree of Life wall patterns in a farmhouse, Saxony, Germany, circa 1910

Fig. 38.5. Electric sockets in a house in England protected by religious images

In many modern houses the Herrgottswinkel is diminished and acknowledged only by a crucifix attached to the corner near the ceiling. The equivalent in traditional Scottish farmhouses was the corner cupboard, protected by amulets, including bundles of rowan twigs

Fig. 38.6. Heart-shaped garland of holeystones, Heacham, Norfolk

(Corrie 1891, 76). Hearths and stoves, connected to the outside by chimneys down which harm might enter the house, must have amuletic protection. Various items, including witch bottles, dried hearts, cats, and wooden amulets, are often found in chimney breasts and in the brickwork of chimneys.

PROTECTING THE OUTSIDE

The outsides of buildings are protected by ornaments disliked by modernist architects. Carved bargeboards and roof elements often have intricate patterns believed to confuse and deter evil spirits. Brickwork can also be laid in particular significant patterns.

Windows and doors are places where harmful people and evil spirits can enter, so the frames are protected by amulets and talismans. The Jewish mezuzah is a parchment talisman fixed to the frame of an entry door. It has the word *shaddai* written on one side, and on the other, two passages from the book of Deuteronomy. White window frames are almost universal all over Great Britain, and the reason is magical. "The Welsh have a custom of whitening all their houses as they think the Devil cannot come through a white door" (Daniels and Stevens 1903, 1246). Door knockers frequently take the form of protective animals, such as lions and dragons.

Fig. 38.7. Nineteenth-century house with brickwork runes,
St. Ives, Cambridgeshire (also see plate 28)

Fig. 38.8. Lion's head door knocker,
made in 2019 (also see plate 29)

Fig. 38.9. Serpentine wall anchor, St. Ives, Cambridgeshire, nineteenth century

Wrought iron wall anchors that tie in beams to brick walls in old buildings have specific forms deemed to deflect lightning. An *S*-shaped wall anchor echoes the luckiest item inside the house—the pothook. Two crossing make a curved swastika-like form.

The outside of buildings is prone to attack, not only by the weather, human intruders, and predatory animals, but also by supernatural beings with bad intent toward the inhabitants. So emblems of magical defense are common throughout the world on traditional buildings. Roofs are protected against supernatural harm by images of birds and dragons as well as spiky projections such as wooden or metal finials.

Fig. 38.10. Pheasant image on thatched roof of cottage at Over, Cambridgeshire

Pennsylvania Dutch barns are famous for their ornate painted roundels. These take numerous forms in bright colors. Many are geometrical, but there are also stars, sunbursts, birds, hearts, tulips, and tree of life motifs. Names are a shorthand way of describing things, and these patterns have particular names in the local German dialect. In the past they were called, among other things *Stern, Blume,* and *Distelfink* (star, flower, and goldfinch), but now they are all known as hex patterns. "Hex" is not the original name; in common with the witches' ladder, the *dag zeichen,* the witch post, and the green man, the present name comes from later writers who gave names to the images, not from their makers (Pennick 2014, 28–29).

Fig. 38.11. Hex signs on farmhouse at Hofgeismar, Germany, 1818

In his 1924 book *Pennsylvania Beautiful,* Wallace Nutting called the signs *Hexafoos* (*Hexenfuss* in standard German) (Nutting 1924, passim). This name is applied generally to the pentagram, but it became generalized as the Pennsylvania barn patterns. In 1928 a scandalous murder connected with witchcraft took place in York County. The press dubbed it the Hex House Murder. This and subsequent "hex murders" in 1929 and 1932 made a connection between the barn emblems and

Fig. 38.12. Eighteenth-century mezuzah on a synagogue

the local tradition of powwowing, which involved traditional healing techniques that used magic, popularly viewed as witchcraft.

As with many ancient patterns, the function and meaning of hex signs is disputed, the argument being over whether they are mere decoration or have an amuletic function. This has been called "the scholars' war" (Yoder and Graves 2000, 11–18). But, as mentioned in the introduction, in the context of Flemish charms, some may be amuletic in their original intention and others may not, but they may be used as amulets nevertheless (Hildburgh 1908b, 200). Gandee, for example, emphasizes their spiritual function as "painted prayers" (Gandee 1971, passim). Undoubtedly many of the patterns are derived from traditional German, Austrian, and Swiss folk art, appearing there on textiles, wooden items, and, in a few cases, on the outside of buildings.

GARGOYLES

Although they are usually described in utilitarian terms as ornate water spouts, gargoyles have a legendary origin. The French *gargouille* means "a gullet or a throat." The English word *gargle* is related and onomatopoeically describes the sound of water gurgling from a gargoyle. In

Fig. 38.13. Twelfth-century dragon head on abbey gatehouse, Bury St. Edmunds, Suffolk

legend gargoyles derive from an event in Rouen, France, around the year 635, when the bishop, Romanus, killed a fire-breathing monster called Gargouille. The carcass was burned, but its neck and head, being fireproof, would not burn. So the head and neck were mounted on the church to scare away evil spirits. Clearly the Gargouille monster was a dragon, and mounting dragons' heads on buildings was common in Norse architecture, such as the stave churches of Norway. So gargoyles are mainly in the form of dragons' heads, although lions come second with humanoid forms, sometimes obscene, third. They are all considered to be amuletic, protecting churches against demonic attack.

Fig. 38.14. Gargoyle, St. John's College, Cambridge

WIND VANES AND WEATHERCOCKS

Wind vanes (or weather vanes), weathercocks, and other animal forms are notable parts of traditional buildings. Blacksmith-made, they are finely balanced artifacts that are driven by the prevailing currents of wind, swiveling on a fixed upright. Wind vanes are important in traditional society because they indicate the likelihood of rain when the wind blows from a certain direction and are also valuable to sailors who want to go to sea. It is significant that the wind vane appears as the final rune of the first *ett* in the Common Germanic Futhark. This is the rune *wunjo* (Anglo-Saxon *wyn*), signifying the function of a wind vane that moves according to the winds yet remains fixed in one place. Its reading is "joy," obtained by having a stable base but being in harmony with the surrounding conditions. In the Viking age gilded metal weather vanes were mounted on ships, and similar ones were set up on stave churches in Norway. A motto depicted with a weathercock in a seventeenth-century emblem book is *officium meum stabile agitare*, "it is my function to turn while remaining stable."

Early records of weather vanes are few. The tomb of the Etruscan leader Lars Porsenna is supposed to have had vanes and bells on it. The triton on the Tower of the Winds at Athens was a vane. The octagonal building, built in 50 BCE by the Macedonian architect Andronikos of Cyrrhus, had a low conical roof with the triton pivoted at its center. In its hand the triton held a wand that pointed at one of eight personified images of the winds, thereby indicating the wind that was blowing at the

Fig. 38.15. Weathercock on church at St. Neots, Cambridgeshire

time. A ninth-century weathercock is known from Brescia, Italy, where Bishop Rampertus had one erected on the Church of San Faustino Maggiore in 820 (Novati 1904, 497). They were in use in Anglo-Saxon England by 862, when Bishop Swithun put a weathercock on Winchester Cathedral. (In England Saint Swithun's Day, July 15, is a weather marker that warns that if it rains on that day, a rainy period lasting forty days will follow; this rarely happens, however.) In 925 the monastery of Saint Gallen had its weathercock stolen by Magyar invaders. Westminster Abbey is depicted in the Bayeux Tapestry, where a man is shown erecting a weathercock upon its completion in 1065.

Vanes and cockerels are not the only forms of traditional wind markers. A medieval saying from France tells us there are lions, eagles, and dragons on top of churches. Swans are features of churches in parts of Germany, especially in Oldenburg and East Frisia. The pavilion of Lord's, the oldest cricket ground in the world, in London, founded 1787, has a vane of Father Time, complete with scythe, removing the bails from the stumps, which marks the close of play in a cricket match.* St. George's Park cricket ground at Port Elizabeth, South Africa, has a griffin holding a cricket bat.

Fig. 38.16. Fox vane, Dry Drayton, Cambridgeshire

---

*When an umpire removes the bails from the cricket stumps, then no more play can take place, so symbolically Father Time determines how long our play in this world shall be.

Chapter 39

Accretional Amulets

The assemblage of amulets and talismans to make powerful objects, either from actual items or assemblages of images as medallions and pendant charms, is a very ancient technique. The crowns of Upper and Lower Egypt, the white *hedjet* and the red *deshret,* were combined in ancient times to create the familiar *pschent* double crowns of the pharaohs.

Similarly three crowns were combined to make the tiara of the popes. European heraldry often depicts collections of symbolic items, as does the

Fig. 39.1. Pharaonic crown, ancient Egypt

traditional Christian image of the cross surrounded by the instruments of the passion—hammer, nails, ladder, and pliers. Magical bottles are filled with disparate amuletic objects. Amulets are collected and sewn with red thread into pouches and bundles. Necklaces of various items, whether seeds, beads, or gems pierced and strung together or chains from which various amulets hang, all are accretional charms.

Fig. 39.2. Accretional necklace with various amulets, 1895

SHRINES AS ACCRETIONAL AMULETS

Shrines of every religion are accretional. The practices of ex-votos, offerings, and images placed in a shrine as a thanks-offering to the deity for some miraculous answer to prayer exist the world over.

Fig. 39.3. Goat ex-voto of aluminum, Crete

From ancient Greece, where tools were left by grateful workmen, to the superannuated military colors that hang in English churches, items taken out of everyday circulation have accumulated. In Cologne Cathedral is an image of Our Lady surrounded by jewelry, including watches that were placed there by grateful supplicants. The practice no longer takes place, so the items are like a museum of pre–World War I artifacts. Shrines filled with ex-votos and other amuletic and talismanic items added when necessary are vibrant with their presence.

Fig. 39.4. Cave shrine of Agios Antonios with bundles of hanging ex-votos, Crete

This practice has often been in conflict with the wishes of priesthood, even those of the religion to which the amuletic objects are addressed. To militant missionaries of other faiths, they have been things to destroy with gusto. In many places this process continues unabated in the twenty-first century.

As in every other land they entered, Christian missionaries in Madagascar attempted to eradicate indigenous religion and beliefs and impose their own on the conquered country. Also, as on previous occasions in other places, they recorded triumphantly in considerable detail the shrines and images they violated and destroyed. The book *Christian Missions in Madagascar* records the destruction in September 1869 of

426. TRÉBEURDEN (C.-du-N.) - Menhir de Penvern
Remarquable à cause de ses dimensions extraordinaires
(8 m. de haut sur 3 m. 50 à la base)   A. B.

Fig. 39.5. Christianized megalith at Trebeurden, Brittany, France,
commercial postcard, circa 1890

the royal ancestral shrine containing the deity Mahavaly and many sacred amulets, talismans, and ex-votos. The missionaries convinced the queen to order its demolition.

"This was the real break with the past," observed Archdeacon McMahon, who quoted the man who carried out the desecration:

> I went up and fetched down the box in which the idol was kept, and all belonging to it, viz. Two large wooden boxes and fifteen baskets with covers, and eleven small baskets with covers, and nine wood cylinders all full. The baskets were all filled with leaves and dust of charms, the cylinders full of wooden charms joined together with silver rings and beads, such as are worn on the neck and head when going out to war; the one box was full of red and purple silk, in the other box was the idol itself, which was called "The Great One." It was made of two pieces of wood each seven inches long and as large as one's wrist. It was wrapped up in different colored cloth, blue, gray, and purple, and covered with oil and incense (ramy) decorated with agate and silver beads; in shape it was like a bird with a red head, and wings glittering with its dressing of beads. When I took hold of it, I thought it was alive, but when I raised it up I saw that it was not.
>
> The contents of the shrine were then burned. The leaves and small things first, then chopped up Mahavaly, which was not easy to do—owing to the amount of oil on him he was slippery, but when he got into the fire he burned like a bundle of dried grass, and I took care that it was all burned, as I was glad of the job. (McMahon 1914, 38–40)

During the uprising against the colonial power in 1895, the holy images of Ravalolona and Masobe, which had been buried to save them from destruction, were unearthed and carried as amulets in battle. They were sprinkled with holy water, and Masobe was wrapped in a white silk frontal taken from the church of All Saints' in Ramainandro and tied up with a Christian priest's stole. Thus the sacred accretional bundles of indigenous Malagsy religion had been re-created using items from churches to accompany local items. The insurgents were defeated and killed (McMahon 1914, 54–55).

NECKLACES AND BRACELETS

The most common accretional amulet is the string of beads. Originally the word *bead* did not describe an object, but a prayer. A *bede,* from the Anglo-Saxon *gebed,* was a ritual petition by the worshipper (Edwards 1968, 32). "Bidding the bedes" was when prayers were offered as a list of intercessions for named individuals and other things such as the harvest or the safe return of a traveler (Edwards 1968, 33). Bedes were "told"; that is, the number of times a prayer was said at any one time was counted. Items on a string were a good way of telling when the stipulated number of prayers had been said. Hence the seeds or wooden, ceramic, glass, or metal items used for telling the prayers became beads.

Fig. 39.6. String of blue beads with peacock feather amulet
(also see plate 30)

The medieval chronicler William of Malmesbury gives an account of Lady Godiva from around the year 1040 that she had a series of gemstones threaded on a cord that she touched one by one as she recited her prayers (Reeves 1997, 194). A fine gold rosary dating from circa 1500 is preserved in the Victoria and Albert Museum in London. It consists of fifty oval beads arranged in tens interspersed with larger marker beads. Each bead bears a sacred image, including the evangelical beasts, saints, and the Agnus Dei, making it a repository of sacred imagery as well as a tool for prayer (Reeves 1997, 195). The Rosary of Mother Julian of Norwich, used in the Norfolk tradition, consists of hazelnuts (Thomas 2019, 101).

Charm bracelets are a common item today. Many have traditional lucky charms such as four-leaf clovers, horseshoes, and birds, although contemporary images such as cartoon characters are available. Earlier accumulations of charms were suspended from pendants, as charm bracelets would have been a hindrance to women performing hard manual labor, as most had to do. A mid-eighteenth-century heart-shaped pendant from Heligoland had a series of metal charms suspended from it, including angels, fish, medallions, and a ship (Gerlach 1971, 206). In eastern England three odd keys on a chain are carried to bring health, wealth, and love (Thomas 2019, 238). These must be keys that cannot open any lock one knows of.

CINCO SEIMÃO

The Portuguese and Brazilian *cinco seimão* is an assemblage of charms that hang around a central piece. Early-twentieth-century versions had a pentagram, a *figa* (fig), a *lua crescent* (a human-faced waxing crescent moon), and a key, all grouped around a heart pierced by two arrows. All of this was surmounted by an image of the Virgin Mary, who had a ring attached to her back for hanging the charm. Others had a cross, an anchor, a lunar crescent, and a small mounted horn made from real horn. Sometimes there was "a four-leaf flower" (Hildburgh 1908a, 221–22). Contemporary ones are similar, although most are without the religious figure. The *figa*, the *corno* (horn), the number thirteen, a four-leaf clover, and a *ferradura* (horseshoe) are often present. The pentagram is often substituted by a *Estrela de Davi,* a hexagram.

THE CHATELAINE

The chatelaine was once a fashionable item, a series of chains attached to a woman's belt and used to carry small bags and useful items such as sewing accessories. The protective and magical uses of pins necessitate them being kept safely. Originally a means of carrying keys, it is named for *la chatelaine,* the lady of the house, the owner or wife of the owner of a grand country estate. Chatelaines have a medallion or roundel at the top, with a hook to fasten them to the belt. They all had some features that were amuletic as well as utilitarian. Georgian chatelaines around 1800 typically had hearts. In later examples pincushions and individual containers for pins, thimbles, and so forth often took the form of acorns, hearts, heart padlocks, or oyster and scallop shells (Cummins and Taunton, 1994, passim). There are overtly charm-bearing chatelaines that have the number thirteen in a carrying roundel. They resemble charm bracelets, but on a larger scale. Characteristically they bear thirteen items. Typically one may have a fish, a lute, a man, a cow, a tankard, a boot, a dog, a teapot, a duck, a heart, a heart padlock, a rooster, and a skull. There may otherwise be turtles, a bottle, or a warding hand sign of either kind.

WATCH CHAINS, FREISENKETTEN, AND CHARIVARI

In Lincolnshire in 1908 folklorist Mabel Peacock noted that elderly countrymen still liked wearing watch chains from which were suspended seals, miniature corkscrews, miniature horseshoes, coins with holes drilled through them, cowrie-shaped shells, and horses' teeth that they had found (Peacock 1908, 87–88). Similarly the Austrian *Freisenkette* strings together various amulets and talismans to protect babies from convulsions. Charms include hairs from a billy goat's beard, metal or coral hands forming warding signs, pierced coins, saints' medallions, and a Breverl, a sewn triangular cloth pouch containing a religious text (Simpson 1987, 117).

The related but well-crafted Bavarian Charivari is a notable part of traditional costumes, both on lederhosen for men and on the dirndl for women. Derived from sets of amulets that serve to help hunters be successful, they appear as striking objects in their own right. The Charivari is a creative form, consisting of a heavy silver chain with various amulets hanging from it. There are always a number of different amulets attached to the chain. They commonly include various organic pieces, generally pieces of antler or horn, claws, tusks, teeth, and bird and animal feet, as well as less commonly silver coins, gems, crystals, and emblems such as boars' heads or crowned skulls. Animal parts are set in silver mounts. These can range from weasel jaws, deer teeth, bear and wolf claws, and a fox's nose and front teeth to tufts of badger hair, a raptor claw, or a *schergraberl* (a mole's foot with its claws). They are clearly powerful amulets.

THE CIMARUTA

Like the mano cornuto hand discussed in chapter 30 (see page 186), the cimaruta is associated with the Italian city of Napoli (Naples). The cimaruta (*cima di ruta*) represents a sprig of the rue plant, *Ruta graveolens,* known in medieval times as "the herb of grace." Frederick Thomas Elworthy states that the cimaruta was "always of silver" and mentions Etruscan examples in the Bologna Museum in his day (Elworthy 1895, 344). Its function is against *jettatura,* the evil eye. As noted in chapter 30 (see page 180), it was believed in former times that the faculty of sight involved sending out rays from the eyes toward the object, which was then perceived. These rays, if projected with hostile intent, caused harm to the object, and the process was called "the evil eye." Scientific studies from the seventeenth century proved this idea to be false, yet the expression "the male gaze," referring to men looking at women, still preserves this mistaken and obsolete view of optics. This is a refined version that runs in parallel with the older conception of the evil eye, which has not completely died out. Turkish glass nazar amulets on sale in 2019 in the market in St. Ives, Cambridgeshire, were labeled as being "against the evil eye."

THE VIRTUOUS HORSESHOE CHARM

An important horseshoe-based accretional amulet made in Mexico is *el secreto de la virtuosa herradura* (the secret of the virtuous horseshoe). It is in the form of a used horseshoe, presented in inverted form and wrapped with rayon thread, usually red but sometimes other colors. In the center of the horseshoe is a *cruz de Caravaca* (cross of Caravaca), and printed images of San Martin Caballero (iconic images of Saint Martin of Tours on horseback) surround the ensemble. The cross of Caravaca

Fig. 39.7. La Ss.* Cruz de Carabaca (cross of Caravaca) printed amulet, eighteenth century

LA SS. CRUZ E CARABACA.

Estan concedidos 3600 dias de Indulgencia, á los devotos que lle-
van consigo y rezaren un Credo, ó un acto de Contricion por los
Señores Eminentísimos Cardenales, Arzazispos y Obispos de España.
Es Abogada contra Rayos, Centellas, y Tempestades.

---

*sanctissima

is a double-barred crucifix depicted with an angel on each side. Legend tells that in Spain in the year 1280, this cross was brought miraculously by two angels to Don Gínes Pérez Chirinos de Cuenca, who was attempting to convert the local Islamic Moorish ruler to Christianity (Fernandes 1722, 200).

THE LOVETT MOTOR MASCOT

Around 1910, as mentioned earlier, the famous London department store, A. W. Gamage, Ltd., commissioned Edward Lovett to design a mascot for motorists. It was a composite of several lucky charms. The

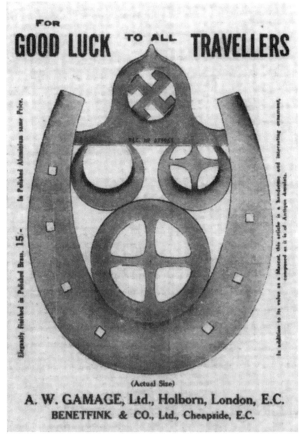

Fig. 39.8. Gamage's store advertisement
for the Lovett Motor Mascot, London, 1912

"Lovett Motor Mascot for good luck to all travelers" was made of metal in the form of a horseshoe with the traditional seven nail holes. It was pointed up, and inside in the lower section was a sun-wheel cross surmounted by a crescent and crescent and star. Above this was a bell-shaped section containing a short-armed swastika.

As a new thing for powered road vehicles, it was still made like a brass horse harness amulet, so common at the time. It was a registered design, an early form of copyright, number 379955. "Elegantly finished in polished brass," it cost fifteen shillings, making it quite expensive in the money of the day. The publicity for the Lovett Motor Mascot stated, "The mascot is, by far, the most powerful one that has ever been devised, consisting as it does of five of the most widely recognized types of amulet in existence, some of which have been in use for more than two thousand years." Production did not last long, and examples of the Lovett Motor Mascot are very rare. Gamage's closed down in 1972, having traded since 1878.

POUCHES, RELIQUARIES, SCAPULARS, AND MOJO HANDS

Religious items are often accretional, bearing a collection of various images, symbols, and formulaic texts. A fifteenth-century gold ring in the British Museum, known as the Coventry Ring, portrays Jesus's five wounds with an inscription: "The five wounds of God are my medicine." There is an image of Jesus standing in the tomb surrounded by the Instruments of the Passion and the names of the three Magi— Caspar, Melchior, Balthazar. Also *TETRAGRAMMATON*, representing the four-letter name of God in Hebrew, and *ANANYZAPTA*, signifying *Antidotum Nazarenem Auferat Necem Intoxicationis Sanctificet Alimenta Pocula Trintas Alma*, "May the antidote of the Nazarene [Jesus] avert death by poisoning and the Trinity sanctify my food and drink."

Another gold religious item is found at Middleham in Yorkshire. It is a portable reliquary intended to be worn around the neck. Dating also from around 1450, it holds a large sapphire and an inscription of the same magical formula, *ANANYZAPTA*. It is engraved with an image of the Christian trinity and a Latin text that translates as "Behold the Lamb of God that takes away the sins of the world" and again the word *TETRAGRAMMATON*. The reverse has a nativity scene surrounded by images of saints (Reeves 1995, 66). A Tau ring with the inscription *ANANIZAPTA* was shown by Octavius Morgan to the Society of Antiquaries on London in June 1873 (Jones 1877, 155–56). The common features of these talismans (for they must have been consecrated by a priest) are an insight into English Christian charms of the period. They were part of a Roman Catholic tradition that was destroyed forcibly as "superstition" by the Protestants.

SCAPULARS AND BREVERLS

The triangular Breverl, mentioned above, is a pouch attached to a necklace or string of other amulets and talismans. Its function is to contain a religious text, as is the devotional scapular. This is composed of two rectangular sewn pieces of cloth containing religious images or texts. Red thread is favored for the sewing. The two rectangular pieces are connected by two cords, which go on either side of the neck, enabling it to be worn with one part in front and one behind. The scapular is a cut-down version of the Carmelite religious habit, which has a large piece of cloth and is worn on front and back of other vestments. The Brown Scapular, otherwise called the Devotional Scapular of Our Lady of Mount Carmel, dates from 1250.

Although unauthorized by the religious authorities, olive leaves from Palm Sunday rites, herbs gathered on Saint John's Eve, wax from church candles, and other materials can be put in a scapular (Paine 2004, 174). There are eighteen distinct forms of scapulars authorized by the Roman Catholic Church. Related to the scapular is the triangular Breverl. From the seventeenth century onward, these printed "minitaure devotionals" took the form of texts and engravings that were folded in a particular way and encased in a protective paper or cardboard envelope printed with symbolic patterns. Known otherwise in Italian as *brevi* or *lettera de pregheria* (prayer letters), the contents included holy names and images of Jesus and saints. Other amulets and talismans were included in the package or added by the owner later to reinforce the amulet's potency. Hung round the neck or carried unseen next to the body, Breverls served to protect the wearer and preempt any harmful influences that he or she might encounter.

During the First World War, Italian army chaplain and medical officer Agostino Gemelli produced a new version of the triangular religious fabric amulet. On the first Friday of 1917, two million Italian soldiers took part in religious services in which they were consecrated by priests to the cult of the Sacred Heart of Jesus. They were issued with triangular fabric amulets inscribed *In Hoc Signo Vinces* (In this sign you shall conquer) and *Protezione del Soldato*. Gemelli produced these triangles in part to counter the use of amulets by Italian soldiers, which of course they continued to carry in addition to the new one (De Simonis and Dei 2010, 82).

EUROPEAN POUCHES AND SACHETS

Red thread is favored for sewing pouches. As noted in chapter 21 (see page 107), the old Scottish adage tells us, "Rowan tree and red threid gar the witches tyne their speid" (Rowan tree and red thread make the witches lose their speed, that is, be disempowered). A dried toad carried against contagious diseases was often carried in such a pouch. Robert

Fig. 39.9. Dried toad from unwrapped bundle, Suffolk

Means Lawrence wrote, "In Tuscany a horse-shoe when found is placed in a small red bag with some hay, which the Tuscans consider also a luck-bringing article, and the twofold charm is kept in its owner's bed" (Lawrence 1898, 112). Pouch charms were made and sold in England and France for luck during World War I. In Rotherham, Yorkshire, Sarah Ann Flint sold pouches to women munitions workers that were found not to contain what she said they did. In France, during the persecution of amulet sellers, Camille Mercier was prosecuted for selling sachets that were supposed to protect soldiers against hostile munitions (Davies 2018, 106).

Fig. 39.10. Bundle containing dried toad, Cambridgeshire

THE ELF BAG

Irish "elf bag that contained a number of amulets: typically three or four flints; a silver coin with a cross on it, called a thirteen pence piece no matter what its face value; three copper coins, often counterfeit halfpennies; seven or eight flint stones, most white, but some black; and four small prehistoric flint arrowheads" (Meehan 1906, 202). These items were used in conjunction with *three-mearne-water*, water taken "in the darkest hour before dawn" from a source on the boundary of three townlands. Juice from the herb lady's mantle (*Alchemilla vulgaris*) was mixed with the three-mearne-water, three coins were put in it, and then a pinch of salt. The water was then given to the animal to drink and some was sprinkled along its spine (Meehan 1906, 207).

THE INSTRUMENTS OF OBEAH

The West Indian Obeah practice has been persecuted by the authorities since the days of slavery, and it is still illegal in Jamaica under the Obeah Act 1898. It was a form of slave resistance, and hence Obeah men were punished without mercy. "The Instruments of Obeah," as material magica is called in legal jargon, have been listed many times in trials of practitioners. Duppy bags and pouches containing amulets belonging to a reputed doctorman or one-eyed man have been exhibited as evidence for the prosecution. In 1891 police officer Herbert Thomas staged an exhibition in Kingston, Jamaica, of "the instruments of Obeah" seized in police raids. He listed "wooden images, dolls' heads, bits of looking glass, the skins of snakes and frogs, the comb and beak of a cock, a pack of cards, a razor, tiny carved calabashes, a bit of brimstone enclosed in a small bag, powdered touchwood, and numerous items of no value in themselves, but all supposed to be endowed with magic power, are to be found in the possession of every obeah man when a 'haul' is made" (Thomas 1891, 6). Thomas mentions the Obi man's snake stick as a significant item. Sticks with spiraled climbing plants that have become embedded in the wood are magical items in many lands. The present author has one he uses, obtained from a shepherd in Germany. Thomas would have had it confiscated. Thomas's *Something about Obeah* catalogs items including "a number of blood-stained pieces of calabash strung together forming what is known as a 'jeggeh,'" and item 16 is "a glass marble" (Thomas 1891, 9, 10). The exhibition ran for ten days in 1891, but then was closed down by order of the Executive Committee.

Knowledge of occult matters was a valuable tool in slaves' resistance against captivity in both the West Indies and the United States. It was one of the few areas of life where slaves had control of something their masters knew little about. In 1842 Charles Colcock Jones wrote about slaves' use of amulets and talismans: "They have, on certain other occasions been made to believe they were invincible; that they might go anywhere and do anything they pleased, and it would be impossible for them to be discovered or known, *in fine,* to will was to do—safely, successfully" [my italics] (Jones 1842, 8). Folktales about characters such as Anansi and High John the Conqueror emphasize the power that can be harnessed from the otherworld. The root by which Frederick Douglass empowered himself is a prime example of what could give strength and hope to enslaved people (Douglass [1845] 1973, 72).

THE MOJO HAND

Many traditions from different cultures teach that luck is a possession that one can be born with, can acquire through appropriate actions, can have bestowed by divine beings including Eshu and Fortuna (Lady Luck), or can buy or lose. Using the card game analogy, a hand is something we are dealt in life. Fate can deal us a winning or losing hand. It is believed that possession of an appropriate charm, amulet, or talisman can override what fate has dealt us.

In the African American tradition, the mojo is a main means of magical empowerment. Called by many names, including conjure hand, nation sack, nature sack, trick bag, gris-gris bag, and toby, it is a bag, customarily made of red flannel, but often green for gamblers, and more rarely, of chamois leather. The bag contains a selection of objects of symbolic and magical potency. Worn around the neck, hung from a belt, kept in a pocket or purse, or concealed in one's underwear, the mojo must be carried at all times and not shown to anyone. It is important culturally, appearing in several famous mid-twentieth-century blues songs. Robert Johnson's "Little Queen of Spades" was a gambling woman who had a mojo, Lightnin' Hopkins sang that he was going to Louisiana to buy a mojo hand, and Muddy Waters told how he activated his mojo but it failed to function as required. To work gris-gris bags must be empowered with a blessing to the voodoo deity Baron Samedi.

The contents of a mojo hand are tailored to the requirements of the user. Particular roots, seeds and herbs, and minerals and bones are assembled to perform designated functions. High John the Conqueror is often an ingredient. A spirit-embodying root, it protects against enemies, assists gamblers, and gives men success with women. The legend of High John the Conqueror has similarities with the acts of the West African Fon and Yoruba deity Gu or Ogun (Alexander and Rucker 2010, 207). It is the tuber of *Ipomoea jalappa,* a species of bindweed, giving it an additional link with binding magic. Another important root is the lucky hand. This is the root of several species of orchid, collectively known as salep (*Orchis* spp.), which resembles a human hand. It often accompanies five-finger grass (a.k.a. silverweed, cinquefoil, *Potentilla erecta*). Shakespeare called salep "dead man's fingers" in his play *Hamlet.* Before tea was introduced to England, salep root made a fine drink. Salep root, growing only in the wild, was much sought after, and the trade in it caused the plant to disappear from most of the country. It is now a rare protected species.

Master root (*Eryngium yuccifolium*) accompanies the lucky hand root. The devil's shoestring (*Nolina lindheimeriana*) and sweet green clover (*Meliotus* spp.) are further herbal components. Five-finger grass, black tobacco soaked in whisky, ginger, a piece of iron pyrites, a lodestone, and magnetic sand and/or anvil dust may compose the contents of a luck-bringing mojo hand. Other materia magica may be cinnamon, allspice berries, ginger, nutmeg, and the resin known as dragon's blood. For winning at cards, a High John the Conqueror root, cinnamon, whisky, tobacco, and a black cat bone will accompany the player, unseen. Another amulet that may be included is a raccoon penis bone wrapped in a twenty-dollar bill. Some practitioners use green material for gambling mojos, green being the color of money. Seeds used include the buckeye nut (*Aesculus glabra*) and the African mojo bean. This is not a rare ingredient. It is the common broad bean or fava bean (*Vicia faba*), which is also the "lucky bean" of English tradition. It is not to be confused with the lucky bean of eastern and southern Africa, a poisonous red fruit of *Erythrina abyssinica.* Once all the items are assembled and put into the bag, the contents are *fixed* by anointing them with special oils and fumigation with incense.

SPROWL BOXES

In the Norfolk tradition in England, people have boxes that contain collections of objects picked up at significant magical places around the county. These items contain *sprowl,* that subtle spiritual virtue known in various European traditions as *pneuma, spirament, önd,* and *väki,* among other things. Academics use the Melanesian word *mana* to describe this virtue. Sprowl items include found items such as pieces of driftwood, shells, fossils, stones, bones, seed heads, and feathers (Thomas 2019, 265–66). The boxes are kept closed with the items in them until there is need for something for a particular purpose.

Fig. 39.11. Amuletic bottles, acorn, and fossil (also see plate 31)

Postscript

A Clash of Worldviews: Magicians and Museums

In Hyderabad in 1921, when the British Empire still ruled India, Dr. E. H. Hunt's laundry worker was threatened by a magic doll made to kill her. So he prepared an amulet to protect her from harm. It was a canister that had once contained film. Inside it was a large garnet, and the container was wrapped in a small Union Flag. She was told to tell no one about it, to carry it on her person, and to make sure the British flag was the right way up (the Union Jack is "handed" and can be flown upside down by mistake). The garnet would rattle in the tin whenever evil was attempting to attack her, she was told, and it would have no power over her. It worked. This ad hoc amulet is preserved in the Pitt-Rivers Museum, Oxford (Paine 2004, 57).

In the British Museum book *Fake? The Art of Deception* is an item described as a "Witch's Wreath." It is a knotted leather thong on which twelve amulets are strung. They are a hollow quill containing a text, sealed with beeswax; a Christian cross of horn; an animal bone; a bone plaque with sigils (undescribed) in red sealing wax; a piece of leather tooled with a six-pointed star; a beeswax image of a heart, covered in red wax and stuck with a pin; an eye of horn; another bone plaque with sigils burned into it with pyrography; a horn skull, also shaped by burning; a "lump of fossilized resin"; an iron staple; and a "fragment of holy writ" on a piece of wood, covered by a sheet of mica. All in all it is a remarkable assemblage of handmade amulets that took time and care in making.

This witch's wreath has all the elements of an authentic amulet, yet it is dismissed as fake because it was sold to the museum in 1941 with a letter apparently written by a Wiltshire woman, Alice Wornum, in 1879 that told how a well-known wise woman, Mary Holt, had made it to cure the writer's mother of the evil eye and her cattle from the plague. Investigations could find no record of Alice Wornum or Mary Holt at Stratton, Wiltshire. Also, unconnected with the witch's wreath, a witch's glove from nearby Wootton Basset had been offered for sale with forged deeds and papers. It was published as a fake in a local archaeological journal in 1940, and this helped in dismissing the witch's wreath. So this remarkable accretional amulet was rejected as inauthentic just because of its dubious provenance. Even if its backstory is a fabrication, as an amulet, the so-called witch's wreath is the real thing. Authenticity in this case is a matter of semantic definitions (Rudoe 1990, 84).

In every time and place there is a generally accepted worldview, accompanied by actions, commonplace things, and ways of being in the world that are taken for granted in the prevailing culture. This is the *habitus*. This is the shared experience of people in any given historical context. Some call it the *zeitgeist*, but this has a more specialized meaning. Each artifact from a particular place and time embodies the habitus of its age. In precommercial times those who created and used amulets and talismans did not make them to be exhibited but to be *used*. To view them as mere commodities, as industrially manufactured items are viewed, is a narrow view of human experience. If we do not have empathy with "ritual specialists," makers, and users, then we discount their very essence.

Spiritual and magical practices operate within specific social relationships. Specific amulets and talismans are embodiments of diverse aggregations of local, regional, and exotic currents. Rudolf Otto observed that natural magic was carried out quite unreflectively and without any basis in theory (Otto [1917] 1936, 121–22). Making amulets and talismans involves accessing unknown realities through an inheritance without instructions. Access to the uncanny realms of human experience can occur through various means. The amulet is

Fig. P.1. Bone and stone head found together in a churchyard in Hertfordshire

more than a mere "object" or "artwork." It is a transcendent communication between human beings and the powers of the natural world that manifests in myriad ways. Amulets are things that radiate presence, empowered by their makers and users.

Fig. P.2. IHS monogram marquetry work on the pulpit of Saint Margaret's church, eighteenth century (also see plate 32)

For an amulet or talisman to be seen as art, it must first be isolated from its context. Many ancient ones have been removed from human remains in graves and tombs and put on display. These had a magical and spiritual function; they were never intended to be seen by human eyes again. Art did not exist as a separate category in traditional society. If a sacred image appears in a museum or art gallery, then it has already lost its sanctity. As André Malraux observed, to the maker, an image of a goddess *was* that goddess (Malraux 1954, 52). Sacred images, like talismans and amulets, were not primarily made to be looked at, subject to the approval or criticism of the observer—their "exhibition value." They were emblematic of the mysteries, containers of spirit, as are those that still serve their original purpose. Items wrenched from their original surroundings have been brought together as natural history collections of the occult. Enthusiasts of the quaint, the weird and wonderful, and "the other within" get great enjoyment from seeing these collections. They may even be inspired by them to become initiates and create and use their own amulets and talismans—the real thing, not replicas.

But essentially amulets, talismans, charms, and mascots on show in museums and galleries now have a different function from their intended one. A Fumsup carried in 1916 by a British soldier whose life was in constant danger on the bloody battlefields of France brought comfort and hope. A century and more later, in a glass case, it cannot have the same meaning to another that it had to its original owner.

Et t Virg. t Ebras
Troncalis na mondo
Cardinal ya manaacadaag
gad natan á intilac na Dios
Ama Dios Anactan Dios
Espto Sto et Sarayan talo
Say ngaran na cat lora nian
amin Inismi sto. ▄

Say ngaray Bay.ᶜᵒ nen

bog calot ni Say a nen ag

Fig. P.3. Filipino printed amulet, nineteenth century

Unless it is a family heirloom, handed down through the generations, it is now a curio with significant "exhibition value," a saleable, collectible item. The afterlife of the amulet in museums and collections tends to diminish and neutralize its meaning.

Things perceived as "heritage" are long since removed from their part in the habitus and become separate objects of curation. They assume meanings far beyond their original status as everyday things in normal, unassuming use. Instead of existing as part of life, they must be maintained in unchanging existence for others—"posterity." Meaning dissolves, and the "preserved" becomes spectator orientated. The objects become citations of what the viewers expect them to be. Museums exist to rescue, preserve, conserve, safeguard, and reassure. But when any culture is no longer empowered by a comprehensive recognition of its inner virtues, then its external relics are frozen in time as exhibits. Individual objects become "iconic" mnemonics for entire cultures. Very famous ones are curated as "world heritage," as if the original makers intended them to be so. Everyday culture disappears and is edited by its curators, who decide at any one time what has "exhibition value" and what does not. Innate virtue has no place in this worldview.

Sometimes their presentation is challenged by those who attempt to reclaim what they view as their own particular heritage. Items taken by or sold to colonial collectors during the nineteenth century have been removed from display and returned to the land where they were made. Frequently only their locations and descriptions are altered. Often they go from one museum to another, where they are then displayed as part of a national heritage rather than being returned to their proper uses. Change is inherent in all existence. Individual amulets and talismans are, in reality, part of a much larger process. *Then* and *now* are not separate; they are part of a continuum. There is no one fixed point in time. Amulets and talismans are continually proliferating, evolving, and being destroyed. But the afterlife of amulets and talismans in museums can mean centuries of languishing in a box in a storeroom. Those on show, wherever the museum is, are always at risk of being transferred from display case to storeroom, there, perhaps, to be mislabeled and mislaid, to decay, be pilfered, "deaccessioned," or thrown in a dumpster out the back and carried away to the landfill. Some may yet escape their museum captivity and resume their proper function.

FINIS

Appendix 1

Collectors and Collections

A large number of amulets, charms, talismans, mascots, and related badges are preserved in European museums. Some collections number many thousands of items and, despite having been collected many years ago, are still not yet fully analyzed and documented. The major collectors in the field included Edward Burnett Tylor (1837–1917; Oxford); Giuseppe Bellucci (1844–1921; Perugia, Italy), who exhibited collections of amulets at the Paris Expositions of 1889 (Bellucci 1889) and 1900 as well as the international exhibitions at Turin and Milan; Edward Lovett (1852–1933; Croydon); Henry Wellcome (1853–1956; London); Lina Eckenstein (1857–1931; London); William J. Clarke (1868–1945: Scarborough, Yorkshire); Adrien de Mortellet (1853–1931; Paris); Lionel Bonnemère (1843–1905; Paris); and H. J. E. van Beuningen (1920–2015; Rotterdam).

These are the most noted European collectors. This list cannot, of course, be comprehensive as the above published some of their material in books and academic journals and much of what they amassed exists, at the time of writing, in museum collections. There have been in the past, and are now, numerous collectors of amulets, talismans, charms, and mascots who are not famous and who did not or have not publicized their collections.

Appendix 2

Glossary of Terms

AGATE: A marble actually made by turning and grinding real agate or, more commonly, a marble made of glass that blends two or more colors, simulating real agate. Used amuletically.

AKRO Agate: A marble made by the Akro Company in Akron, Ohio, established 1911.

BULL'S Pestle: Penis of a bull carried by British Army officers in the North African campaign in World War II.

CANGACEIRO: In northeastern Brazil in the 1920s and 1930s. Known for their flamboyant outfits covered with amulets.

CAUL: An amniotic membrane some babies are born with. Used as an amulet against drowning or gunshot.

CINCO Seimão: Portuguese amulet with five different charms.

CORN: The traditional Scottish ceremonial drinking cup, an aurochs horn with a lip of chased silver.

EINHEILEN: The implantation under the skin of religious texts, consecrated hosts, or lichen from an unburied skull. Used as battle-magic and protection against gunshot.

Elf bag: Pouch containing items used in healing animals sick from attacks by elves; Irish practice.

Er Ger Fong (1851–1935): The King of Gamblers, founder of a gambling empire in Thailand. His image appears on amulets used by gamblers in Thailand.

Evil Eye: Belief that a person can "overlook" someone or something with evil intent, causing ill to the person or thing.

Ghost Shirts: Sacred shirts of the Ghost Shirt cult, supposed to be bulletproof, worn by Sioux warriors at the Wounded Knee massacre, 1890.

Haly or **Sely How:** Scottish names for the caul, an amniotic membrane some babies are born with. Used as an amulet against drowning or gunshot.

Hard-Shot: The ability to withstand gunshot magically.

High John the Conqueror Root: Tuber of *Ipomoea jalappa*. Spirit-embodying item used in mojos.

Mezuzah (plural Mezuzot): Jewish parchment talisman bearing on one side two passages from Deuteronomy and the word *shaddai* on the other.

Mojo (Mojo Hand): Pouch containing various materials produced for particular uses.

Ostentum: An unexpected but meaningful happening.

Overlook: To overlook someone is to use the evil eye against that person.

Pouch: Fabric bag of various forms used to hold amuletic objects (see Elf Bag, Mojo).

Punter: Person who lays out money in gambling.

Ramus Feralis: The wild branch, a straight branch of a tree that never bore leaves.

RELIC: A fragment of human body, such as a skull, bones, blood, or a garment from a person regarded as holy. Enshrined as an object of worship in a temple or church, a continuation of the cult of ancestors of the Elder Faith.

SCAPULAR: A talismanic consecrated fabric item worn by Roman Catholics over the shoulders that contains religious items.

SEWEL (Sewell): String with feathers woven into it, used to scare deer and herd them into specific areas. Identical in structure to the witches' ladder (q.v.).

SHOT-FREE: The ability to withstand gunshot magically.

SISTRUM (plural Sistra): Bell rattle used in ancient Egypt in the rites and ceremonies of the goddess Isis.

SPIRAMENT: Subtle energy, cosmic breath.

VALKNUT (Valknútr): A glyph of three interlaced equilateral triangles, associated with the god Odin as "the knot of the slain."

VULCAN: Roman god of smithcraft.

WARLOCK: Man with the power of binding spirits.

WARLOCK Fecket: Magically protective jacket woven from water-snake skins; Scottish practice.

WEB of Wyrd: The interwoven fabric of things, places, events, actions, and persons that makes up our world as we experience it.

WITCHES' Ladder: String with feathers woven into it (but see Sewel).

WOUNDPROOF: Having magical protection that prevents one from being wounded or killed by an edged metal weapon.

WYRD: That which comes to happen.

Bibliography

Abbott, Lynne, and Doug Seroff, eds. 2009. *Ragged but Right: Black Traveling Shows, Coon Songs, and the Dark Pathway to Blues and Jazz*. Jackson: University Press of Mississippi.

Abulafia, David, and Nora Berend, eds. 2002. *Medieval Frontiers: Concepts and Practices*. Aldershot, England: Ashgate.

Ackerman, John Yonge. 1885. *Remains of Pagan Saxondom*. London: John Russell Smith.

Adams, Max. 2010. *The Prometheans: John Martin and the Generation that Stole the Future*. London: Quercus.

Adams, W. H. Davenport. 1895. *Witch, Warlock, and Magician: Historical Sketches of Magic and Witchcraft in England and Scotland*. London: Chatto & Windus.

Adorno, Theodor W. 1981. *Prisms*. Translated by Samuel Weber and Shierry Weber. Cambridge, Mass.: MIT Press.

Agrell, Sigurd. 1934. *Lapptrummor och Runmagi*. Lund, Sweden: Glerup.

Ahrens, W. 1918. "War Charms and Kindred Amulets." *The Open Court*, January: 51–59.

Aladel, M. 1890. *The Miraculous Medal: Origin, History, Circulation, Results*. Philadelphia, Pa.: H. L. Kilner & Co.

Albaum, Charlet. 1972. *Ojo de Dios: Eye of God*. New York: Grosset & Dunlap.

Alexander, Leslie M., and Walter C. Rucker Jr. 2010. *Encyclopedia of African-American History*. 3 vols. Santa Barbara, Calif.: ABC-CLIO.

Alvarado, D. 2011. *The Voodoo Hoodoo Spellbook*. San Francisco: Weiser Books.

Anawalt, Patricia Rieff. 2014. *Shamanic Regalia in the Far North*. London: Thames & Hudson.

Anderson, Jeffrey Elton. 2007. *Conjure in African-American Society.* Baton Rouge: Louisiana State University Press.

Anderson, Rasmus Bjørn. 1875. *Norse Mythology, or the Religion of Our Forefathers: Containing All the Mythology of the Eddas, Systematized and Interpreted.* Chicago: S. C. Griggs.

Anon. 1899. "The Trick Bone of a Black Cat." *The Journal of American Folk-Lore* 12 (46): 228–29.

Anon. 1995. *Im Zeichen des Kreuzes.* Körperkult. Tätowier Magazin, Ethno-Sonderband. Mannheim, Germany: Huber Verlag.

Anon. 2006. *Conjuration and an Excellent Discourse of the Nature and Substance of Devils and Spirits in Two Books.* Hinckley, England: Society of Esoteric Endeavour.

Appadurai, Arjun. 1986. *The Social Life of Things: Commodities in Cultural Perspective.* Cambridge, England: Cambridge University Press.

Armstrong, Edward A. 1969. *The Folklore of Birds.* Boston: Houghton Mifflin Co.

Arntz, Helmut. 1944. *Handbuch der Runenkunde.* Halle an der Saale, Germany: Niemeyer.

Arwas, Victor. 1978. *Berthon & Grasset.* London: Academy Editions.

Ashton, John. 1896. *The Devil in Britain and America.* London: Ward and Downing.

Astruc, Michel. 1999. *Bijoux d'Auvergne et de Velay: Orfevrerie profane at sacreé.* Paris: ASPMCC.

Aswynn, Freya. 1988. *Leaves of Yggdrasil.* London: Aswynn.

Aubrey, John. 1857. *Miscellanies upon Various Subjects.* 4th ed. London: John Russell Smith.

Ayres, James. 1977. *British Folk Art.* London: Thames & Hudson.

Bächtold-Stäubli, Hanns, ed. 1927–1942. *Handwörterbuch des Deutschen Aberglaubens.* 9 vols. Berlin: Koehler & Amerlang.

Baillie, Scott Mackay Hugh. 1906. *Houses and Gardens.* London: George Newnes.

Bales, E. G. 1939. "Folklore from West Norfolk." *Folklore* 50 (1): 66–75.

Baring-Gould, Sabine. (1893) 1905. *Mrs. Curgenven of Curgenven.* London: Methuen & Co.

Bariş, İlhan. 2007. *The Astrology of the Ottoman Empire.* Istanbul, Turkey: İbariş Ilban.

Barratt, William. 1926. *Deathbed Visions.* London: Methuen.

Barrett, Francis. (1801) 2007. *The Magus, or Celestial Intelligencer.* Stroud, England: Nonsuch Publishing.

Bärtsch, Albert. 1993. *Holz Masken: Fastnachts- und Maskenbrauchtum in der Schweiz, in Süddeutschland und Österrech.* Aarau, Switzerland: AT Verlag.

Bassett, M. G. 1982. *Formed Stones—Folklore and Fossils.* Cardiff: The National Museum of Wales.

Bell, Henry Hesketh J. 1889. *Obeah: Witchcraft in the West Indies.* London: Sampson Low, Marston, Searle & Rivington.

Bell, Quentin. 1948. *On Human Finery.* London: The Hogarth Press.

Bellucci, Giuseppe. 1881. *Catalogo della collezione di amulet inviata all'Expositione National di Milano.* Perugia, Italy: Tipografia di Vincenzo Bartelli.

Bellucci, Joseph [Giuseppe]. 1889. *Catalogue descriptif d'une collection d'amulettes Italiennes, envoyeé à l'Exposition Universelle de Paris 1889.* Perugia, Italy: Imprimerie Boncompagni.

———. 1907. *Il feticismo primitivo in Italia e le sue forme de adattamento.* Perugia, Italy: Unione Tipografica Cooperative.

———. 1920. *Folk-lore di guerra.* Perugia, Italy: Unione Tipografica Cooperative.

Bennett, Gillian. 1991. *English Folklore and the Land of Lost Content. The Folklore Historian* 8: 26–37.

Berners, Dame Juliana. 1905. *Boke of St Albans.* London: Elliot Stock.

Besant, Annie, and C. W. Leadbeater. 1901. *Thought-Forms.* London: The Theosophical Publishing House.

Billingsley, John, Jeremy Harte, and Brian Hoggard, eds. 2017. *Hidden Charms.* Mytholmroyd, England: Northern Earth Books.

Bills, Mark. 2010. *Watts Chapel: A Guide to the Symbols of Mary Watts' Arts and Crafts Masterpiece.* London: Philip Wilson Publishers.

Binder, Pearl. 1973. *Magic Symbols of the World: Talismans, Charms, Fertility Symbols.* London, New York, Sydney, Toronto: Hamlyn.

Blick, Sarah, ed. 2007. *Beyond Pilgrim Souvenirs and Secular Badges: Essays in Honour of Brian Spencer.* Oxford, England: Oxbow Books.

Blinkenberg, C. 1911. *The Thunderweapon in Religion and Folklore: A Study in Comparative Archaeology.* Cambridge: Cambridge University Press.

Blount, Godfrey. 1905. *The Science of Symbols: Setting Forth the True Reason for Symbolism and Ritual.* London: A. C. Fifield.

———. 1910. *Arbor Vitæ. On the Nature and Development of Imaginative Design.* London: A. C. Fifield.

Blumler, Martinus Fredericus. (1710) 1887. *A History of Amulets.* Edinburgh: E. & G. Goldsmid.

Boehm, Barbara. 1997. "Body-Part Reliquaries: The State of Research." *Gesta* 36 (1): 8–19.

Bortoft, Henri. 1996. *The Wholeness of Nature: Goethe's Way toward a Science of Conscious Participation in Nature*. Hudson, N.Y.: Lindisfarne Press.

Bottrell, William. 1880. *Stories and Folk-Lore of West Cornwall*. Penzance, England: F. Rodda.

Bouquet, Mary, and Nuno Porto. 2005. *Science, Magic, and Religion: The Ritual Processes of Museum Magic*. Oxford, England: Berghahn Books.

Boutellier, Marcelle. 1966. "L'œuvre et les collections folkloriques de Lionel Bonnemère (1843–1905)." *Arts et Traditions Populaires* 1/2: 17–42.

Bradley, Jude, and Cheré Dastugue Coen. 2010. *Magic's in the Bag: Creating Spellbinding Gris-Gris and Sachets*. Woodbury, Minn.: Llewellyn.

Braekman, Willy L. 1997. *Middeleeuwse witte en zwarte magie in het Nederlands taalgebied*. Gent, Belgium: Koninklijke Academie voor Nederlandse Taal-en Letterkunde.

Brears, Peter. 1981. *Horse Brasses*. London: Country Life Books.

Briggs, Asa. 1979. *Iron Bridge to Crystal Palace: Impact and Images of the Industrial Revolution*. London: Thames & Hudson.

Brink, Stefan, and Lisa Collinson, eds. 2017. *Theorizing Old Norse Myth*. Turnhout, Belgium: Brepols.

Brinton, Daniel G. 1890. "Folk-Lore of the Bones." *Journal of American Folklore* 3 (8): 17–22.

Broadbent. Geoffrey. 1977. "A Plain Man's Guide to the Theory of Signs in Architecture." *Architectural Design*: 474–82.

Brockie, William. 1886. *Legends and Superstitions of the County of Durham*. Sunderland, England: B. Williams.

Brown, Bill. 2001. "Thing Theory." *Critical Enquiry* 28: 1–22.

Brown, Calum G. 2001. *The Death of Christian Britain*. London: Routledge.

Brown, David H. 1990. "Conjure/Doctors: An Exploration of a Black Discourse in America, Antebellum to 1940." *Folklore Forum* 23 (1/2): 3–46.

Browne, Sir Thomas. (1635) 1927. *Pseudodoxia (Works)*. Edinburgh: John Grant.

Bryan, Patrick E. 2000. *The Jamaican People, 1880–1902: Race, Class, and Social Control*. Kingston, Jamaica: The University of the West Indies Press.

Budge, Sir E. A. Wallis. 1930. *Amulets and Superstitions*. London: Humphrey Milford.

Bulwer, John. 1653. *Anthropometamorphosis: Man Transformed, or the Artificial Changeling . . .* London: William Hunt.

Bunn, Ivan. 1975. "Mummified Cats!" *Lantern* 12 (Winter): 9.

———. 1991. "'A Devil's Shield . . .' Notes on Suffolk Witch Bottles." *Lantern* 39 (Autumn): 3–7.

Burdick, Lewis Dayton. 1901. *Foundation Rites with Some Kindred Ceremonies: A Contribution to the Study of Beliefs, Customs, and Legends Connected with Buildings, Locations, Landmarks, etc.* New York: Abbey Press.

Burne, Charlotte Sophie, and Georgina F. Jackson. 1883. *Shropshire Folk-Lore.* London: Trübner.

Burridge, Frank. 1975. *Nameplates of the Big Four Including British Railways.* Poole, England: Oxford Publishing Company.

Burton, Robert. (1621) 1926. *The Anatomy of Melancholy.* 3 vols. London: Bell and Sons.

Buschan, Georg. 1926. *Illustrierte Völkerkunde.* Stuttgart, Germany: Strecker and Schröder.

Butler, Bill. 1975. *The Definitive Tarot: The Origins of Tarot and Its Inner Meaning.* London: Rider.

Cadbury, Tabitha. 2012. "The Charms of Scarborough, London, etc.: The Collecting Networks of Charles Clarke and Edward Lovett." *Journal of Museum Ethnology* 25: 119–137.

———. 2015. "Amulets: The Material Evidence." In *Physical Evidence for Ritual Acts: Sorcery and Witchcraft in Christian Britain,* edited by Ronald Hutton, 188–208. Basingstoke, England: Palgrave Macmillan.

Campbell, John Gregorson. 1900. *Superstitions of the Highlands and Islands.* Glasgow, Scotland: J. MacLehose.

Caplan, Jane, ed. 2000. *Written on the Body: The Tattoo in European and American History.* London: Reaktion Books.

Carew, Richard. (1602) 1969. *The Survey of Cornwall.* London: Adams & Dart.

Carman, Bliss. 1896. *More Songs from Vagabondia.* Boston: Copeland & Day.

Carpenter, Edward. 1912. *The Art of Creation: Essays on the Self and Its Powers.* London: George Allan.

Carr-Gomm, Philip, and Sir Richard Heygate. 2010. *The Book of English Magic.* London: John Murray.

Carter, H. R. 1916. "English Horse Amulets." *The Connoisseur,* July: xxx.

Cassecanarie, Myal Djumboh. n.d. *Obeah Simplified: The True Wanga.* Port of Spain, Trinidad and Tobago: Mirror Office. Reprinted by The Society of Esoteric Endeavour.

Cassidy, F. S., and R. B. Le Page. 2002. *Dictionary of Jamaican English.* Kingston, Jamaica: University of the West Indies Press.

Cheape, Hugh. 1993. "The Red Book of Appin: Medicine as Magic and Magic as Medicine." *Folklore* 104 (1/2): 111–23.

Cielo, Astra. 1918. *Signs, Omens, and Superstitions.* New York: George Sully.

Chadwick, H. M. 1899. *The Cult of Othin.* Cambridge: Cambridge University Press.

Champeaux, J. 1982. *Fortuna: Recherches sur le culte de la Fortuna à Rome et dans le monde romaine des origines à la mort de César.* Vol. I. Rome: École Française de Rome.

———. 1987. *Fortuna: Les transformations de Fortuna sous le république.* Vol. II. Rome: École Française de Rome.

Chapman, Rod. 2007. *Seven: An Idiosyncratic Look at the Number Seven.* North Elmham, England: Seven Star Publishing.

Chireau, Yvonne P. 2003. *Black Magic: Religion and the African-American Conjuring Tradition.* Berkeley: University of California Press.

Chishti, Fazlullāh Sābri. 2011. *The Permissability of Amulets and Ruqya in Islam.* Mumbai, India: Raza Publications.

Chomsky, Noam. 1977. "Objectivity and Liberal Scholarship." *Cienfuegos Press Anarchist Review* 1 (3): 38–58.

Christian, Paul. (1870) 1972. *The History and Practice of Magic.* Translated and edited by James Kirkup, Julian Shaw, and Ross Nichols. Secaucus, N.J.: The Citadel Press.

Chumbley, Andrew. 2000. *Grimoire of the Golden Toad.* London: Xoanon Publishing.

Clark, H. P. (ca. 1820) 1930. "Old Sussex Harvest Customs." *The Sussex County Magazine* IV: 796–97.

Clarke, Mike, and Sam Yates. 2009. *Brightwork: Traditional Paintwork on Leeds and Liverpool Canal Boats.* Barnoldswick, England: Milepost Research.

Colles, Abraham. 1887. "A Witches' Ladder." *The Folk-Lore Journal* 5: 1–5.

Colquhoun, Ithell. 1957. *The Living Stones.* London: Peter Owen.

Cook, Martin Godfrey. 2015. *Edward Prior: Arts and Crafts Architect.* Marlborough, England: Crowood Press.

Coombs, Rose E. B. 1983. *Before Endeavours Fade.* London: After the Battle.

Cooper, Emmanuel. 1994. *People's Art: Working-Class Art from 1750 to the Present Day.* Edinburgh and London: Mainstream Publishing.

Cooper, Robert L. D. 2006. *Cracking the Freemasons' Code.* London: Rider.

Corrie, John. 1891. "Folk-Lore of Glencairn." *Transactions of the Dumfries and Galloway Natural History and Antiquarian Society (1890–1891):* 37–45, 75–83.

Corso, Raffaele. 1926. "La rinascita della superstizione nell'Ultra Guerra." *Bylichnis* 9: 81–98. Cramer, Daniel. (1617) 1991. *The Rosicrucian Emblems of Daniel Cramer.* Translated by Fiona Tait. Introduction and commentary by Adam McLean. Grand Rapids, Mich.: Phanes Press.

Croker, T. Crofton. 1826–1828. *Fairy Legends and Traditions of the South of Ireland.* 3 vols. London: John Murray.

Crowley, Aleister. (1911) 2018. *The Book of Lies.* In *Diary of a Drug Fiend and Other Works by Aleister Crowley,* 624–822. London: Arcturus.

Crupi, Gianfranco. 2016. "Mirabili Visioni: From Movable Books to Movable Texts." *Italian Journal of Library Information* 7: 26–86.

Cummins, Genevieve, and Nerylla D. Taunton. 1994. *Chatelaines: Utility to Glorious Extravagance.* Boston: Museum of Fine Arts.

Cumont, F. 1919. "Mithra ou Serapis Kosmokrator." Comptes Rendus des séances de l'Academie des Inscriptions et Belles-Lettres, 1919: 322.

Dalyell, John Graham. 1834. *The Darker Superstitions of Scotland: Illustrated from History and Practice.* Edinburgh: Waugh and Innes.

Dancik, Robert. 2009. *Amulets and Talismans: Simple Techniques for Creating Meaningful Jewelry.* Cincinnati, Ohio: North Light Books.

Daniels, Cora Lynn, and C. M. Stevens, eds. 1903. *Encyclopedia of Superstitions, Folk-Lore, and the Occult Sciences of the World.* 2 vols. Chicago: J. H. Yewdale & Sons.

Dasen, Véronique, and Árpád Nagy. 2019. *Gems.* In *Guide to the Study of Ancient Magic,* edited by David Frankfurter, 416–55. Leiden, the Netherlands: Brill.

Da Silva, Francesco Vaz. 2013. "Charming the Moon: Moon Charms for Sick Children in Portuguese Ethnography." In *The Power of Words: Studies in Charms and Charming in Europe,* edited by James Alexander Kapaló, Éva Pócs, and William Francis Ryan, 257–63. Budapest, Hungary, and New York: Central Europe University Press.

Dauzat, Albert. 1919. *Legendes, prophéties, et superstition de la guerre.* Paris: Le Renaissance du Livre.

Davidson, Hilda Ellis. 1988. *Myths and Symbols in Pagan Europe.* Syracuse, N.Y.: Syracuse University Press.

Davídsson, Ólafur. 1903. "Isländischer Zauberzeichen und Zauberbücher." *Zeitschrift des Vereins für Volkskunde* 13: 150–67.

Davies, Owen. 1996. "Healing Charms Used in England and Wales 1700–1950." *Folklore* 107: 19–32.

———. 2003. *Cunning Folk: Popular Magic in English History*. London: Hambledon.

———. 2018. *A Supernatural War: Magic, Divination, and Faith during the First World War*. Oxford: Oxford University Press.

Davis, Francis. 2003. *The History of the Blues*. Cambridge, Mass.: Da Capo Press.

Dawson, Warren R. 1927. *Mummy as a Drug. Proceedings of the Royal Society of Medicine* 21 (1): 34–39.

Day, George. 1894. "Notes on the Essex Dialect and Folk-Lore, with Some Account of the Divining Rod." *The Essex Naturalist* 8: 71–85.

De Cuba, Johannes. Circa 1490. *Hortus Santitatis*. Paris: n.p.

De La Salle, Laisnel. 1875. *Croyances et légendes du centre de la France*. Paris: Imprimerie et Librairie Centrale des Chemins de Fer.

De Martino, Ernesto. 1948. *Il mondo magico: Prolegemeni a una storia del magismo*. Turin, Italy: Einaudi.

De Mello, Margo. 2000. *Bodies of Inscription: A Cultural History of the Modern Tattoo Community*. Durham, N.C., and London: Duke University Press.

Dennis, Victoria Solt. 2005. *Discovering Friendly and Fraternal Societies*. Shire, England: Prince's Risborough.

Dent, A. 1964. *The Lost Beasts of Britain*. London: Harrap.

Deren, Maya. 1975. *The Voodoo Gods*. London: Paladin.

De Simonis, Paolo, and Fabio Dei. 2010. "Wartime Folklore: Italian Anthropology and the First World War." In *Doing Anthropology in Wartime and War Zones—World War I and the Cultural Sciences in Europe*, edited by Reinhard Johler, Christian Marchett, and Monique Scheer, 75–99. Bielefeld, Germany: Transcript Verlag.

Dickens, Bruce. 1915. *Runic and Heroic Poems*. Cambridge: Cambridge University Press.

Diószegi, V., ed. 1968. *Popular Beliefs in Siberia*. Bloomington: Indiana University Press.

Diprose, Ted. 2006. "Hanging a Horseshoe." *Silver Wheel* 77: 18–19.

Di Signano, Giuseppe, and David Sulzberger. 1977. *Car Mascots: An Enthusiast's Guide*. New York: Crescent Books.

Douglass, Frederick. (1845) 1973. *Narrative of the Life of Frederick Douglass: An American Slave*. Garden City, N.Y.: Anchor Books.

Drake-Carnell, F. J. 1938. *Old English Customs and Ceremonies*. London: Batsford.

Duffin. Christopher John. 2013. "Chelidonius: The Swallow Stone." *Folklore* 124: 81–103.

Dyer, T. F. Thisleton. 1881. *Domestic Folk-Lore.* London, Cassell.

———. 1911. *British Popular Customs Present and Past.* London: George Bell and Sons.

Eckenstein, Lina. 1906. "Horse Brasses." *The Reliquary and Illustrated Archaeologist,* n.s., XII: 248–62.

Edwards, Gillian. 1968. *Uncumber and Pantaloon: Some Words with Stories.* London: Geoffrey Bles.

Eliason, Eric A., and Tad Tuleja, eds. 2012. *Warrior Ways: Explorations in Modern Military Folk Lore.* Logan: Utah State University Press.

Elliott, Ralph. 1959. *Runes: An Introduction.* Manchester, England: Manchester University Press.

Ellis, Bill. 2002. "Why Is a Lucky Rabbit's Foot Lucky? Body Parts as Fetishes." *Journal of Folklore Research* 39 (1): 58–59.

Elworthy, Frederick Thomas. 1895. *The Evil Eye: An Account of this Ancient and Widespread Superstition.* London: John Murray.

Ennemoser, Joseph. 1854. *The History of Magic.* 2 vols. Translated by William Howitt. London: H. C. Bohn.

Ettlinger, Ellen. 1939. "British Amulets in London Museums." *Folklore* 50 (2): 148–75.

———. 1943. "Documents of British Superstition in Oxford." *Folklore* 54 (March): 227–49.

———. 1965. "The Hildburgh Collection of Austrian and Bavarian Amulets in the Wellcome Historical Medical Museum." *Folklore* 76: 104–17.

Evans, E. P. 1896. *Animal Symbolism in Ecclesiastical Architecture.* New York: Henry Holt & Co.

———. 1906. *The Criminal Prosecution and Capital Punishment of Animals.* London: William Heinemann.

Evans, J. 1897. *Ancient Stone Implements, Weapons, and Ornaments.* London: Longmans, Green & Co.

Evans, Stewart P. 2009. *Executioner: The Chronicles of a Victorian Hangman.* Stroud, England: The History Press.

Evans-Wentz, W. Y. 1911. *The Fairy Faith in Celtic Countries.* Oxford: Oxford University Press.

Falk, A. B. 2006. *My Home Is My Castle: Protection against Evil in Medieval Times.* In *Old Norse Religion in Long-Term Perspectives: Origins, Changes, and Interactions,* edited by A. Andrén, K. Jennbert, and C. Raudvere, 200–205. Lund, Sweden: Nordic Academic Press.

Fanger, Clare, ed. 1998. *Conjuring Spirits: Texts and Traditions of Medieval Ritual Magic.* London: Thrupp.

Farelli, Marie Helena. 1977. *O livro dos amuletos e dos talismãs.* Rio de Janiero, Brazil: Pallas.

Farrell, Nick. 2001. *Making Talismans: Living Entities of Power.* St. Paul, Minn.: Llewellyn Publications.

Felix, Richard. 1998. *Derby: The Crossroads of History.* Derby, England: Derby Heritage Centre.

Fernandes. Martin de Cuenca. 1722. *Historia sagrada de la Santissima Cruz de Caravaca.* Madrid, Spain: Juan Garcia Infançon.

Fiske, Willard. 1905. *Chess in Iceland and in Icelandic Literature: With Historical Notes on Other Table Games.* Florence, Italy: The Florentine Typographical Society.

Fleming, Juliet. 2000. "The Renaissance Tattoo." In *Written on the Body: The Tattoo in European and American History,* edited by Jane Caplan, 61–82. London: Reaktion Books.

Flowers, Stephen. 1989. *The Galdrabók: An Icelandic Grimoire.* York Beach, Maine: Samuel Weiser.

———. 2011. *Runes and Magic: Magical Formulaic Elements in the Older Runic Tradition.* Bastrop, Tex.: Lodestar.

———. 2016. *Icelandic Magic: Practical Secrets of the Northern Grimoires.* Rochester, Vt.: Inner Traditions.

Frankfurter, David, ed. 2019. *Guide to the Study of Ancient Magic.* Leiden, the Netherlands: Brill.

Franklin, Anna. 2002. *The Illustrated Encyclopedia of Fairies.* London: Vega.

Frazier, Paul. 1952. "Some Lore of Hexing and Powwowing." *Midwest Folklore* 2 (2): 101–7.

Freeman, Charles. 2011. *Holy Bones, Holy Dust: How Relics Shaped the History of Medieval Europe.* New Haven, Conn., and London: Yale University Press.

Gandee, Lee R. 1971. *Strange Experiences: The Autobiography of a Hexenmeister.* Englewood Cliffs, N.J.: Prentice-Hall.

Gerish, W. B. 1895. "A Churchyard Charm." *Folk-Lore* 6: 200.

Gerlach, Martin, ed. 1971. *Primitive and Folk Jewelry.* New York: Dover.

Gerner, Manfred. 1983. *Farbiges Fachwerk.* Stuttgart, Germany: Deutsche Verlaganstalt.

———. 2003. *Formen, Schmuck, und Symbolik in Fachwerbau.* Stuttgart, Germany: Fraunhofer Informationszentrum Raum und Bau.

Gettings, Fred. 1981. *Dictionary of Occult, Hermetic, and Alchemical Sigils.* London: Routledge & Kegan Paul.

Gimelli, Agostino. 1917. *Il nostro soldato: Saggi di psicologia miltare.* Milan, Italy: Treves.

Glanvil, Joseph. 1681. *Saducismus Triumphatus, or Full and Plain Evidence Concerning Witches and Apparitions.* London: Thomas Newcombe.

Glazier, Ken. 1995. *The Last Years of the General.* Harrow Weald, England: Capital Transport Publishing.

González-Wippler, Migene. 2003. *The Complete Book of Amulets and Talismans.* St. Paul, Minn.: Llewellyn Publications.

Goodrich-Freer, A. 1899. "The Powers of Evil in the Outer Hebrides." *Folk-Lore* 10, no. 3 (September): 259–82.

Grambo, Ronald. 1979. *Norsk trollformer og magiske ritualer.* Oslo, Norway: Universitetsforlaget.

Green, C. 1968. *Out-of-the-Body Experiences.* Oxford, England: Institute of Psychophysical Research.

Gregor, Walter. 1881. *Notes on the Folk-Lore of North-East Scotland.* London: The Folk-Lore Society.

Grieve, Maud. 1931. *A Modern Herbal.* London: Jonathan Cape, Ltd.

Griffinhoofe, H. G. 1894. "Breeding Stone." *The Essex Review* III: 144.

Grist, Tony, and Aileen Grist. 2000. *The Illustrated Guide to Witchcraft: The Secrets of Wicca and Paganism Revealed.* Newton Abbot, England: Godsfield Press.

Groves, Derham. 1991. *Feng-Shui and Western Building Ceremonies.* Singapore and Lutterworth, England: Graham Brash and Tynron Press.

Guichard, Bernardette. 1991. *Amulettes et talismans—La collection Lionel Bonnemère.* Paris: Réunion des Museés Nationaux.

Guidon. (Rome, 1670) 2011. *Magic Secrets and Counter-Charms.* Hinckley, England: The Society of Esoteric Endeavour.

Gunston, Bill. 1982. *Aircraft of World War II.* London: Octopus Books.

Gunther, R. T. 1905. "The Cimaruta: Its Structure and Development." *Folk-Lore* 16 (2): 132–61.

Gurdon, Lady Camilla. 1892. "Folk-Lore from South-East Suffolk." *Folk-Lore* 3 (4): 558–60.

Gutch, Mrs., coll. and ed. 1901. *Folk-Lore of Yorkshire. North Riding. Publications of the Folk-Lore Society County Folk-Lore.* Vol. II. London: David Nutt.

———. 1911. *Folk-Lore of Yorkshire. East Riding. Publications of the Folk-Lore Society County Folk-Lore.* Vol. VI. London: David Nutt.

Hall, Alaric. 2007. *Elves in Anglo-Saxon England: Matters of Belief, Health, Gender, and Identity.* Woodbridge, England: Boydell Press.

Hallowell, A. Irving. 1926. "Bear Ceremonialism in the Northern Hemisphere." *American Anthropologist,* n.s., 28 (1): 1–175.

Hamerman, Eric J., and Carey K. Morwedge. 2015. "Reliance on Luck: Identifying Which Achievement Goals Elicit Superstitious Behaviour." *Personality and Social Psychology Bulletin* 41 (3): 323–35.

Hargrave, John. 1920. *The Boys' Book of Signs and Symbols.* London: C. A. Pearson.

Harland, John, and T. T. Wilkinson. 1867. *Lancashire Folk-Lore.* London: Frederick Warne.

Hart, Cyril. 2004. "Edward (Saint Edward, Called Edward the Martyr)." In *The Oxford Dictionary of National Biography:* 783–85. Oxford: Oxford University Press.

Harvey, David Allan. 2005. "Fortune-Tellers in the French Courts: Antidivination Prosecutions in France in the Nineteenth and Twentieth Centuries." *French Historical Studies* 28 (1): 131–57.

Hasenfratz, Hans-Peter. 2011. *Barbarian Rites: The Spiritual World of the Vikings and the Germanic Tribes.* Translated by Michael Moynihan. Rochester, Vt.: Inner Traditions.

Healy, Margaret. 2016. "Wearing Powerful Words and Objects: Healing Prosthetics." *Textual Practice* 30 (7): 1233–51.

Heather, P. J. 1903. "Transmigration Belief in East Anglia." *Folk-Lore* 14: 63–64.

Hegele, A. 1997. "Belemniten in Volksglauben und Volksmedizin." *Fossilien* 1: 21–26.

Heidegger, Martin. 1927. *Sein und Zeit.* Halle, Germany: Max Niemeyer.

———. 1967. *What Is a Thing?* Chicago: Henry Regnery and Co.

———. 1987. *Being and Time.* London: Blackwell.

Henderson, William. 1879. *Notes on the Folk-Lore of the Northern Counties of England and the Borders: A New Edition with Many Additional Notes.* London: W. Satchell, Peyton and Co.

Hennels, C. E. 1972. "The Wild Herb Men." *The East Anglian Magazine* 32: 79–80.

Hermann, Paul. 1929. *Das altgermanische Priesterwesen.* Jena, Germany: Diederichs.

Herr, Karl. 2002. *Hex and Spellwork: The Magic Practices of the Pennsylvania Dutch*. York Beach, Maine: Red Wheel/ Weiser.

Herrick, Robert. (1648) 1902. *The Poems of Robert Herrick*. London: Grant Richards.

Hewett, Sarah. 1900. *Nummits and Crummits: Devonshire Customs*. London: Thomas Burleigh.

Hieronymussen, Paul. 1967. *Orders, Medals, and Decorations of Britain and Europe*. London: Blandford Press.

Hildburgh, W. L. 1906. "Notes on Spanish Amulets." *Folk-Lore* 17: 454–71.

———. 1908a. "Notes on Contemporary Portuguese Amulets." *Folk-Lore* 19: 213–24.

———. 1908b. "Notes on Some Flemish Amulets and Beliefs." *Folk-Lore* 19: 200–13.

———. 1944. "Indeterminability and Confusion as Apotropaic Elements in Italy and Spain." *Folk-Lore* 55: 133–49.

Hill, Douglas, and Pat Williams. 1965. *The Supernatural*. London: Aldus Books.

Hobsbawm, E. J., and G. Rudé. 1969. *Captain Swing*. London: Lawrence and Wishart.

Hodson, Geoffrey. 1925. *Fairies at Work and Play*. London: Theosophical Publishing House.

Hoggard, Brian. 2004. "The Archaeology of Counter-Witchcraft and Popular Magic." In *Beyond the Witch Trials: Witchcraft and Magic in Enlightenment Europe*. Edited by Owen Davies and William De Blécourt, 167–86. Manchester, England: Manchester University Press.

———. 2019. *Magical House Protection: The Archaeology of Counter-Witchcraft*. New York and Oxford, England: Berghahn Books.

Hole, Christina. 1977. "Protective Symbols in the Home." In *Symbols of Power*, edited by H. R. Ellis-Davidson, 124–36. London: The Folklore Society.

Horst, Georg Conrad. 1821–1826. *Zauber Bibliothek. Von Zauberei, Theurgie und Mantik, Zauberen, Hexen und Hexenprozessen, Dämonen, Gespenstern, und Geistererscheinigungen*. 7 vols. Mainz, Germany: Florian Kupferberg.

Houlbrook, Ceri, and Rebecca Shawcross. 2018. "Revealing the Ritually Concealed: Custodians, Conservators, and the Concealed Shoe." *Material Religion: The Journal of Objects, Art, and Belief* 14: 163–82.

Howard, Margaret. 1951. "Dried Cats." *Man* 61: 149–51.

Howat, Polly. 1998. *Ghosts and Legends of Cambridgeshire*. Newbury, England: Countryside Books.

Howe, Ellic. 1964. *Raphael, or the Royal Merlin*. London: Arborfield.

Hukantaival, Sonja. 2015. "Frogs in Miniature Coffins from Churches in Finland." *Mirator* 16 (1): 192–220.

———. 2018. "The Materiality of Finnish Folk Magic: Objects in the Collections of the National Museums of Finland." *Material Religion: The Journal of Objects, Art, and Belief* 14: 183–98.

Hultkrantz, Åke. 1961. *The Supernatural Owners of Nature*. Stockholm, Sweden: Almqvist & Wiksell.

Hurston, Zora N. 1931. "Hoodoo in America." *The Journal of American Folklore* 44: 317–417.

———. 1943. "High John de Conker." *American Mercury* 57: 450–59.

Hutton, Ronald, ed. 2015. *Physical Evidence for Ritual Acts, Sorcery, and Witchcraft in Christian Britain*. Basingstoke, England: Palgrave Macmillan.

Hyatt, Harry Middleton. 1970–1978. *Hoodoo, Conjuration, Witchcraft, Rootwork*. 5 vols. New York: Memoirs of the Alma Egan Hyatt Foundation.

Inman, Thomas. 1875. *Ancient Pagan and Modern Christian Symbolism, with an Essay on Baal Worship, on the Assyrian Sacred "Grove" and Other Allied Symbols*. New York: J. W. Bouton.

Ivanits, Linda J. 1989. *Russian Folk Belief*. Armonk, N.Y.: M. E. Sharpe.

Ivanov, S. V. 1978. "Elementy zaschitnogo dospekha v shamanskoi odedzhdo narodov zapadnoi i luzhnoi Sibiri" (Shamanic costume of the western and southern Siberian tribes as protective armor). In *Etnografiia narodov Altaia i zapadnoi Sibir,* edited by A. P. Okladnikov, 136–68. Novosibirsk, Russia: Nauka.

Jacobsen-Widding, Anita. 1979. *Red-White-Black as a Mode of Thought*. Uppsala Studies in Cultural Anthropology I. Stockholm, Sweden: Almqvist and Wiksell.

Jaguer, Jeff. 1990. *The Tattoo: A Pictorial History*. Horndean, England: Milestone.

Jayne, Caroline Furness. 1906. *String Figures: A Study of Cats' Cradles in Many Lands*. New York: Charles Scribner's Sons.

Jekyll, Gertrude. 1904. *Old West Surrey*. London: Longmans, Green & Co.

Johnston, Walter. 1912. *Byways in British Archaeology*. Cambridge: Cambridge University Press.

Jones-Baker, Doris. 1977. *Folklore of Herfordshire*. London: B. T. Batsford.

Jones, Ben. 2018. *X-Trains: Pushing the Boundaries of Railway Technology*. Horncastle, England: Mortons Media Group Ltd.

Jones, Charles Colcock. 1842. *The Religious Instruction of the Negroes in the United States*. Savannah, Ga.: n.p.

Jones, C. O. 2000. "Stigma and Tattoo." In *Written on the Body: The Tattoo in European and American History*, edited by Jane Caplan, 1–16. London: Reaktion Books.

Jones, Melvyn. 2004. *The Making of Sheffield*. Barnsley, England: Wharncliffe Books.

Jones, Nigel. 2004. *The Birth of the Nazis: How the Freikorps Blazed a Trail For Hitler*. London: Robinson.

Jones, Prudence. 1982. *Eight and Nine: Sacred Numbers of Sun and Moon in the Pagan North*. Fenris-Wolf Pagan Paper 2. Bar Hill, England: Fenris-Wolf.

Jones, Prudence, and Nigel Pennick. 1995. *A History of Pagan Europe*. London: Routledge.

Jones, Thomas Gwynn. 1930. *Welsh Folklore and Folk Customs*. London: Methuen.

Jones, William. 1877. *Finger Ring Lore: Historical, Legendary, Anecdotal*. London: Chatto & Windus.

———. 1880. *Credulities Past and Present: Including the Sea, Miners, Amulets, and Talismans*. London: Chatto & Windus.

Jung, Carl G. 1972. *Synchronicity: An Acausal Connecting Principle*. London: Routledge & Kegan Paul.

Kapaló, James Alexander, Éva Pócs, and William Francis Ryan, eds. 2013. *The Power of Words: Studies in Charms and Charming in Europe*. Budapest, Hungary, and New York: Central Europe University Press.

Kay, David, and Kay Springate. 2018. *Automotive Mascots: A Collector's Guide to British Marques, Corporate and Accessory Mascots*. Dorchester, England: Veloce Publishing.

Keegan, Terry. 1973. *The Heavy Horse: Its Harness and Harness Decoration*. London: Pelham Books.

Keyhoe, Alice Beck. 2006. *The Ghost Dance: Ethnohistory and Revitalization*. Long Grove, Ill.: Waveland Press Inc.

Kieckhefer, Richard. 1997. *Forbidden Rites: A Necromancer's Manual of the Fifteenth Century*. University Park: Pennsylvania University Press.

King, Francis. 1971. *Rites of Modern Occult Magic*. New York: Macmillan.

Kirwin, W. Chandler. 1997. *Powers Matchless: The Pontificate of Urban VIII, the Baldachin, and Gian Lorenzo Bernini*. New York: Peter Lang.

Klotz, David. 2006. *Adoration of the Ram: Five Hymns to Amun-Re from Hibis Temple*. New Haven, Conn.: Yale Egyptological Studies.

Knutson, Sarah Ann. 2019. "The Materiality of Myth: Divine Objects in Norse Mythology." *Temenos* 55 (1): 29–53.

Koch, Rudolf. 1930. *The Book of Signs.* London: The First Edition Club.

Kodolányi, J., Jr. 1968. *Khanty (Ostyak) Sheds for Sacrificial Objects.* In *Popular Beliefs in Siberia,* edited by V. Diószegi, 103–6. Bloomington: Indiana University Press.

Köhler, Johann August Ernst. 1867. *Volksbrauch, Abergalauben, Sagen, und andere alter Nieberlieferungen im Voigtlande.* Leipzig, Germany: Verlag von Fr Fleischer.

Koudounaris, Paul. 2013. *Heavenly Bodies: Cult Treasures and Spectacular Saints from the Catacombs.* New York and London: Thames & Hudson.

Kõuts, Eric, and Heinz Valk. 1998. *Rist ja raud* (Cross and iron). Tallinn, Estonia: SE & JS.

Krappe, Alexander H. 1941. "Irish Earth." *Folklore* 52 (3): 229–36.

Krause, Rhett. 1996. "Traditional and Invented Sword Locks." *Rattle Up My Boys* 6 (1): 1–7.

Krutak, Lars, and Aaron Deter-Wolf. 2017. *Ancient Ink: The Archaeology of Tattooing.* Seattle and London: University of Washington Press.

Kummer, Siegfried. 1993. *Rune Magic.* Smithville, Tex.: Rûna-Raven.

Kunz, George Frederick. 1913. *The Curious Lore of Precious Stones: Being a Description of their Sentiments and Folk Lore, Superstitions, Symbolism . . .* Philadelphia and London: J. B. Lippincott Company.

Kürzdeder, Christoph. 2005. *Als die Dinge heilig waren: Gelebte Frömmigkeit im Zeitalter des Barock.* Regensburg, Germany: Schnell & Steiner.

Lachatañere, Romulu. 1942. *Manual de Santeria.* Havana, Cuba: Editorial Caribe.

Lakoff, George, and Mark Johnson. 1980. *Metaphors We Live By.* Chicago: Chicago University Press.

Lambert, Margaret, and Enid Marx. 1989. *English Popular Art.* London: Merlin Press.

Lambeth, M. 1969. *A Golden Dolly: The Art, Mystery, and History of Corn Dollies.* London: John Baker.

Lane, Edward William. (1836) 1908. *The Manners and Customs of the Modern Egyptians.* New York: E. P. Dutton.

Langford, J. A. 1875. "Warwickshire Folk-Lore and Superstitions." *Transactions of the Birmingham and Midlands Institute* 6: 9–24.

Larwood, Jacob, and John Camden Hotten. (1908) 1985. *The History of*

Signboards: From the Earliest Times to the Present Day. New York: Arco Publishing.

Latham, Charlotte. 1878. "Some West Sussex Superstitions Lingering in 1868." *Folk-Lore Record* 1: 1–67.

Laurie, William Alexander. 1859. *History of Freemasonry and the Grand Lodge of Scotland.* London: E. Spencer; Calcutta, India: R. C. Lepage and Co.

Lawrence, Robert Means. 1898. *The Magic of the Horse Shoe: With Other Folk-Lore Notes.* Boston: Houghton Mifflin.

Leather, Ella Mary. 1912. *The Folk-Lore of Herefordshire.* Hereford, England: Jakeman and Carver; London: Sidgwick and Jackson.

———. 1914. "Foundation Sacrifice." *Folk-Lore* 24: 110.

Le Braz, Anatole. 1982. *La légende de la mort chez les Bretons Armoricains.* Marseille, France: Lafitte.

Lecouteux, Claude. 2013. *The Tradition of Household Spirits.* Rochester, Vt.: Inner Traditions.

———. 2014. *The High Magic of Talismans and Amulets: Tradition and Craft.* Rochester, Vt.: Inner Traditions.

———. 2015. *Demons and Spirits of the Land.* Rochester, Vt.: Inner Traditions.

Lee, Rev. Frederick George, ed. 1875. *Glimpses of the Supernatural.* 2 vols. London: Henry S. King and Co.

Lefévre-Pontalis, Pierre. 1900. *Receuil de talismans Laotiens.* Paris: Ernest Leroux.

Leland, Charles Godfrey. 1887. "The Witches' Ladder." *The Folk-Lore Journal* 5: 257–59.

———. 1891. *Gypsy Sorcery and Fortune Telling: Illustrated by Numerous Incantations, Specimens of Medical Magic, Anecdotes, and Tales.* New York: Charles Scribner's Sons.

Lethaby, William Richard. 1891. *Architecture, Mysticism and Myth.* New York: Macmillan.

———. 1911. *Architecture: An Introduction to the History and Theory of the Art of Building.* London: Williams & Norgate.

Lewery, A. J. 1991. *Popular Art: Past and Present.* Newton Abbot, England: David and Charles.

Lidén, H. 1969. "From Pagan Sanctuary to Christian Church: The Excavation of Maere Church, Trondelag." *Norwegian Archaeological Review* 2: 23–32.

Lilly, William. 1822. *William Lilly's History of His Life and Times from the Year 1602 to 1681.* London: Charles Baldwyn.

Lindig, Erika. 1987. *Hausgeister: Die Vorstellung übernaturlicher Schützer und Helfer in der deutschen Sagenüberlieferung.* Frankfurt and Bern, Germany: Peter Lang.

Lip, Evelyn. 1979. *Chinese Geomancy.* Singapore: Times Books International.

Lithgow, William. (1640) 1906. *The Totall Discourse of the Rare Adventures and Painefull Peregrinations of Long Nineteen Yeares Travayles form Scotland to the Most Famous Kingdomes in Europe, Asia and Affrica.* Glasgow, Scotland: J. MacLehose.

Livingstone, Karen. 2011. *The Bookplates and Badges of C. F. A. Voysey Architect and Designer of the Arts and Crafts Movement.* Woodbridge, England: The Antiques Collectors' Club.

———. 2013. *V&A Patterns: C. F. A. Voysey.* London: Victoria and Albert Museum.

Livingstone, Karen, Max Donnelly, and Linda Parry. 2016. *C. F. A. Voysey: Arts and Crafts Designer.* London: Victoria and Albert Museum.

Long, Edward. 1774. *The History of Jamaica.* 3 vols. London: Lowndes.

Loomis, C. Grant. 1948. *White Magic: An Introduction to the Folklore of Christian Legend.* Cambridge, Mass.: Medieval Academy of America.

Louandre, Charles Leopold. 1853. *La sorcellarie.* Paris: Librairie de L. Hachette et Cie.

Lovett, Edward. 1903. "Fetish Worship in Central Africa." *Folk-Lore* 14: 60–63.

———. 1909. "Amulets from Costers' Barrows in London, Rome, and Naples." *Folk-Lore* 20: 70-71.

———. 1925. *Magic in Modern London.* Croydon, England: Croydon Advertiser.

———. 1928. *Folklore and Legends of the Surrey Hills and of the Sussex Downs and Forests.* Caterham, England: Caterham Printing Works.

Lupton, Thomas, Edward Somerset, Worcester, and George Edwards. 1815. *A Thousand Notable Things on Various Subjects.* London: Walker, Edwards and Reynolds.

Lyndoe, Edward. 1935. *Everybody's Book of Fate and Fortune.* London: Odhams.

MacAldowie, Alex. 1896. "Personal Experiences in Witchcraft." *Folk-Lore* 7 (3): 309–14.

Mackenzie, William. 1895. *Gaelic Incantations, Charms, and Blessings of the Hebrides.* Inverness, Scotland: Northern Counties Newspaper.

Macleod, Mindy, and Bernard Mees. 2006. *Runic Amulets and Magic Objects.* Woodbridge, England: The Boydell Press.

Macleod, Sharon Pace. 2018. *Celtic Cosmology and the Otherworld: Mythic*

Origins, Sovereignty, and Liminality. Jefferson, N.C.: McFarland & Co., Inc.

MacPherson, Joseph McKenzie. 1929. *Primitive Beliefs in the North East of Scotland.* Edinburgh, Scotland: Longmans, Green & Co.

Madden, R. R. 1835. *A Twelve Months' Residence in the West Indies.* London: Cochrane.

Malaguzzi, Silvia. 2008. *Bijoux, pierres, et objets précieux: Representation et symbole.* Paris: Editions Hazan.

Malraux, André. 1954. *The Voices of Silence.* London: Secker & Warburg.

March, H. Colley. 1899. "Dorset Folk-Lore Collected in 1897." *Folk-Lore* 10 (4): 478–89.

Marquis, Amy. 2009. *Lumière: Lithographs by Odilon Redon.* Cambridge, England: Fitzwilliam Museum.

Martin, Stephen A., ed. 2001: *Archibald Knox.* London, Artmedia Press.

Martinot, Lucien, George Weber, and Philippe George. 1996. *Le clé de Saint Hubert: Feuillets de la Cathédrale de Liège.* Liège, Belgium: Trésor de la Cathédrale de Liège.

Mason, Hugo. 2001. *All Saints' Church, Brockhampton, Herefordshire.* Brockhampton, England: Brockhampton Parochial Church Council.

Mathers, Samuel Liddel MacGregor. 1997. *The Goetia: The Lesser Key of Solomon the King.* Edited by Aleister Crowley. York Beach, Maine: Samuel Weiser.

Mayhew, Henry. 1861–1862. *London Labour and the London Poor: Cyclopedia of the Conduct and Earnings of Those That Will Work, Those That Cannot Work, and Those That Will Not Work.* 4 vols. London: Griffin, Bohn and Co.

Mayr, Rolf. 1934. "Hausmarken von Kobern." *Germanien* 1934: 101–9.

McAdoo, W. G. 1913. Treasury Decisions under Customs and Other Laws, 24, January–June 1913. Washington, D.C.: Government Printing Office.

McFadzean, Patrick. 1984. "Heraldry and the Planetary Colours." *The Symbol* 4: 19–20.

McMahon, E. O. 1914. *Christian Missions in Madagascar.* London: The Society for the Propagation of the Gospel in Foreign Parts.

McMahon, Seán. 2005: *The Story of the Claddagh Ring.* Cork, Ireland: Mercier Press.

McNamara, Kenneth J. 2007. *Shepherds' Crowns, Fairy Loaves, and Thunderstones: The Mythology of Fossil Echinoids.* In *Myth and Geology,* edited by L. Piccardi and B. W. Masse, 270–94. London: The Geological Society of London, Special Publications, no. 273.

McNeill, F. Marian. 1957–1968. *The Silver Bough.* 4 vols. Glasgow, Scotland: William MacLellan.

Meany, A. L. 1981. *Anglo-Saxon Amulets and Curing Stones.* London: BAR British Series, no. 94.

Meehan, Fr. Joseph. 1906. "The Cure of Elf-Shooting in the North West of Ireland." *Folk-Lore* 17: 200–210.

Merrifield, Ralph. 1988. *The Archaeology of Ritual and Magic.* New York: New Amsterdam Books.

Mitchell, Stephen. 2011. *Witchcraft and Magic in the Nordic Middle Ages.* Philadelphia: University of Pennsylvania Press.

Miranda, Michelle D. 2016. *Forensic Analysis of Tattoos and Tattoo Inks.* Boca Raton, La., New York, and London: CRC Press.

Mooney, James. 1896. *The Ghost-Dance: Religion and the Sioux Outbreak of 1890.* Washington, D.C.: The Government Printing Office.

Morgan, A. 1995. *Toads and Toadstools: The Natural History, Folklore, and Cultural Oddities of a Strange Association.* Berkeley, Calif.: Celestial Arts.

Morgan, Prys. 1983. "A Welsh Snakestone, Its Tradition and Folklore." *Folklore* 94 (2): 184–91.

Morgan, W. E. T. 1895a. "Charms." *Folk-Lore* 6, no. 2 (June): 202–4.

———. 1895b. "Charms." *Folk-Lore* 6, no. 3 (September): 304.

Morris, Desmond. 1999. *Body Guards: Protective Amulets and Charms.* Shaftesbury, England: Element.

Mortimer, Bishop Robert. 1972. *Exorcism: The Report of a Commission Convened by the Bishop of Exeter.* Edited by Dom Robert Petitpierre. London: The Society for Promoting Christian Knowledge.

Moss, Fletcher. 1898. *Folk-Lore, Old Customs, and Tales of My Neighbours.* Didsbury, England: The Old Parsonage.

Mota, Jordi, and Maria Infiesta. 1995. *Das Werk Richard Wagners im Spiegel der Kunst.* Tübingen, Germany: Grabert Verlag.

Mowl, Tim, and Brian Earnshaw. 1988. *John Wood: Architect of Obsession.* Bath, England: Millstream Books.

Mullen, Redmond. 1978. *Miracles and Magic.* London and Oxford: Mowbray.

Munro, Jane. 2006. *Chasing Happiness: Maurice Maeterlinck, the Blue Bird, and England.* Cambridge, England: The Fitzwilliam Museum.

Napier, A. David. 1986. *Marks, Transformation, and Paradox*. Berkeley: University of California Press.

Nataf, André. 1994. *Dictionary of the Occult*. Translated by John Davidson. Ware, England: Wordsworth Editions.

Neat, Timothy. 2002. *The Horseman's Word*. Edinburgh, Scotland: Birlinn.

Nesbit, Edith. 1906. *The Story of the Amulet*. London: T. Fisher Unwin.

Neville-Rolfe, Eustace, and Holcombe Ingleby. 1899. *Naples in 1888*. Napoli, Italy: E. Prass.

Newall, Venetia. 1978. "Some Examples of the Practice of Obeah by West Indian Immigrants in London." *Folklore* 89: 29–51.

Newman, Leslie. 1940. "Notes on Some Rural and Trade Initiation Ceremonies in the Eastern Counties." *Folklore* 51 (3): 32–42.

Nicholson, John. 1890. *Folk-Lore of East Yorkshire*. London: Simpkin Marshall.

Nioradze, Georg. 1925. *Der Schamanismus bei den sibirischen Völkern*. Stuttgart, Germany: Strecker und Schröder.

Novati, Francesco. 1904. *Studi Medievali*. Torino: E. Loescher.

Nutting, Wallace. 1924. *Pennsylvania Beautiful*. Framingham, Mass.: Old America Co.

Nylén, Erik, and Jan Peter Lamm. 1981. *Bildsteine auf Gotland*. Neumünster, Germany: Karl Wachholz Verlag.

Oakilia [Helene Mobius]. 2006. *Herblore: Treelore—A Different Branch*. Alconbury Weston, England: Molecatcher's Cottage Crafts.

Oakley, E. R. 1991. *London County Council Tramways*. Vol. 2, *North London*. London: The London Tramways History Group.

Oakley, K. P. 1965. "The Folklore of Fossils." 2 parts. *Antiquity* 39: 9–17, 117–25.

Oatman-Stanford, Hunter. 2013. "The Killer Mobile Device for Victorian Women." *Collectors' Weekly*, May 23.

O'London, John. 1926. *London Stories Old and New*. London: George Newnes Ltd.

Otto, Rudolf. (1917) 1936. *The Idea of the Holy: An Enquiry into the Non-Rational Factor in the Idea of the Divine and Its Relation to the Rational*. London: Oxford University Press.

Page, R. I. 1973. *An Introduction to English Runes*. London: Methuen.

Paine, Sheila. 2004. *Amulets: A World of Secret Powers, Charms, and Magic*. London: Thames & Hudson.

Papanek, Victor. 1995. *The Green Impaerative*. London: Thames & Hudson.

Pavitt, William Thomas, and Kate Pavitt. 1922. *The Book of Talismans, Amulets, and Zodiacal Gems*. 2nd ed. London: Rider.

Peacock, Mabel Geraldine W. 1896. "Executed Criminals and Folk Medicine." *Folk-Lore* 6: 268–83.

———. 1897. "Omens of Death." *Folk-Lore* 8: 377–78.

———. 1908. "Amulets Used in Lincolnshire." *Folk-Lore* 19: 87–88.

Peacock, Mabel Geraldine W., Katherine Carson, and Charlotte Burne. 1901. "Customs Relating to Iron." *Folk-Lore* 12: 472–75.

Peesch, Reinhard. 1993. *The Ornament in European Folk Art*. London: Alpine Fine Arts.

Pelton, Robert. 1973. *Voodoo Charms and Talismans*. New York: Drake Publications.

Pennick, Nigel. 1986. *Skulls, Cats, and Witch Bottles*. Bar Hill, England: Nigel Pennick Editions.

———. 1989. *Practical Magic in the Northern Tradition*. Wellingboro, England: Aquarian Press.

———. 1990. *Das Runen Orakel*. With cards by Hermann Haindl. Munich, Germany: Knaur Esoterik.

———. 1991. *The Secret Lore of Runes and Other Ancient Alphabets*. London: Rider.

———. 1992a. *Magical Alphabets*. York Beach, Maine: Samuel Weiser.

———. 1992b. *Rune Magic: The History and Practice of Ancient Runic Traditions*. London: Aquarian Press.

———. 1994. *Practical Magic in the Northern Tradition*. Loughborough, England: Thoth Publications.

———. 1997. *The Celtic Saints: An Illustrated and Authoritative Guide to These Extraordinary Men and Women*. London: Thorsons.

———. 2002. "The Goddess Zisa." *Tyr* 1: 107–9.

———. 2006. *The Eldritch World*. London: Earl Shilton.

———. 2011a. *The Toadman*. Hinckley, England: The Society of Esoteric Endeavour.

———. 2011b. "The Bogey Man." *Silver Wheel* 3: 25–29.

———. 2012. "The Overlooked Histories of Snakes' Eyes and the Ace of Spades." In *The Starry Rubric Set*, edited by Gareth Bell-Jones and an Endless Supply, 22. Bourn, England: Wysing Arts Centre.

———. 2013. "The Ensouled World." *Silver Wheel* 4: 138–44.

———. 2014: *The Book of Primal Signs: The High Magic of Symbols*. Rochester, Vt.: Destiny Books.

———. 2018. "Northern Cosmology: The World Tree and Irminsul." In *Tyr: Myth—Culture—Tradition,* edited by Joshua Buckley and Michael Moynihan, 104–20. Vol. 5.

———. 2019. *Witchcraft and Secret Societies of Rural England: The Magic of Toadmen, Plough Witches, Mummers, and Bonesmen.* Rochester, Vt.: Destiny Books.

Pennick, Nigel, and Helen Field. 2003. *A Book of Beasts.* Milverton, England: Capall Bann Publishing.

Pennick, Nigel and Prof. Ir Marinus Gout. 2004. *Sacrale Geometrie: Verborgen Lijnen in de Bouwkunst.* Den Haag, the Netherlands: Synthese.

Pentikäinen, Juha. 2007. *Golden King of the Forest: The Lore of the Northern Bear.* Helsinki, Finland: Etnika Og.

Pentz, Peter. 2018. "Viking Art: Snorri Sturluson and Some Recent Metal Detector Finds." *Fornvännen Journal of Swedish Antiquarian Research* 113: 17–33.

Petrie, W. M. Flinders. 1914. *Amulets.* London: Constable & Co.

Pigorini-Beri, Catherine. 1891. *Le tatouage religieux et amoureux au pèlerinage de N.D. de Loreto.* Archives de l'Anthropologie Criminelle et des Sciences Pénales, XVI.

Pinch, G., and E. A. Waraksa. 2007. "Votive Practices." In *UCLA Encyclopedia of Egyptology,* edited by J. Dielman and W. Wendrich, 1–9. Los Angeles: UCLA Press.

Pipe, Marian. 1985. *Myths and Legends of Northamptonshire.* Stamford, England: Spiegl Press.

Pocock, W. Innes. 1906. "Cat's Cradle." *Folk-Lore* 17: 73–93.

Pokropek, M. 1988. "Interior." In *Folk Art in Poland.* Edited by Aleksandra Czeszunist-Cicha, 46–75. Warsaw, Poland: Arkady.

Pollington, Stephen. 2011. *The Elder Gods: The Otherworld in Early England.* Hockwold cum Wilton, England: Anglo-Saxon Books.

Porter, Enid. 1969. *Cambridgeshire Customs and Folklore.* Fenland material provided by W. H. Barrett. London: Routledge & Kegan Paul.

Post, W. Ellwood. 1970. *Saints, Signs, and Symbols.* London: The Society for Promoting Christian Knowledge.

Potter, Carole. 1983. *Knock on Wood: An Encyclopedia of Talismans, Charms, Superstitions, and Symbols.* New York and Toronto: Beaufort Books.

Price, A. Grenfell. 1971. *The Explorations of James Cook in the Pacific as Told by Selections of His Own Journals, 1768–1779.* New York: Dover Publications.

Pritchard, Violet. 1967. *English Medieval Graffiti.* Cambridge: Cambridge University Press.

Pull, J. H. 2003. "Shepherds' Crowns—The Survival of Belief in the Magical Virtues in Sussex." *West Sussex Geological Society Occasional Publications* 3: 33–35.

Puvel, Martin. 1976. "The Mystery of the Cross-Road." *Folklore* 87 (2): 167–77.

Quayle, Eric. 1972. *The Collector's Book of Detective Fiction.* London: November Books.

Quinn, George. 1970. "The Claddagh Ring." *The Mantle* 13: 9–13.

Radford, Edwin, and Mona Radford. 1949. *Encyclopedia of Superstitions.* New York: The Philosophical Library.

Randall, Arthur. 1966. *Sixty Years a Fenman.* Edited by Enid Porter. London: Routledge & Kegan Paul.

Randolph, Charles Brewster. 1905. "The Mandragora of the Ancients in Folk-Lore and Medicine." *Proceedings of the American Academy of Arts and Sciences* 40 (12): 487–537.

Rashford, John. 1984. "Plants, Spirits, and the Meaning of 'John' in Jamaica." *Jamaican Journal* 17 (2): 62–70.

Rayson, George. 1865a. "East Anglian Folk-Lore, no. 1. 'Weather Proverbs.'" *The East Anglian, or, Notes and Queries on Subjects Connected with the Counties of Suffolk, Cambridgeshire, Essex, and Norfolk* I: 155–62.

———. 1865b. "East Anglian Folk-Lore, no. 2. 'Omens.'" *The East Anglian, or, Notes and Queries on Subjects Connected with the Counties of Suffolk, Cambridgeshire, Essex, and Norfolk* I: 185–86.

———. 1865c. "East Anglian Folk-Lore, no. 3. 'Charms.'" *The East Anglian, or, Notes and Queries on Subjects Connected with the Counties of Suffolk, Cambridgeshire, Essex, and Norfolk* I: 214–17.

Reeves, Compton. 1997. *Pleasures and Pastimes in Medieval England.* Stroud, England: Allan Sutton Publishing.

Regardie, Israel. 1936. *The Golden Dawn.* Chicago: Aries.

———. 1972. *How to Make and Use Talismans.* London: Aquarian Press.

Reid, Anna. 2006. *The Shaman's Coat: A Native History of Siberia.* New York: Public Affairs.

Reid, Elspeth, and Flora Davidson. 1995. *The Fortunes of Cynicus: Victorian Cartoonist and Postcard Designer.* Dykehead by Kirriemuir, Scotland: Forest Lodge.

Reisner, M. G. A. 1907. *Amulets.* Cairo: Imprimerie de l'Institut Français d'Archeologie Orientale.

Rennie, William, et al. 2009. *The Society of the Horseman's Word.* Hinckley, England: The Society of Esoteric Endeavour.

Reuter, Otto Sigfrid. 1934. *Germanische Himmelskunde.* Jena, Germany: Koehler & Amerlang.

Richards, H. S. 1970. *All about Horse Brasses.* London: Drew & Hopwood.

Rider, Catherine. 2002: *Magic and Religion in Medieval England.* London: Routledge.

Robinson, May, and M. J. Walhouse. 1893. "Obeah Worship in East and West Indies." *Folk-Lore* 4, no. 2 (June): 207–18.

Roper, Charles. 1883. "On Witchcraft Superstition in Norfolk." *Harper's New Monthly Magazine* 87, no. 521 (October): 792–97.

Rosecrans, Jennipher Allan. 2000. "Wearing the Universe: Symbolic Markings in Early Modern England." In *Written on the Body: The Tattoo in European and American History,* edited by Jane Caplan. London: Reaktion Books, 46–60.

Rosen, Barbara, ed. 1991. *Witchcraft in England, 1558–1618.* New York: Taplingen.

Ross, Cathy, and Oliver Bennett. 2015. *Designing Utopia: John Hargrave and the Kibbo Kift.* London and New York: Philip Wilson Publishers.

Roud, Steve. 2003. *The Penguin Guide to the Superstitions of Britain and Ireland.* London: Penguin.

Routledge, Martin, and Elspeth Wills. 2018. *The Beautiful Badge: The Stories behind the Football Club Badge.* Durrington, England: Pitch Publishing.

Rudenko, S. I. 1970. *Frozen Tombs of Siberia: The Pazyryk Burials of Iron Age Horsemen.* London: Dent.

Rudkin, Ethel. 1936. *Lincolnshire Folklore.* Gainsborough, England: Beltons.

Rudoe, Judy. 1990. "The Limits of Belief: Religion, Magic, Myth, and Science." In *Fake? The Art of Deception,* edited by Mark Jones. London: British Museum Publications, 79–80.

Rushen, Joyce. 1984. "Folklore and Witchcraft in Tudor and Stuart England." *Popular Archaeology,* April 1984, 33–36.

Russell, Jeffrey. 1972. *Witchcraft in the Middle Ages.* Ithaca, N.Y.: Cornell University Press.

Rysdyk, Evelyn C. 2016. *The Norse Shaman: Ancient Spiritual Practices of the Northern Tradition.* Rochester Vt.: Destiny Books.

Sæmundsson, Mattias Viðar. 1992. *Galdrar á Íslandi: Íslensk galdrabók.* Reykjavík, Iceland: Almenna bókafélagið.

Sandford, Lettice. 1983. *Straw Work and Corn Dollies*. London: Batsford.

Sapere, Aude. n.d. *The Chaldaean Oracles of Zoroaster*. Edited by W. Wynn Westcott. London: Neptune Press.

Sartori, Paul. 1898. "Ueber das Bauopfer." *Zeitschrift für Ethnologie* 30: 1–54.

Saxo Grammaticus. 1905. *The Nine Books of the Danish History of Saxo Grammaticus*. Translated by Oliver Elton. New York: Norroena Society.

Schnippel, E. 1926. "Die Englische Kalenderstäbe." *Leipziger Beiträge zur Englischen Philologie:* 24–105.

Scott, Sir Walter. 1885. *Letters on Demonology and Witchcraft*. 2nd ed. London and New York: George Routledge & Sons.

Seymour, John D. 1913. *Irish Witchcraft and Demonology*. Dublin: Hodges Figgis.

Shorter, A. 1931. "Notes on Some Funerary Amulets." *Journal of Egyptian Archaeology* 21: 171–76.

Siliotti, Alberto. 1996. *Guide to the Valley of the Kings, and to the Theban Necropolises and Temples*. Luxor, Egypt: A. A. Gaddis & Sons.

Simpkins, John E. 1912. *Country Folk-Lore: Fife*. London: The Folk-Lore Society.

Simpson, Jacqueline. 1975. *Legends of Icelandic Magicians*. Cambridge, England: D. S. Brewer.

———. 1987. *European Mythology*. London: Hamlyn.

Sinclair, Sir John. 1795. *The Statistical Account of Scotland Drawn Up from the Communications of the Ministers of the Different Parishes*. Volume XIV. Edinburgh: William Creech.

Skemer, Don C. 2006. *Binding Words: Textual Amulets in the Middle Ages*. University Park: Pennsylvania State University.

Smeeton, C. S. 1986. *The Metropolitan Electric Tramways*. Vol. 2. *1921–1933*. London: The Light Rail Transit Association.

Smylie, Adolphe E. 1919. *The Marines, and Other War Verse*. New York: Knickerbocker Press.

Snodgrass, Mary Ellen. 2004. *Encyclopedia of Kitchen History*. New York and London: Fitzroy Dearborn.

Smylie, Adolphe E. 1919. *The Marines, and Other War Verse*. New York: Knickerbocker Press.

Sousa, R. 2007. "The Meaning of Heart Amulets in Egyptian Art." *Journal of the American Research Center in Egypt* 43: 59–70.

Speth, G. W. 1894. *Builders' Rites and Ceremonies*. Margate, England: Keeble's Gazette.

Spinner, Alice. 1896. *A Reluctant Evangelist and Other Stories.* New York: Edward Arnold.

Stammers, Michael. 2005. *Figureheads and Ship Carving.* London: Chatham Publishing.

Starck, Adolf Taylor. 1916. *Der Alraun ein Beitrag zur Pflanzrnsagenkunde.* Baltimore, Md.: J. H. Furst Co.

Stauff, Philipp. 1921. *Runenhäuser.* Berlin: Guido-von-List Verlag.

Sternberg, Thomas. 1851. *The Dialect and Folk-Lore of Northamptonshire.* London: John Russell Smith.

Storms, G. 1948. *Anglo-Saxon Magic.* The Hague, the Netherlands: Nijhoff.

Story, George Morland, W. J. Kirwin, and John David Allinson Widdowson. 1982. *Dictionary of Newfoundland English.* Toronto: University of Toronto Press.

Ström, Ake V. 1975. *Germanische Religion.* Die Religion der Menschheit 19, part I. Stuttgart, Germany: Kohlhammer.

Strygell, Anna-Lisa. 1974. "Kyrkans teken och årets gång." *Finnska fornminnesförenigens tidskrift* 77: 46.

Stuart, Kathy. 1999. *Defiled Trades and Social Outcasts: Honour and Ritual Pollution in Early Modern Germany.* Cambridge: Cambridge University Press.

Stübe, R. "Passauer Kunst." 1927–1942. In *Handwörterbuch des Deutschen Aberglaubens,* edited by Hanns Bächtold-Stäubli, vol. 6, 1460–1461. Berlin: Koehler & Amerlang.

Sturluson, Snorri. 1967. *Heimskringla: From the Sagas of the Norse Kings.* Translated by Erling Monson and Gudmund Sandvik. Oslo, Norway: Dreyers Forlag.

———. 1987. *The Edda.* Translated by Anthony Faulkes. London: J. M. Dent.

Summers, Martin. 1990. *Bluebird, a Dream of a Boat in Six Acts (after Maeterlinck).* London: Collectors' Books Ltd.

Swinnerton, Frank. 1954. "Sherlock Holmes—World Figure." In *The Sherlock Holmes Scrapbook.* Edited by Peter Haining. London: Treasure Press, 13.

Sykes, Wirt. 1880. *British Goblins: Welsh Folk-Lore, Fairy Mythology, Legends, and Traditions.* London: Samson Low, Marston, Searle & Rivington.

Taylor, Alison. 1999. *Cambridge: The Hidden History.* Stroud, England: Tempus.

Taylor, Stephen. 2006: *The Fylfot File.* Cambridge, England: Perfect Publishers.

Terry, Quinlan. 1993. *Quinlan Terry: Selected Works.* Architectural Monographs, no. 27. London: Academy Editions.

Thomas, Herbert, 1891. *Something about Obeah.* Kingston, Jamaica: Mortimer C. deSouza.

Thomas, Val. 2019. *Of Chalk and Flint: A Way of Norfolk Magic.* London: Troy Books.

Thompson, C. J. S. 1927. *The Mysteries and Science of Magic.* London. John Lane at the Bodley Head.

———. 1932. *The Hand of Destiny.* London: Rider.

———. 1934. *The Mystic Mandrake.* London: Rider.

Thorsson, Edred.1984. *Handbook of Rune Magic.* York Beach, Maine. Samuel Weiser.

———. 1992. *Northern Magic.* St. Paul, Minn.: Llewellyn.

———. 2004. *Rune Might: History and Practices of the Early 20th Century German Magicians.* Smithville, Tex.: Rúna-Raven.

———. 2016. *The Nine Doors of Midgard.* South Burlington, Vt.: The Rune-Gild.

Thwaite, Annie. 2019. "A History of Amulets in Ten Objects." *Science Museum Journal* 11.

Tlusty, Ann. 2015. "Invincible Blades and Invulnerable Bodies: Weapons Magic in Early-Modern Germany." *European Review of History* 22: 658–79.

———. 2019. "Bravado: Martial Magic and Masculine Performance in Early Modern Germany." In *Rethinking Europe: War and Peace in Early Modern German Lands,* edited by Gerhild Scholz Williams, Sigrun Haude, and Christian Schneider, 9–38. Leiden, the Netherlands, and Boston: Brill Rodopi.

Tribe, Tania Costa, ed. 2001. *Heroes and Artists: Popular Art and the Brazilian Imagination.* Cambridge, England: The Fitzwilliam Museum.

Trigg, B. 1973. *Gypsy Demons and Divinities: The Magical and Supernatural Practices of the Gypsies.* London: Sheldon Press.

Trubshaw, Bob. 1995. "The Metaphors and Rituals of Place and Time: An Introduction to Liminality." *Mercian Mysteries* 22: 1–8.

Tyack, George S. 1899. *Lore and Legend of the English Church.* London: William Andrews.

Tylor, E. B. 1890. "Notes on the Survival of Ancient Amulets against the Evil Eye." *Journal of the Royal Anthropological Institute* 19: 54–56.

Usener, H. 1905. "Sol Invictus." *Rheinisches Museum für Philologie* LX: 465–80.

Van der Geer, Alexandra, and Michael Dermitzakis. 2010. "Fossils in Pharmacy: Form 'Snake's Eggs' to 'Saints' Bones.'" *Hellennic Journal of Geosciences* 45: 323–32.

Van der Klift-Tellegen, Henriette. 1987. *Knitting from the Netherlands: Traditional Dutch Fishermen's Sweaters*. London: Dryad Press.

Vaneigem, Raoul. 1975. *The Revolution of Everyday Life*. London: Practical Paradise.

Veblen, Thorsten. 1973. *The Theory of the Leisure Class: An Economic Study of Institutions*. Boston: Houghton Mifflin.

Vickery, Roy. 2019. *Vickery's Folk Flora: An A to Z of the Folklore and Uses of British and Irish Plants*. London: Weidenfeld & Nicolson.

Villiers, Elizabeth. 1923. *The Mascot Book*. London: T. Werner Laurie.

Vinci, Leo. 1977. *Talismans, Amulets, and Charms*. New York: Regency Press.

Von List, Guido. 1912. *Das Geheimnis der Runen*. Vienna, Austria: Guido-von-List Gesellschaft.

Von Zaborsky, Oskar. 1936. *Urväter-Erbe in Deutscher Volkskunst*. Leipzig, Germany: Koehler & Amerlang.

Waite, Arthur Edward. 1911. *The Book of Ceremonial Magic: Including the Rites and Mysteries of Goëtic Theurgy, Sorcery, and Infernal Necromancy*. London: Rider.

Wall, J. Charles. 1905. *Shrines of British Saints*. London: Methuen.

Ward Williams, Howard. 1865. *The Superstitions of Witchcraft*. London: Longman, Roberts and Green.

Warrack, Alexander. (1911) 1988. *The Scots Dialect Dictionary*. Poole, England: New Orchard Editions.

Watts, Mary Seton. 1898. *The Word in the Pattern*. London: William H. Ward.

Webb, Denzil. 1969. "Irish Charms in Northern England." *Folklore* 80: 262–65.

Webb, Wilfred Mark. 1907. *The Heritage of Dress: Being Notes on the History and Evolution of Clothes*. London: E. Grant Richards.

Webster, D., ed. 1820. *Collection of Rare and Curious Tracts on Witchcraft*. Edinburgh, Scotland: T. Webster.

Weeks, W. Self. 1910. "Witch Stones and Charms in Clitheroe and District." *Transactions of the Lancashire and Cheshire Antiquarian Society* 27: 104–10.

Weiner, G. G. 2017. *Unique Lalique Mascots*. Vol. 2, *The Automotive Radiator Hood and Desk Ornaments of Master Glass Artisan R. Lalique*. London: Grosvenor House.

Weinhold, Karl. 1856. *Altnordisches Leben*. Berlin: Weidmannsche Buchhandlung.

Weiser-Aal, Lily. 1947. "Magiske tegn på Norske trekar?" *By og byd årbok:* 117–44.

Wenzel, Siegfried, ed. 1989. *Fosciculus morum: A Fourteenth Century Preachers' Handbook*. University Park: Pennsylvania State University.

Whittick, Arnold. 1971. *Symbolic Signs and Their Meaning and Use in Design*. London: Leonard Hill.

Wilde, Lady Jane Francesca [Speranza]. 1887. *Ancient Legends, Mystic Charms, and Superstitions of Ireland*. Boston: Ticknor and Co.

Wilkes, John, ed. 1812. *Encylopædia Londinensis: Universal Dictionary of Art, Sciences, and Literature*. 11 vols. London: J. Adlard.

Williams, Gareth, Peter Pentz, and Matthias Wemhofff. 2014. *Vikings: Life and Legend*. London: The British Museum.

Williams, Gerhild Scholz, Sigrun Haude, and Christian Schneider, eds. 2019. *Rethinking Europe: War and Peace in Early Modern German Lands*. Leiden, the Netherlands, and Boston: Brill Rodopi.

Williams, Joseph J. 1932. *Voodoos and Obeahs: Phases of West Indian Witchcraft*. New York: Dial Press.

Wilson, Thomas. 1891. "Anthropology at the Paris Exposition in 1889." *Annual Report of the Board of Registrars of the Smithsonian Institution. Year Ending June 30, 1890*, 641–80. Washington, D.C.: Government Printing Office.

Wilstach, Frank J. 1926. *William Butler Hickok: The Prince of Pistoleers*. New York: Garden City Publications.

Wirth, Hermann. 1934. *Die heilige Urschrift der Menschheit*. Leipzig, Germany: Koehler & Amerlang.

Wordsworth, Rev. Christopher. 1903. "Two Yorks. Charms or Amulets: Exorcisms and Adjurations." *The Yorkshire Archaeological and Topographical Journal* XVII: 376–412.

Wright, A. R. 1928. *English Folklore*. London: Ernest Benn Ltd.

Wright, A.R., and E. Lovett. 1908. "Specimens of Modern Mascots and Ancient Amulets of the British Isles." *Folk-Lore* 19 (3): 283–303.

Wright, A. R., and W. Aldis Wright. 1912. "Seventeenth Century Cures and Charms." *Folk-Lore* 23 (4): 90–97.

Wunn, Ina. 2000. "Beginning of Religion." *Numen* 47 (4): 434–35.

W. W. N. 1899. "Negro Superstitions of European Origin." *The Journal of American Folk-Lore* 12, no. 47 (October–December): 294–95.

Yoder, Don. 1974. "Toward a Definition of Folk Religion." *Western Folklore* 33: 2–15.

Yoder, Don, and Tomas E. Graves. 2000. *Hex Signs: Pennsylvania Dutch Barn Symbols and Their Meaning.* Mechanicsburg, Penn.: Stackpole Books.

Zammit-Maempfel, G. 1989. "The Folklore of Maltese Fossils." *Papers in Mediterranean Social Studies* 1: 1–29.

Zook, Jacob, and Jane Zook. 1990. *Hexology: The History and the Meaning of Hex Symbols.* Paradise, Penn.: Jacob Zook.

Index

Page numbers in *italics* refer to illustrations.
Numbers in *italics* preceded by *pl.* refer to color insert plate numbers.

sun amulets, *pl. 15,* 94–96
  with face, *96*
  South American, *96*
superstition, 7–8
swastika, 208–10, *208, 209*
Sykes, Wirt, 77, 92

Talazac, Jean, 57
talismans. *See also* amulets
  as art, 278
  consecrated, 9–10
  defined, 2–3
  functions, 1–5
  with magic square, *pl. 5, 31*
  meanings of, 4
  meant to be used, 276–80
  Safety Talisman, 101
  wartime, 22
tango, 46–47
tattooing, 174–77
Tau cross, *78,* 162, 242
Tau ring, 268
taweez, 17
teddy bear, 138–39
"Teddy Bears' Picnic," 139
teeth, 154–55
  wolf's, 159
Terry, Quinlan, *207*
Tetrad, 27
Teutonic knights, 163
Thai gambling amulets, 233–34, *233*
Theodore of Samos, 79
Theodul, Saint, 166
theopeaea, 195
thirteen, 38
thirty-five, 30
thirty-six, 30
Thirty Years' War, 167

Thompson, C. J. S., 21, 22, 86, 107, 184
Thor, Hammer of, 78
Thorir, 222
three-legs emblem, *54*
Tibetan amulet with nine emblems, *30*
tiger, 140
tilsimli gōmlek, 222
Tilsters, 17
tin, 40
tincture, 41
toad bones, 145–46
  toad bone locket, *145*
toad-doctors, 143
toadmanry, 145–46
toads, 143–46
  dried toad from bundle, *269, 270*
  toad amulet, *144*
toadstone, 143–45
  toadstone ring, *144*
Tolkien, J. R. R., 65, 204
touching wood, 106, 201
Tower of the Wind, 254
Tree of Life, 105, *247*
trees, 105–14
  plane tree, 106
  rowan, 106–7
Triad, 27
triskele, 54
troll knots, 49, *50*
truth, and the invisible, 1
Tubal Cain, 76
turquoise, 70
twenty-three, 38–39
twenty-seven, 30
twenty-eight, 30
Tylor, Edward Burnett, 55, 281